RIDING TOWARDS ME

RIDING TOWARDS ME

A Thousand-Day Journey from
Chicago to Delhi

JAY KANNAIYAN

HarperCollins *Publishers* India

First published in India by
HarperCollins *Publishers* in 2019
A-75, Sector 57, Noida, Uttar Pradesh 201301, India
www.harpercollins.co.in

2 4 6 8 10 9 7 5 3 1

P-ISBN: 978-93-5277-670-2
E-ISBN: 978-93-5277-671-9

Typeset in 11/14.2 Aldine401 BT at
Manipal Digital Systems, Manipal

Printed and bound at
Thomson Press (India) Ltd

To the friends I made on this journey

CONTENTS

INTRODUCTION

PULLING OFF INTO a clearing, I celebrated my first successful border crossing. I was now on a one-way trip out of the United States. Here, in the Sonoran Desert in northern Mexico, surrounded by dry squat shrubs and cacti and amidst the clinging grey dust, I had severed the cord with my previous life. Sitting atop sanDRina, my motorcycle, I felt a weight lift from my shoulders. I was alone, free and heading overland to India.

A white delivery van's sudden dust-laden arrival awoke me from my thoughts. Immediately, trying to gauge whether I was in any trouble, I was assaulted from the van's window by the driver hollering in rapid Spanish, '¿Es este el camino a Chihuahua?' Stunned momentarily, I took a second to answer. I knew that 'camino' meant road from the Spanish audio tapes I had played on my way to the border, and guessed the rest – he was asking if this was the road to the city of Chihuahua. I quickly replied, 'Sí, señor!' Satisfied, the van sped off. Fortunately, in the right direction.

It was hardly a baptism of fire but I was proud of my first Spanish interaction, and over the next two weeks, riding through Mexico, I realized I was being taken for a Mexican whenever I spoke Spanish. Being an Indian with brown skin might actually be a virtue on a long motorcycle journey through Latin America. If I could pass for a local and blend in as best as I could, then the situation regarding my security would vastly improve. But what I didn't know then was that in my effort to hide my identity, I was to discover more of it.

In the months and years prior to this, I had been in Chicago and working in the technology sector, steadily pursuing the Indian-American dream of getting a Green Card. But whose dream was that? Not mine, at least. Evenings and weekends were spent reading motorcycle travel books and blogs, watching *The Motorcycle Diaries* over and over again, wondering how I could get out of the rat race. To go on an extended motorcycle journey was my dream.

At home in Chicago, I felt my life was on pause. Out on the road, chasing down a distant destination, I felt at home. This told me a long journey lay in my immediate future, but how could I pull it off? Could I possibly wrap up my life in the US and not come back?

I had lived in the US for over ten years and thoroughly enjoyed it, so maybe it was time to move on, to look for a new home. Maybe even go back to incredible India? That last thought crept up and the more I dwelt on it, the more I realized my exciting prospects there. The West was slowing me down and I sure could use more dosas in my life. But was India really home for me?

I was born in India but spent my childhood shuttling between home in Zambia and a boarding school in southern India. From a young age, for me, home was wherever I was at the moment, so who was I fooling by saying I was going back home? For what it was worth, I had an Indian passport but I wasn't sure how much I associated with being an Indian. I couldn't speak Hindi and I could barely speak my mother tongue, Telegu, as the grimaces of my relatives often testified to. Regardless, it was time I discovered what being an Indian in the twenty-first century meant to me. Perhaps this motorcycle journey, through the frontiers of Latin America and Africa, would shed some light on that. I didn't really need a purpose for this trip, but for whoever asked why I was going, they themselves had an answer. I knew my reason for going – to be free. Free from schedules, from obligations and from rigidity. Pulling off a long motorcycle journey, with no sponsors or support vehicle, was going to be a tough task, but this was a challenge that I discovered I had been preparing for my whole life.

1

TRIP PREPARATION

THE SHUTTER DOOR rose, spilling the early autumn light into the garage. I rode sanDRina up the driveway and turned her engine off. Kicking down the stand, I smiled. My big trip was finally going to happen. The years of dreaming and preparing for it were coming to a close. I was leaving behind this life in America for a life on the road, for this departure was the start of a journey whose end I could not see.

It was the middle of September 2009 and I had just returned from a journey down the Continental Divide. The two-week trip had taken my motorcycle, sanDRina, and I down the entire length of the Rocky Mountains. From the Canadian to the Mexican borders, we had travelled most of it through small forest roads and it was deservedly one of America's motorcycling treasures. But for me, the Continental Divide ride was the final dry run before I started my real journey.

The plan was to sell everything I had in Chicago, quit my corporate engineering job, give up on my Green Card application, hop onto a motorcycle and ride away. I fell in love with this idea the day it dawned on me that it was actually quite possible. But I had been, and in many ways remained, a 'good boy' in my mother's eyes. All through my schooling and college years, I had been doing the 'right' things to live a better life in America, while not knowing where this biker alter ego had come from and how it overtook my corporate ladder-climbing persona.

There was no sudden transformation but it was a desire from a young age that slowly found its place in my world. A desire to understand more. A desire to connect. A desire to be free. And now, I was one step closer to realizing that.

But was I ready? Was I really going to commit to this? Could I really quit my work and leave behind the life I had nurtured in Chicago? Yet, everything was coming together. sanDRina, my gear and my own riding skills had performed as well as I had hoped they would.

I still had to sell my townhouse, my car, my other motorcycle and rid myself of everything else that gets accumulated when you settle in one place. I had a feeling everything would go as per my plan, but even then, a few months before my planned departure, there were many evenings when I sat in my cavernous living room and questioned, from the comfort of my couch, whether I was really going through with this. At the same time, was I ready to give up the thrill of my motorcycle track days? Was I going to miss the yearly ski trips with my friends? Was I ready to give up the convenience of living in a developed society for the uncertainty of travelling through those still in a flux? The right side of my brain, the free-thinking one, gave an emphatic 'Yes!' while the more subdued left side of my brain sat stubbornly on the fence. Whether I decided to go or not on this journey, I felt a momentum carrying me closer to the point where the decision would be made for me.

As winter approached, I had thought through most of the tangible hurdles that I envisioned would come across my path on this journey. I figured travelling on an Indian passport wasn't going to be an issue and I had enough funds saved up to travel for two years at least. I had a motorcycle that I trusted and knew how to repair and maintain. I had figured out how to maintain a website and share my journey as I went along. Yet, I wasn't ready to commit, or at least that was what I kept reassuring my left brain with.

There was another element that I had to contend with in addition to all the usual jangling of nerves which come before leaving on a long overland journey. This distinct thorn came from being an Indian child. How could I tell my parents? It might seem strange for those who have grown up in the West or have more open-minded parents, but I was an adult who feared telling his parents about going on a motorcycle journey. It wasn't so much a fear as it was a sense of engendering great disrespect by not following their wishes. In Indian culture, there are cases where children and parents don't share such open relationships. It's more centred on respect and reverence. And a good Indian boy would listen to his parents, but not this one.

I had been preparing them the past few months by talking about how I wanted to return to India and why it was a good idea. The financial crisis was still unravelling in the West while India was booming. I tried to find other anecdotes to first convince them of my return. I brought up how the West is a more individualistic culture, which I thrived on, but told them how raising a family in India would be better. When they saw the logic in this, it was time to drop the bomb. On one unsuspecting Skype call, I revealed to them the plan, adding that I was coming to India not on a plane but on a motorcycle. I was met with silence. Video calling was a boon to my communication with my parents as it allowed me to read their facial expressions, and they looked shell-shocked. They simply could not even fathom what I was planning.

Quickly, I explained how I had been planning it all these years, had discussed it with close friends, including my sister, and how it would be good for my future. While I tried to coax them, they tried to dissuade me, begging me not to go ahead with it. Of course, I felt some remorse in the fact that my parents had toiled to give my sister and I an excellent education in the hope that it would build a secure foundation for our lives. But whose life was I living? Theirs or mine? I had an opportunity in the next few months to make a massive life change. Could I live with myself if I looked the other way and continued on the safe, prescribed path? But then, would I really have a safe and predictable life if I continued in my job in Chicago?

My status as a foreign worker in America, after the financial crisis of 2008, was much more unpredictable compared to the heyday when I joined. The company I worked for was already failing to impress the investors of Wall Street and now, with such low confidence in the markets, weak companies had it worse. Layoffs were a constant threat at work and every few weeks, a whole group would be let go. When other foreign colleagues were being asked to leave, I realized my situation wasn't secure. I was hired as a specialized employee and my terms with the US immigration department were that in the event that I was laid off, I had exactly thirty days to find a similar position with another company or I would be deported. The other companies I could have joined didn't look like they were hiring high-skilled foreign workers, looking instead to hire more US citizens. So my choice was either to live in fear of suddenly having thirty days to find a new job or leave on my own terms.

This realization gave me the power to choose my own path. I would leave with my head held high. I was going to do this.

In the middle of February, I was called in for my annual performance review. I had always been rated effective and was excited when I found out that I had actually been rated excellent for the previous year. But that didn't matter. I had a great relationship with my manager, Thomas. He was a fair leader, a good friend and it had been tough to keep the secret from him. So when he asked me if I had anything to add, I gave him my two weeks' notice.

I went back to my cubicle and hit the 'send' button on the e-mail I had been dreaming of writing ever since I was bitten by the travel bug. Within seconds, my inbox flooded with shocked reactions of colleagues and friends. The closest of them came over, beamed huge smiles and congratulated me for finally doing what I had been talking about for years. My boss's boss called me to his office and expressed his shock and amazement at what I was getting ready to do. He asked if there was any way I could be convinced to stay. More pay? Better benefits? Nope. This journey had already begun.

My confidence and conviction were unshakable. The ball was now officially rolling for my trip departure.

I got home that evening and gave sanDRina a pat. We were going to leave this garage soon and there would be no turning back. As much as I was smiling, I was trembling at the gravity of my decision.

With the decision to go made, I turned my focus back to getting ready to leave. There were two weeks to go before I was to leave on 1 March and I still had a long task list of things to get done on sanDRina. I had spent the winter months rebuilding her engine and replacing parts such as wheel bearings and the drive chain. Now, there was a skip in my step every time I entered the garage and sanded a piece of Lexan, a kind of hard plastic sheet, for a headlight cover, or drilled holes for my solar panel. From here on, this motorcycle and whatever could fit in her panniers were all that I was going to own in this world. And I could not wait.

Much before I had decided whether or not I was actually going, I had begun clearing up my life so that I would be ready if and when the time came. A year ago, I scoured through my townhouse and got rid of things I was no longer using. This trip was going to be funded just through my savings, so whatever additional funds I could raise through selling my accumulated junk would allow me to choose a $10 hotel over a $5 one in Bolivia, somewhere down the road. I used eBay, Craigslist and local classified sites to sell all sorts of things; from a spare helmet that I got $50 for to an unused laptop for $200, and whatever else I could do without, thus raising a few thousand dollars.

The journey was going to be an exercise in minimalism. Space and weight are a premium on a motorcycle, so I thought long and hard about every single piece of gear I would take with me. However, I didn't have to go through this exercise as my departure neared. I had already figured out what kind of gear I would be taking thanks to all my previous trips.

That dry run down the Continental Divide showed me that one pair of cargo pants and four dry-fit t-shirts would be enough for my wardrobe on the road. My trip to Alaska the previous year showed me that I was carrying all the right tools to do simple as well as complex maintenance while on the road. When I went to Mexico in 2007, I tested my riding suit, a Kevlar-threaded mesh jacket and pants which were custom-fit and felt extremely comfortable in hot weather and offered a high level of safety. I knew that because I had crashed on that trip and got away with just a light scrape.

Once the gear questions were answered, I wondered how I would handle being detached from the convenience of America's consumerism. If one has enough money, the latest goods can be bought on a credit card with fraud protection and delivered to your door the next day. I would be saying goodbye to all of that once I crossed the border into Mexico.

The grand plan was to ride south from the US, through Mexico and Central America and then cross into South America through Colombia. From there, I would head south till Bolivia and turn north to cross the Amazon rainforest and explore Brazil. I would then head south for Patagonia before leaving the Americas at Buenos Aires. The next destination would be Africa. I wanted to enter at Morocco and circumnavigate counter-clockwise around the continent. Exiting through Egypt into the Middle East, I would make the last leg across Iran and Pakistan into India. That was the plan. Whether it would play out just like that or not, I had no idea. I had to accept that this journey was going to be more than just an extended motorcycle trip. It was going to be a life-changing experience. I wanted this trip to transform my life. A transformation from a corporate engineer into someone more involved with our generation's big questions, and I had faith that this journey would show me the way. But to help this, I wanted to first learn about the big challenges that we as a global society are facing.

There was a distance master's degree in sustainable development from the University of London that was possible to undertake while on the road. I would have courses which focused on climate change, poverty reduction and food security. I could study from a laptop and take exams along the way. I envisioned that this would give me deeper context about the places I was travelling through. The study materials arrived and I made digital copies of them all.

Items were quickly being checked off my master task list. Helmet painted: check. Website up and running: check. iPod playlists created for the first few days: check. And then it was time for my farewell party on 28 February 2010. It was a bittersweet moment to say goodbye to all the close friends I had made through my five years in Chicago. Everyone there was exultant that my dream was finally coming alive, especially after having been my sounding board all these years. But it was a false departure.

1 March came and went, and I still hadn't left. sanDRina's engine temperature gauge was registering very high numbers in my final test runs and I wasn't feeling confident about her newly rebuilt engine. The complex installation back into the chassis had gone smoothly but something was off in the carburettor settings. She wasn't firing as I expected. I wasn't going to leave until I was comfortable with the bike. I posted on motorcycle forums, talked to mechanics and made some adjustments to the main jet inside the carburettor till the engine temperature finally seemed acceptable. Then on 2 March, my birthday, sanDRina blew a big electrical fuse in the garage. I had installed many new electrical accessories and was very meticulous in my work, but an exposed wire had shorted

a circuit and tripped the fuse. This was not boding well on the eve of my grand departure.

On the 3rd, I decided at the last minute to instal a quick-release pin for the front sprocket of the drive chain. I reasoned that this would make changing the chain and sprockets a rapid job while on the road. But in my haste, I set the chain too tight. Feeling sanDRina was finally ready to go, I went for a test ride at around 11 p.m. and speeding over a railway crossing near my house, the bike rose up over the rails and came down hard. The landing generated extreme force on the tight chain and broke it.

Rescued by my close friend Allen and his rusty red Toyota Tacoma pickup, he and I made light of the situation with a good laugh, although he was surprised at the number of difficulties I was having with sanDRina right before I was supposed to leave. But I didn't think for one moment that these signs indicated I should not go. There was no turning back now.

On 4 March, I finally had sanDRina running just right. Test ride finished, I packed her panniers and this was it. I had one last dinner with Allen and thanked him for his tremendous help. We used his pickup truck to clear the house of anything that wasn't sold and sent it all over to the Salvation Army. I also gave Allen the power of attorney to finish up the sale of my house and any legal matter that may have remained. I was privileged to have such a trusted, dependable and supportive friend.

I had no bed and lay on the carpeted floor of my bedroom at night. The house was empty. There were still boxes everywhere and extra tools in the garage, which Allen was going to clear once I had left. But the house was empty of the life I had blown into it during my four years there. I couldn't fall asleep and my mind was packed with images and memories. I thought about how in the morning, I would be getting on sanDRina and riding south. I knew from a long time ago that I had to go on this journey. My life had led me right here. But on the surface, on the night before leaving, I was still questioning my conviction. What would happen to my career?

What was going to happen when I reached India? Was I really never coming back to the US? What if I died in the next country? These nervous thoughts finally gave way to happier ones and I thought back to the Thanksgiving dinners, the barbeques, the Formula 1 viewing parties and hanging out in the garage, drinking beers with friends. For all the good times I had spent here, the house had my thanks and it finally granted me a few hours of sleep.

2

A RUN FOR THE BORDER

I WAS STANDING ON the footpegs. sanDRina was purring in fourth gear. We were riding across Patagonia, the landscape was bleak and the winds chilling. I looked down to see that the alarm on my phone had sounded.

I'd had that dream many times in the past few years, but today, it was coming into being. I woke up and went about my morning rituals, while my passport, driver's licence and sanDRina's keys seemingly watched me from the bathroom counter. I donned my riding jacket and pants, soaking in the realization that this suit was going to be my home and comfort from here on. Over one last bowl of warm oatmeal as I sat at the breakfast counter, I bid farewell to this home.

sanDRina was ready the previous night and after stashing my Keen sandals in the left pannier, that was it. There was nothing more in this house I was taking with me. There was no time to second-guess what I was about to do. It had already begun. Turning the key, I fired up sanDRina. Letting her engine warm up from the freezing overnight temperatures, I rolled her out of the garage and down my short driveway. I had left the house keys inside and Allen had the spare set. He would be coming by later and clearing up for me. So I hit the close button on the garage door remote and flicked it under the closing door.

I kicked up my right leg and slid across sanDRina's high seat, sitting myself down on her saddle. I traded a home with four walls for one with a panoramic vista. Rolling the throttle, I felt connected to the guttural music that came out of the exhaust pipe. The kickstand went up, the gear-shift lever clicked down into first and we were on the move. I rode out of my cul-de-sac, turned onto the main road and crossed the railroad tracks which had bordered my house for the last four years, one last time.

I placed my left hand over the inner pocket of my jacket and felt my passport over my heart that was beating heavily. Money and credit cards were in my quick-access pocket on the right and there was nothing else to worry about. The playlist on my iPod had the Eagles playing. '*Take it easy*' always signalled the start of a road trip and a huge smile stretched across my face as I realized what was happening. I navigated through the northern suburbs of Chicago and merged onto Interstate 94, heading south.

I started around 6 a.m. in early March of 2010. Winter still had a tight grip over the region and the morning temperatures hovered around 5°C (41°F). The skies were clear with the winter's haze near the horizon, and it was blisteringly cold.

I had a long ride planned for the first day of the trip. It was nearly 1,000 km (620 miles) south from Chicago to Memphis. I wanted to escape the winter's wrath as quickly as possible, aiming to be in San Francisco in one week's time. It usually takes only a few days, but crossing the snowy Rocky Mountains in Colorado in early March was going to be no fun on a motorcycle. I opted for a route that headed straight south to Memphis and then cut west across Texas and Arizona before heading up to the Bay Area.

The temperatures rose through the day as I headed further south. By the time I crossed into Tennessee, I was comfortable, enjoying the ride and smiling with glee at having actually started the journey. I had read many other traveller's tales and a common message I gleaned was that to start is the hardest part of an extended trip. Many people dream of going on such a journey, and plan and save for it. But to actually go takes massive commitment. And I had done it.

From Memphis, I cut across the state of Arkansas and thought back to the first long weekend ride that I had made to the northwest of this state five years prior. It was on that journey I realized my love for travelling by motorcycle. I was just cruising by on the interstate this time through but smiled knowing that deep behind those forests lay remote areas and twisting roads that only I knew.

Texas is a huge state and can rightly be a country in its own right, but I crossed its breadth in one day. Dark rain clouds were hanging in the air and heavy winds were whipping at me throughout the ride. Riding a motorcycle means being in and amongst the elements of nature. Enjoying the sun when it shines strong and accepting the cold when it rains. So I carry my rain gear wherever I go. The rain finally eased as I left Texas and entered New Mexico, enjoying the warm colours of the fresh, setting sun.

The next day, it was very windy as I left Las Cruces, battling a heavy headwind all the way into Phoenix. Following my GPS, I arrived at Mike's house and was warmly greeted by his young daughters. I had contacted him through the Adventure Rider Tent Space List, an online directory of motorcycle owners willing to host passing travellers. Many such networks exist, such as CouchSurfing, and I planned to make full use of them throughout my journey. This would not only allow me to stretch my dollars but also allow me to meet interesting locals instead of being an anonymous tourist at a hotel.

Mike was a police officer in the local service and asked if I would be travelling with any kind of weapon for my safety through all the dangerous countries of Latin America. All I had was a Leatherman Wave multi-tool and its pocket knife. It was the only weapon I had ever carried with me and fortunately all I ever needed, with the exception of bear spray in Alaska.

Leaving Phoenix the next day and entering California, I ran head first into a cold front. There were bone-chilling winds and smatterings of rain as I passed through Joshua Tree National Park. I happened to look down and noticed that engine oil was spraying onto my right boot. I immediately pulled over and saw that a screw cap on the engine had fallen out. I rummaged through my bag of bolts and found a replacement, and was back underway in just a few minutes. I told the voice in the back of my head to keep quiet about this being a possible problem in the future.

The cold front over California kept the temperatures low for my ride across this beautiful state. I went up and over Tehachapi Pass and saw snow at only 1,220 m (4,000 ft). I wasn't expecting this and instead of warming up at a restaurant at the summit, I descended to warmer climes. It was beautiful to see acres and acres of farmland and be able to understand the economic might of this state. By late afternoon, I reached San Jose and rode up a steep hill to Chris's house.

I had met Chris at a campsite on my trip to Alaska back in 2008, and we spent many days riding together from the Yukon up to Prudhoe Bay in the Arctic Circle. He runs a successful termite extermination business and his preferred bike is the BMW R1200GS Adventure. It's the most sophisticated, purpose-built motorcycle for adventure touring. The popular Suzuki DR650, on the other hand, is a decent off-road bike that needs many modifications to transform it into an adventure touring motorcycle. Some riders prefer the first option but I prefer the second since it allows you to create your own version of how an adventure motorcycle should be. Chris and I have had an ongoing fun sparring ever since we met about how I should give up on my DR and get a 'proper' motorcycle like his GS. It didn't help my case when my first DR650 experienced a serious tyre issue and then a catastrophic engine breakdown, leading me to abandon that bike in Anchorage and fly home to Chicago. It irked Chris so much that I went ahead regardless and bought another DR, my present motorcycle, sanDRina, having a good laugh about how he'd tried his best to change my mind.

Northern California is prime motorcycling country with many hills leading to twisting roads and great views of forests and the ocean. I entered San Francisco and pulled up at Shridhar's place. The first leg of my journey had come to a close and this was how I would manage the multi-year sojourn: small chunks at a time.

Shri was part of the support team I had created to assist me along the way with logistics, moral support, and maybe even a financial bailout, if it came to that. We bonded a few years ago when we realized how similarly we were leading our lives. We were both Indians from a Telegu background, working in the technology sector, riding the same bikes and yearning to travel the world. There were other facets too that deepened our friendship and over the years, he became my main partner as the concept for this journey grew. When I would be overly inspired, I would ring Shri up and throw an idea at him, such as crossing from Alaska to Siberia and then riding down to India. But he would temper me and suggest I first ride through South America and then see where the journey took me. At other times, when I would be swallowed up in self-doubt and low on belief, Shri would ratchet up the inspiration.

This is why I wanted to pass through San Francisco even though it was not on the route between Chicago and Mexico. Shri let me use his place as the last staging point in the US before I crossed over the border into Mexico. As the date approached for me to leave Chicago, I didn't receive certain items for the trip that I had ordered, such as a global SIM card and filters for my camera lenses. These were sent ahead to Shri. He was also extremely gracious and bought me a new set of tyres. After a few days of relaxing and taking in the sights of the Bay Area, I set about servicing sanDRina. Stewart was a friend of Shri's and a mechanic, and together, we changed the tyres, mounted a new chain and did a valve check on the engine.

As I was inspecting the engine, I found the original screw cap that I had replaced in Joshua Tree National Park lodged in a crevice on the crankcase. Though there were no issues with the replacement bolt, I felt it was best to put the original screw cap back on. I finger-tightened it and used my wrench to secure the screw on the engine. My mind was not fully focused on the task and I applied one too many revolutions to the wrench and a sense of dread came over me. I had stripped the threads. The spiral thread on a bolt is designed to match its mating thread in the bolt-hole, and there comes a point where the threads finish and the bolt is considered locked. But extra force that continues to spin the bolt beyond its design limit can destroy the threads and leave the bolt spinning endlessly, preventing it from acting as an oil seal. This is what I had just done.

Stripping a thread is not so grave an issue but it must be addressed, otherwise an engine doesn't function as designed and can continue leaking oil. I proceeded to remove the part of the engine with this bolt-hole, the cam chain tensioner housing, and inspected the damaged threads. Stewart looked over it and saw that only half the threads were damaged and I could salvage the situation by putting my replacement bolt, that had longer threads, back on. I was delighted that my maintenance mistake had an easy fix, but in my glee, I overlooked an important procedure that would haunt me later.

The cam chain tensioner is a spring-loaded bolt that applies the right amount of pressure on the cam chain inside the engine. This chain connects the upper and lower parts of the engine and is vital for all the intricate functioning that takes place inside it. If the tensioner is removed from the engine, its bolt needs to be wound up, and only after the tensioner is mounted on the engine should the bolt be released to apply the correct amount of pressure.

Even though I was a mechanical engineer, my experience as a mechanic was still growing. One can be taught the theory in schools, but mechanics are the ones who learn by doing. Before the trip, I tried to learn as much as I could with Gus, my mechanic mentor, in Chicago. He had shown me how to properly instal the tensioner back on the engine, but in my moment of elation, I had forgotten to wind up the spring-loaded bolt and proceeded to assemble the tensioner with the bolt fully extended, forcing it on. Experienced mechanics will know that one should never force anything as that is a sign something isn't right. I wasn't an experienced mechanic, yet.

I fired up sanDRina and went for a test ride. I was immediately worried when the engine temperature sensor on my dash computer registered a very high reading. Previously, the sensor would register around 104°C (220°F) but was now shooting past 149°C (300°F). I stopped and let sanDRina cool down thinking that riding in the city was leading to the high temperatures, as she has an air-cooled engine and needs good air flow to keep the engine cool. I went back to Stewart and asked him for his advice. He wasn't familiar with these kinds of motorcycles and just shrugged, saying that maybe it would get better as I rode longer. That's all I had to go with it.

I spent a few more days with Shri, going over the route plan, setting up my GoPro helmet camera, printing out sheets of passport photos, and getting in touch with motorcyclists to stay with on my way to the Mexican border. On a lovely Wednesday morning in the middle of March, I set off from San Francisco. Rush hour had passed, allowing for an easy cruise on the wide, concrete highways. My thoughts fell on the journey ahead. While the dreamer side of me fantasized about small roads through the Andes and the Amazon, the side of me that worried kept looking at the engine temperature reading. It was hovering around 149°C (300°F). It wasn't rising, so I reckoned it was just the new normal. It's strange how the mind can convince itself of whatever it wants to believe.

The interstate got left behind for the famed Pacific Coast Highway along the California coast. I passed the charming little town of Half Moon Bay and then came San Gregorio. As I got through its traffic, I saw the temperature rising again and heard sanDRina's plea for more speed so that the fins on her air-cooled engine could get some relief. We left the town behind as I moved up the gears. Third gear was engaged and I twisted the throttle, enjoying a wide curve as I passed Pomponio State Beach. The road straightened up and I shifted into fourth with my mind anticipating fifth. As I twisted up fourth, all of a sudden, the engine shut down. sanDRina had lost drive. I eased her over to the shoulder and stopped under some shade.

I cranked the engine over a few times but it would not start. There was power in the battery and the lights were working but something wasn't allowing the engine to fire up. I felt my heart sink. But instead of throwing my gloves on the ground and venting at the birthing pains of this journey, I thought back to a quote that all adventure riders know: 'The adventure begins when things stop going to plan.' And I made sure to remember this quote as well: 'The difference between an ordeal and an adventure is attitude.'

So this was my first major hurdle. I opened up my tool roll and after removing the massive fuel tank, I opened up the valve check covers on top of the engine to get a look inside and confirmed what I had feared. The cam chain had broken. This was catastrophic. I realized right away that my mistake of not putting the proper tension on the cam chain by winding up that bolt had resulted in this failure. The cam chain had been tightened to the point that it was causing excessive heat through friction that was picked up by the sensor. After 65 km (40 miles) of running this way, the cam chain gave up. It was a very unusual failure as an engine can cover a million miles before needing its cam chain replaced – if it's maintained properly.

Luckily, I was still in the US where expert mechanics and parts are available. I called up Shri and he arranged for a friend with a pickup truck to come and rescue me. As I waited by the side of the road, a few people stopped to check if I was alright and I assured them that help was on the way. It was reassuring to know that people in this day and age do stop for stranded strangers to offer a helping hand. Though I was, of course, in a very friendly part of the world.

Jul pulled up in a white pickup truck and we rolled sanDRina onto the back. He was an older riding friend of Shri's and I thanked him profusely for coming out to rescue me. He had been stranded and saved many times in his life during his travels and felt this was his way of repaying the kindness. Regaling me with his motorcycle travel stories, my mind had no time to wallow in the dire situation that I was in: sanDRina's engine was destroyed.

We dropped sanDRina off at Werkstatt, a specialist motorcycle workshop. The next day, they opened up her heart and revealed the bad news. The damage was extensive and it would cost over $2,000 to repair. I had bought a used sanDRina for only $1,200. The mechanic told me the smarter thing to do would be to find a replacement engine. I immediately posted on various motorcycle forums looking for a used Suzuki DR650 engine, but I couldn't find any. There were parts of the engines available but I needed the whole unit. If I waited long enough, I was sure I could find one for sale but unfortunately, time was not on my side. I had to leave the US soon as my visa for Mexico was already close to expiry.

Shri also rode a Suzuki DR650. In an astonishing display of friendship and taking into account my time constraint, he offered to sell me his engine and he would then find a replacement for his motorcycle when one became available. I was blown over by this gesture. Of course, I still had to pay him but that was beside the point. Finding an engine on such short notice was a boon.

Using Mike's help, a forum member on ADVrider.com, the primary adventure motorcycling forum in the US, we performed a heart transplant surgery on the two bikes. I was well versed in the process of this delicate operation having worked on my original engine. We went about it methodically, first removing the electrical connectors, then the fuel connectors, and finally the engine mounting bolts. I labelled the bolts so there would be no extra ones remaining after the operation. The engine from Shri's bike was fitted into sanDRina's frame and after nine hours of diligent work, we were ready. She fired up on the first go. We were elated that nothing seemed amiss. My mechanic experience was ratcheting up a few notches. Downing a few beers, we patted ourselves on the back.

I was ready to hit the road the very next day but Shri asked me to slow down. His advice was to spend the day going for a test ride and ensuring there were no problems. The engine was misfiring occasionally and the boys at Werkstatt showed me how to tweak the settings on the carburettor to get her running smoothly. One last evening with Shri and I was back on the Pacific Coast Highway.

As I passed the site of the breakdown, the engine temperature sensor was displaying a cool 104°C (220°F). sanDRina was happy with her new heart. I grinned at how quickly I was able to bounce back from a potentially trip-ending incident. This was a good sign for the journey ahead. Shri joked that now that I had a major incident under my belt, there couldn't be anything worse ahead.

I had driven along the coast of California back in my college days when I was first interested in motorcycles. I told myself then that some day, I would ride here again. Passing San Luis Obispo, the cliffs were jagged and the road undulated to a beautiful rhythm. sanDRina was heavy, laden with about 80 kg (176 lbs) of kit but she was well balanced and proved to be an exciting motorcycle in tight corners. The new engine was purring along through the gears and my state of despair from a few days ago was a long way away.

Grey clouds hovered off the coast as strong waves broke against the rocky shore. I was soaking in this ride along one of the most beautiful roads in the world but was cold to the bone. Warmer climes were thankfully up ahead.

The gentle two-lane coastal route was swallowed up by the giant that is Los Angeles. I soon found myself on a fourteen-lane highway jam-packed with traffic. And it wasn't even rush hour! If I was running away from anything, it was this. At least in California, motorcycles are allowed to lane-split. This is banned almost everywhere else in the United States for safety reasons. As the four-wheelers slowed to a stop in front of me, I continued forward and threaded my way through the sea of oversized vehicles. Passing Los Angeles, I found the coastal route again and continued down to San Diego. Mexico was just a stone's throw away now. But I wasn't crossing through just yet.

The border between San Diego and Tijuana is one of the busiest land borders in the world and the threat of illegal migration and drug trafficking leads to a very heavy security presence. I had heard about this from other travellers and decided to head east into Arizona and cross at a smaller, less busy border. Not that I had anything to hide but I was just seeking low-stress situations.

I had planned to spend only one night in Ajo, a small frontier town on the edge of the Sonoran Desert, south of Phoenix. Gayle, a host I contacted through CouchSurfing, was extremely excited about my journey and upon hearing about my sustainability studies, convinced me to spend an extra day. She retired here with her husband, John, from Wisconsin and both were deeply involved with the local community and its activities that she took me to visit in her golf cart. I had to hang on as we sped around corners and squeezed through barriers just wide enough. She was an old lady with a lot of zeal.

The community of Ajo was dealing with troubled youths as many of them had emigrated from across the border and did not have elders to guide them. Gayle and I met with one of her friends who was a teacher, giving a special lesson to some of the kids about gardening in an effort to rehabilitate them from juvenile prison. The kids looked hip and modern with their tattered jeans and piercings, but had found a connection with the soil and proudly showed off their tomato plants and healthy carrot leaves. We stayed on for another class in which they were being taught to make salsa. It's a simple preparation, but these kids probably only knew the salsa that came from bottles. They took genuine interest and enjoyed the process of making food from their own gardens. I feel many of us who live in cities have lost touch with where our food comes from and expect to find everything at the supermarket. Some intangible part of humanity is lost when we lose sight of our food origins. These troubled kids were finding a way to reconnect with themselves through getting their hands dirty. I suspect more of us could use that.

That evening, Gayle invited a few of her close friends over for a meal that we prepared together. They were eager to taste Indian food and I prepared a lentil curry that went well with the fried rice and grilled steak made by John. The mood of collaboration and engaging conversation was what I was expecting, and hoped for, out of this journey. I had traversed varied landscapes, overcome an adversity, made many new friends, all the while learning about interesting community projects; and I hadn't even left the US yet. From here, I was entering Latin America.

3

THE FIRST CHICKEN CURRY

S AN CRISTOBAL DE las Casas is a tourist magnet. Perched in a valley atop the Central Highlands of Mexico's Chiapas state, the cool weather draws people from the warmer plains. The Spanish left behind an architectural feast for the eyes with a grand cathedral and red-tiled roofs. Today, the pedestrianized town centre and cobblestone streets are lined with chic cafés, while the throngs of tourists have created a demand for boutique hotels and guest houses clustered around the central plaza.

I too was escaping the heat of the plains and I sighed with relief as the cool air penetrated my mesh suit. But I was not a tourist here. Jose Luis, a friend I had not yet met, had opened up his ranch house to me a few kilometres outside of town. I followed my GPS and rode sanDRina away from the town centre and turned towards a hilly street that was flanked by giant eucalyptus trees. Even now, if I inhale that refreshing scent, I'm transported to the Palani Hills of southern India and my childhood. Though meeting me for the first time, Jose Luis greeted me with open arms like an old friend.

His white beard, matching hair and slightly rotund figure made for a warm, all-embracing welcome.

I was exhausted, more mentally than physically. The pace of my journey over the last two weeks had been intense. For some reason, I was rushing; perhaps to make up for the time I lost during my disastrous engine failure, or maybe I was still winding down from running my life to a schedule. The long hours in the saddle down Mexico's Pacific Coast let me cover ground, but now, I needed a break. Even Jose Luis could see it on my face.

He lived in a tile-roofed cottage that had a grand ranch house as a backdrop, in front of which horses leisurely ambled. Here on the porch of his cottage, we sat drinking Sol beers with Mario and Lucas. They were two Argentine travellers who Jose Luis, true to his spirit, had picked up from a bakery earlier in the day having overheard that they were looking for a place to stay. I was enjoying this free-spirited environment, where anyone with a warm soul was invited to be a part of Jose Luis's life for a short while. That's why, he later explained, he had signed up on the CouchSurfing website, so interesting people would come into his life. He had had enough of managing nightclubs and being involved in Mexican politics, and just wanted to escape the bustle of the capital city and found his solace in these hills.

I could see the appeal. I was still in my riding gear, enjoying the fading sun and drinking cold beer while Lucas strummed his guitar. Belting out rich melodies, he harboured a warm spirit. A Spanish Literature teacher, he told us he'd play and sing at bars in the evenings. He and Mario had just flown into Mexico from Cordoba, central Argentina, with the idea of travelling back home overland, however long it took. Their English, like my Spanish, was not strong and it took only a couple of beers before we decided on some mutual language training. It was an idea roundly endorsed by Jose Luis, who welcomed us to stay as long as we needed.

Neither of us having taught languages before, it was at times the blind leading the blind when we started the next day, but thrown into a CouchSurfing group event that same afternoon in the sunny central square of San Cristobal, we had no time to waste and quickly exchanged some basic phrases. A fair-skinned girl with long dreadlocks bouncing off her hip taped a sign to my shirt that said 'Abrazos Gratis', Spanish for 'Free Hugs'. Selva, a traveller staying with another CouchSurfing host in town, explained that we were here to give free hugs to passers-by, which I learned later was a common group activity in CouchSurfing culture. It's a wonderfully simple concept. The afternoon was spent doling out hugs and smiles with the thirty other CouchSurfing hosts and travellers. It was a social experiment in spreading bonhomie that took but a warm smile and open arms to break through to even the coldest of hearts and leave strangers walking away with a smile.

As the afternoon wound on, our group found a courtyard serving 'cervezas', Spanish for beer, and unbeknownst to me, word spread that this 'Indian guy' was cooking a chicken curry that night at 'Casa de Luis'. I had mentioned earlier to Jose Luis, Mario and Lucas that I would cook them a curry that evening and it seems they extended that invitation to everyone there. The news was broken to me at the end of the afternoon that I would, in fact, be cooking for over thirty that night. Faced with a crowd hungry for my curry and calculating that it's only a question of scale, I accepted the honour and challenge. Beers finished, we decamped en masse led by Jose Luis and a slightly nervous cook, with over thirty chicken curry groupies in tow.

This, I told the guests, was a participatory dinner, meaning their time and energy was needed to prep the vegetables and help out in the kitchen. But first, I showered. I like to shower and shave my bald head as a way to bring some good energy into the food before I start cooking it. While Mario and Lucas ran out for additional groceries, I scanned the kitchen for everything I would need to host a small banquet.

I would require some very large pots for the six chickens I was to curry. Jose Luis smiled wide and rushed into the ranch house, returning with an industrial-sized pot that could hold maybe thirty chickens. That was great but it wasn't going to fit on one burner and instead, would be sitting on all four. We were definitely going to need another stove. Maurizio, another tenant who was living on the first floor of the ranch house, opened his kitchen to us as the number of mouths to feed slowly crept up.

More guests started arriving as the evening chill set in and I shuttled back and forth between the two kitchens. I had a team chopping onions here, another dicing tomatoes there, while I took on my favourite task of cutting the chickens up to cook. I've never liked buying pre-cut chicken, believing there's greater quality in the curry when the pieces are carved up from the whole bird. I took a deeper interest in cooking a few years earlier, not just to satisfy my taste buds but, as Robert M. Pirsig described in *Zen and the Art of Motorcycle Maintenance*, to satisfy my philosophical pursuit of quality.

Kal, a traveller from Seoul, had connected with me a day earlier and was busy preparing a vegetable fried rice to go with my curry. Besides sharing a passion for cooking, we also shared our pursuit of a deeper understanding of the universe. Training with a Zen master in the forests of Japan, he told me how he was routinely blindfolded and had to find his way out of the dense woods by making sense of his surroundings rather than seeing or touching. He was now sensing the right ratio of carrots to peas for his rice.

Jose Luis was entertaining the guests and stopped me one time as I was rushing out to Maurizio's kitchen. He said he was very happy to see me running the evening like I was at my own house. It was a moment of great satisfaction for me as I realized that more than an act of showing gratitude to my hosts, cooking was a way for me to connect with home and the good times I had enjoyed cooking with friends so often before leaving Chicago. Throughout my travels, it became a conscious decision to always cook when I could to help ward off feeling homesick. This became even more important to me as my time on the road grew.

The party was centred in Jose Luis's kitchen while I focused in Maurizio's. I wanted to be a part of the social atmosphere, but I now had a duty to deliver this chicken curry to our hungry guests. With sweat forming over my brow, I leaned over the giant pot to inhale the rich aroma of caramelized onions infused with roasted garlic and ginger. Selva looked in and said she could sense an aura around me. I told her it was the aura of my mother, whose spices I was using, and we smiled. Blonde-haired Melody, standing behind her, asked if she could marry me as she didn't know anything about cooking. These two hippies were travelling together, but being vegetarians, they quickly left the scene along with the marriage proposal once the smell of frying chicken filled the air. Just for them, I had a small pot of potato curry going on in Jose Luis's kitchen.

Cooking for thirty, as most chefs might tell you, takes longer than you might think and it was four hours before dinner was finally served. An untested hand at cooking for so many people, I felt this wasn't my best curry. My hungry audience, on the other hand, shielded me from any judgement. The vat of chicken curry and pot of potato curry were quickly emptied, with many diners going back for seconds and thirds.

Mission accomplished. I slumped, replete in an empty chair at the dining table on the porch, basking in the happy smiles plastered on my guests' faces. Ikura, a Japanese traveller sitting next to me, leaned over. She possessed a Type A personality and had goals for everything in life, including life itself, and quizzically inquired about the purpose of my journey. I paused, irritated perhaps at the intrusion into my thoughts, before simply pointing to her plate and saying, 'If there had to be a purpose to my journey, let it be cooking curries.' She forced a strained smile, perhaps looking for a more rational answer, but carried on eating.

Bellies full, the mood of the party remained warm and intimate. Lucas began to serenade the ladies with his wholesome baritone voice as a bonfire lit by Maurizio blazed in the courtyard under a starlit night. I wanted to take Lucas along with me, maybe in a sidecar, so he could create a soundtrack as my journey through Latin America unfolded. He reminded me of Alberto Granado, Ernesto Guevara's travel companion in *The Motorcycle Diaries*, a jovial, effervescent character who always attracted the ladies. But I soon decided against it. Without denying all the great characters of past motorcycle adventures any delusions of grandeur, I was committed to my sanDRina. She was my companion on this journey and this, I swore, was going to be our story. I wouldn't know it then, but a new character would soon be forming inside me, and it all began with that curry.

Many of the travellers who came for the dinner party were charmed by Jose Luis's hospitality and asked if they could spend a few nights there. It was decided by Jose Luis that we would open the doors to all on the sole condition that everyone cooked at least once. There would be no exceptions. His condition was met with smiling faces and on that Mexican patio in the hills above San Cristobal and we soon began an international culinary tour. Over the next few evenings, we had a hearty Czech goulash, coconut chicken from Réunion and delicious mole from Mexico made by Jose Luis.

Between these feasts, Lucas and I continued our language lessons. Through our time spent speaking on the patio or walking around the grounds of the ranch, Lucas was impressed at how quickly I was grasping Spanish. He still struggled to get a hold over the nuances of the English language. He loved some of the similarities with Spanish, but failed to understand how words could have several different meanings depending on their context and tone.

One afternoon, as we joked about how Spanish had lost out to English in the race to global language dominance, Selva and Melody arrived with bags full of vegetables and fruit, preparing to cook a vegetarian feast. Their enthusiasm was tempered, however, by their lack of experience in the kitchen. I was immediately conscripted as the de facto chef-in-residence. Cheered on by Jose

Luis, who continued to revel in his role as host, I rolled up my sleeves and prepped the menu with them both. Mashed potatoes, rice with broccoli and a green bean tomato sauce, ending with a fruit salad. Melody and Lucas prepared the fruit salad and Selva helped me by the stove. As the frying onions crackled with the tomatoes, she started telling me her story. Her father was a prominent engineer in Germany and her mother was from an upper-class family from Lima. Selva shunned her privileged life and instead of attending college, decided to travel and work odd jobs to stay on the road. From rolling spliffs faster than machines could in Amsterdam to making necklaces out of beads in Bali, she managed to survive without calling on her parents for financial help. She hitchhiked around India, became inspired to teach yoga and had just finished a training course on it on Mexico's coast before coming up to San Cristobal. During her training, she had taken on her new name, Selva, which means 'forest' in Spanish. She believed a free spirit connected us all and said people should do whatever makes them happy.

Our conversation continued through the cooking and over dinner. We were left talking alone at the table once the crowd had dispersed. After weeks on the road, I was thankful for the company and the interest. I suspect she was too, and soon had me signed up for a trip to a remote Mayan village on the way to Palenque, a few hours east of San Cristobal. She and Melody were leaving in the morning. It was not an easy decision, but one I was grateful for. Up until this point, I had been sticking religiously to a preordained allocation of days, scheduled to take me through Mexico and Central America into Brazil. I was struggling to drop the engineer within, finding comfort in order and structure. 'What's a few days when you'll be travelling for years?' she asked with a smile. The penny dropped as I realized right then that my plans and philosophies had shifted.

The air was cold with the scent of dew on the pine trees early the next morning when I met the girls at the bus station. I was to follow them on sanDRina. I could have left her behind, but all my belongings were stashed away in various places on the bike and I was not set up to travel without her. Nor was I willing to shake off the reluctance of not sharing my adventure.

In trailing their bus, I descended from San Cristobal's pine forests to the market town of Ocosingo. Here, the girls had arranged to catch a colectivo, a pickup truck with bench seating in the back. The tarmac deteriorated as the road descended further, taking on an appearance as if it had been shelled by mortars. Large potholes straddled the road, forcing the colectivo driver to swing wildly from side to side as he tried to find the smoothest path. Times like these made me relish being on a motorcycle. I needed less than a foot in width of good tarmac for a smooth ride, while the colectivo passengers endured mile after mile of back-crunching jolts.

Turning away from the main road, we drove down a dirt track towards the jungle, where the road was relatively smoother. With the constant throttle-on, throttle-off riding of the past few hours navigating the potholed main road, it was a relief to finally just open the throttle to higher speeds on sanDRina as we ripped along the hard-packed mud road. Beneath an interlaced canopy of trees and vines that blocked the sunlight, sanDRina carried me past the colectivo, escaping its cloud of red clay dust as the girls screamed in encouragement.

After nearly three sublime hours of riding deep into the jungle, far from the routes of any map I had, we arrived at Naha. This Mayan village of a few scattered houses and an abandoned airstrip extended past no more than two bends in the road. Selva had heard of it from other travellers and instead of staying in the fancy ecolodge away from the village centre, we opted for a homestay.

I parked sanDRina under some trees, after which we walked over a makeshift bridge fastened with pieces from a wooden crate. This led us to a simple cottage in which we would stay a few nights. Sunlight shot through gaps in the planks of its walls and ceiling, slicing through the musty air and illuminating the mosquito nets covering our beds.

While the toilet was sanitary and the water in the cistern looked clean enough to drink, living conditions in the village were simple. Selva was fluent in Spanish and tried to converse with the ladies of the house, but they spoke Mayan, so communication was limited. We were in the common room, which was the largest structure on the property and host to a raised open fire without a chimney at its centre. The black soot covering the walls and ceiling explained the deep wracking coughs of the residents, including the two young girls who rushed up to greet us, from presumably years of sitting around the fire.

While walking through the village, we befriended Bor, a deaf man in our host family who was shunned by the other villagers and his family, probably due to his condition. He accompanied us on our tour and to the only store that sold basic rations of rice, pasta, lentils and flavoured soda. There was more soda than water and this was clear from the attendant's smiling mouthful of rotting teeth.

We rejoined the family next to the fire as we prepared a simple meal of rice and lentils with cabbage. Over the next few days, we observed that our host family ate corn tortillas for breakfast, lunch and dinner – with eggs for breakfast and lunch, and with beans for dinner. Selva asked if they ever ate other kinds of food. They recounted the time they visited San Cristobal and had white bread sandwiches. Since their stomachs were not used to it, they immediately felt sick. From then on, they hadn't tried it again and preferred to stick to what their stomachs knew – good old corn tortilla. We learned that they grew corn in jungle plots called 'milpas', that they had to shift every few years since tropical soils lose their nutrients quickly. It was refreshing to see people living so close to the earth. There was beauty in the simplicity of their lives and I wondered how soon it would be before the outside world of progress would interfere with it. Of course, that's where we were from, but I hoped we were not disturbing their way of life.

Over the next few days, we explored a nearby lake, a coffee plantation and just lazed about in the tranquillity. On our last night in Naha, Bor joined us for dinner. He was a jovial character and had a warm spirit about him, always smiling. He tried on my helmet and motioned with outstretched hands, making a 'vroom vroom' sound. For a deaf man, he had a rich sense of sound. As we laughed at his antics, Selva, Melody and I acknowledged that we were out there laughing in the jungle, connecting with villagers who had hardly stepped out of their world, whereas a few nights prior, we were laughing with travellers from faraway lands. It was becoming clear that it did not matter where one was from, but it was one's positive attitude to life that determined their ability to connect with others and as a result, feel contented. I was extremely satisfied with my experience through Mexico and now, the rest of Central America was calling. The girls were heading further east to the ruins at Palenque, and it was time for me to get back on the road down south.

4

STAHLRATTE CROSSING

ICOULDN'T CALL MYSELF the breakfast chef. In my eyes, working under the gentle giant Rolli meant that I was barely even the sous chef. While I sliced tomatoes and cheese, made orange juice and espressos, he made omelettes, grilled the meat and raised the anchor. The galley hierarchy was firmly established. I was, however, Rolli's right-hand man on a magnificent 40 m (131 ft) century-old twin-mast schooner.

The *Stahlratte* plied the azure Caribbean waters between Panama and Colombia. A majestic and breathtaking vessel, the current route she plied was, however, just a holding pattern. Much like her captain, Ludwig, she was waiting to continue their voyage around the world. It was in contemplating my journey from Central to South America that her rising masts had caught my attention.

In early April, as I was whiling away time at Casa de Luis in San Cristobal, I was confronted in my planning by thoughts of passing through the Darien Gap. Since I had left Chicago, I had known it was out there. I was finally facing the inevitable decision that all travellers treading this path have to make – just how to get past it?

The Darien Gap has garnered a certain reputation amongst overland travellers. It is one of the few places on Earth that is still considered 'impassable', with the exception of a few dedicated and hard-worn adventurers. It was, to many human migrations in history, the final gateway before entering the promised new worlds. It lies at the exact point at which Panama latches itself onto the northwest of Colombia, the gateway to the North and South American continents, depending on which direction one is travelling.

In spite of being just 50 km (31 miles) wide and 160 km (100 miles) long, it is formidable terrain. A road has never been built through this jungle of mountains, marsh and swamps. While such a feat remains considerably possible today, it remains hard to achieve. The jungles on the gap's southern flank in Colombia remain FARC territory. This particular rebel group has financed its operations largely via the cocaine trade and kidnappings. To build a road connecting their territories with nations to the north would only make the drug trade swing in favour of the rebels. So, while the drug war rages, the Darien Gap remains closed to almost all.

'Almost all' because some hardy adventurers had indeed managed to cross the Gap from way back in 1924 onward. But with the exception of a British cyclist in 1971, it wasn't until 1975 that a motorcyclist managed the first recorded feat. But that involved dragging the bike through the jungle and finding enough canoes to traverse the multitude of rivers and creeks that barred the path. It is a journey that has taken its toll on its challengers and is certainly one that seasoned adventurers can be forgiven for blanching at.

This typically leaves us with two options: to fly or swim. Well, sail. The purist amongst adventurers will seldom permit their feet to leave terra firma. I was determined to do the same.

My first request to Ludwig was politely declined on account of a group of sixteen bicycle travellers and their friends who had booked the whole boat. The boat was scheduled for three months of major dry-dock repairs in Cartagena, which made this departure my last chance to escape Panama without flying and hit Colombia before hurricane season left me at the mercy of washed-out roads and landslides. I *had* to get on the *Stahlratte* and make the crossing with sanDRina.

Necessity is the mother of bargaining while travelling, and my appeal to Ludwig of how I had sold everything I had to go on this trip, earned me an invitation on board as a deckhand due to the full passenger load. Since I was part of his crew for the journey, I was only required to pay for transporting sanDRina. The rest of my expenses, in exchange for my labour, would be covered. It was a good deal by any standard.

There are many 'captains' offering to take passengers and cargo across the sea to Cartagena. However, I had read one too many stories of travellers being stranded on remote islands because captains didn't have the correct paperwork to pull into port and thus, offloaded their 'cargo' before coming under Colombian jurisdiction. Fortunately, Ludwig's reputation was solid and I had little to worry about as sanDRina and I prepared to embark upon the *Stahlratte*.

With hurricane season looming, my departure from the US delayed and my stay in Mexico extended, I now had just two weeks to travel nearly 3,500 km (2,175 miles) through Central America. It left me with barely any time to do justice to the archaeological and natural sites, but at least I managed to spend a few days in each country.

When travelling in a rush, schedules and deadlines rarely work out as planned. While I took in the major sites, including the impressive pyramids of Guatemala's Tikal and the massive locks of the Panama Canal, I arrived in Panama City a day earlier than planned. I used the day to travel to the end of the Pan-American Highway at Yaviza, after which the jungles of the Darien Gap block the way south.

The road there is empty, lined by tall trees and dense jungle. From that point, looking back, I reflected on the many months of

travel, thousands of kilometres ridden and countless memories of
my old home in Chicago. The end of my world did indeed lie at
the start of the Darien Gap.

In order to reach the *Stahlratte* the following morning, Ludwig
directed me to Carti. This port lay on the banks of the Rio Carti
Grande in the Gulf of San Blas, northeast of Panama City. My
journey there on sanDRina was a typical Central American one.

Under a light rain, I paid a toll to the Kona people to pass
through a nature reserve controlled by their tribe. Lush forests
on steep hills surrounded its road. sanDRina growled and roared
her way through the ascents and descents before I emerged on the
banks of the Rio Carti Grande, where we were suddenly thrust
back into the din of the modern world. Surrounded by jeeps and
people, a mass of labourers in loose, sodden clothing waited in the
rain for the weather to abate. The pillions of a bridge on which
they were waiting could be seen above the mud-grey torrent.

Having ridden through the mud and rain, I wondered if my
canoe pickup crew would be waiting on the other side. Luckily, they
found me within a few minutes. A long wooden canoe pulled up
at the quay and the headsman asked if I was going to the *Stahlratte*.
Damp but relieved, I rolled sanDRina down to the water. A team
of five, lean-muscled and tanned Kona Indian men, dressed in just
shorts and their smiles, jumped ashore after securing the canoe on
the banks. With no ramp in sight, we would be lifting sanDRina
onto the canoe. This was not at all an easy feat as the canoe had a
half-metre-high stern. I detached her side panniers, and alongside
one of the crew members holding her at the back for balance, it
took three of us to lift her front tyre onto the canoe. A plank would
have made this much easier but we had to make do without it. I
jumped onto the canoe to steady her by the handlebars and then
motioned for the rest of the crew to lift the rear tyre and get her on
board. I sat astride her with two planks pushed in under her engine
to keep her upright, and we pushed off from shore as the canoe's
motor fired up.

Leaving land to sail on water with a motorbike is what adventures are made of. I felt like an explorer sitting on my perch, inspecting mysterious forested shores on both sides of the bow. But my fantasies had little time to play out. The river took us to the sea, and from the brown, murky currents, we transitioned almost suddenly to the clear, turquoise waters of the Caribbean Sea. On the horizon, the *Stahlratte* slowly rose into view. Her two masts punctured the sky and her white, chipped hull spoke of the proven credentials that came with her storied journey around the world.

As our canoe pulled up alongside the schooner, Ludwig was the first to greet me, waving from the deck. He inspected both his cargo and new deckhand. As I wondered how we were going to get sanDRina aboard, a blonde-haired, shirtless, lithe giant of a man swung out a small crane from the ship and lowered ropes into the canoe. Rolli swung down and fastened sanDRina by her frame in sturdy knots. He climbed back to the ship just as quickly as he had descended from it. Just then, a wave rocked the canoe, pushing it away and sanDRina started tipping over. Horrified, I watched in near slow motion from the bow – if sanDRina fell into the salt water, she and I were finished. Even if I could fetch her from the sea, I would be facing weeks of cleaning out all the salt and replacing most of her electricals. Luckily, the boatmen grabbed the ropes and pulled us back close to the side of the hull. sanDRina was righted. A laugh of relief went around and sanDRina was hoisted onto the deck. I paid the boatmen and boarded the *Stahlratte* like a deckhand reporting for duty.

I was thrilled to be on board because I wasn't just a passenger; I was part of the crew. While Rolli proceeded to tie sanDRina to the deck, Ludwig led me inside. The main deck structure consisted of a cramped seating area with an adjacent kitchen, a small and efficient bathroom behind it, and a large lounge area that had enough sofa seating for ten people. A computer in the corner made up Ludwig's office. Downstairs, in the fore of the ship, eight bunk beds constituted the passenger sleeping quarters. The engine room, along with a small desalination unit, was in the middle, and behind it was a cramped private room with a mattress and a high porthole. This was to be my quarters. Rolli usually slept here but he gave up his bed to me for this journey, electing to sleep in a hammock up on deck instead. I could understand why. Soon after spending time on any boat, you accept the inescapable nature of certain smells, and the mix of diesel with the sea was ever-present back there. Having lugged my panniers into the cabin, I joined the rest of the crew for lunch. We all sat at the large wooden table on the upper deck, adjacent to the bridge and ship's wheel. Ludwig gave me the rundown of what he expected of me. My duties were to help prepare the meals, clean the ship once or twice a day, and help out Rolli when required. My duties were to start the next day.

I was up bright and early the following morning and began my duties straight away. The cabin was swept, beers were packed in the fridge and the fresh produce was placed out back. Our passengers arrived by noon. The anchor was raised and the *Stahlratte* put her prow out to sea. Even though she had sails, the *Stahlratte* ran primarily on her diesel engine. When using sails, a ship has to move perpendicular to the winds, which even a motorcyclist knows is not a very efficient way to move forward. It is a more leisurely and romantic method of locomotion, but on our first day, Ludwig really just wanted to get us away from shore and into the San Blas Archipelago.

These waters would have witnessed Spanish ships in search of the New World. Columbus's folly in thinking that he had reached India gave rise to centuries of Native Americans being wrongly called 'Indians'. Many a time, during my decade in America, I had to elaborate that I was actually an Indian from India. Having to constantly repeat this explanation to strangers deeply troubled me. I was more than just a national; I associated myself with many cultures and wanted to shed the nationalist label. In the West, Indians are perceived as head-wobbling, heavily-accented tech workers. I may have been the latter, but I was certainly not the former.

Admittedly, my many years growing up in Zambia and being cocooned in an international school in India left me with a hard-to-place neutral accent. Living in America and having to stress that I wasn't an Indian from a reservation, but actually from India, made me want to shed this forced label even more. But in all honesty, in my experience, America is a place where your origin isn't as important as what you are capable of doing and who you are as an individual. You are who you make yourself to be, as you do on any journey, and I soon felt that way with this group of American travellers aboard the *Stahlratte*.

As the diesel engine hummed along, producing a piercing yet lyrical tone characteristic of small ships, the passengers gathered on the upper deck for a late lunch. Serving them lasagna, I mused on what might be their impressions of me. Brown and bald, with features that allowed me to blend in with most other brown people of the world, they probably thought I was a native employed to work on the ship.

One of them, who I presumed to be leading the group, broke the silence by asking me my name and where I was from. When I mentioned India, everyone's eyes turned towards me followed by a volley of questions.

How did I get there from India? What was I doing there and were all Indians vegetarians? When I revealed to them that the motorcycle strapped on deck was my vehicle for a journey back to India, they were all very impressed and invited me to sit with them and tell them more about my journey. As we exchanged stories, I found out that two of them, Seth and Parker, were on a bicycle journey from Alaska to Argentina and had invited their friends and girlfriends to join them for this special section of their trip. They also happened to meet another bicycle-touring couple, Martin and Nessa from Ireland, who had joined their party. So we were all long-distance travellers, or at least friends or girlfriends of travellers.

I'm always impressed when I meet long-distance bicycle travellers, but this bunch was more impressed with me than I was with them. They saw me as an equal and were actually jealous that I was able to work for my passage. In reality, my work on the ship was very limited, especially when everyone on board was expected to help out in preparing meals and manning the ropes when the sails went up or down.

Just before dusk, Ludwig got us to our destination. In front of us lay an uninhabited tropical island. The white sandy beach was flanked by a trove of coconut trees and thicker jungle behind it. All around us were small islands with outcrops of coconut trees. This was the San Blas Archipelago, a group of hundreds of little to large islands off the Caribbean coast of Panama. In the distance behind us, we could make out the faint, craggy Cordillera de San Blas mountains on the mainland.

As soon as the anchor was dropped, Seth dived off the ship, swimming ashore, and the others followed. Rolli and I, encumbered by a BBQ and supplies for dinner, came ashore on a dinghy. As we sat on the beach, fanning the BBQ coals in a sandpit, I took in the magical setting. Dark clouds gripped the horizon, behind which the setting sun broke through a few scant gaps. Regal and silhouetted, the *Stahlratte* was anchored just a few metres offshore. Around me, bikini-clad beauties roamed the beach collecting shells. And then, Rolli handed me a beer. It was a surreal moment and only a few beers have ever tasted better in my life. Once the sun had set, the chicken devoured and the beers drunk, we left behind no trace.

I was awoken from my slumber when Rolli poked his head in the trapdoor and called out to me. I made sure to keep my distance from the exposed fan blades spinning next to my feet. Through the porthole near the ceiling, I could make out that it was dawn and the ship had stopped moving. I climbed up and as I was relieving myself in the phonebooth-sized bathroom, I looked through the porthole and saw small groups of coconut trees huddled together in the distance, anchored in their white sand beds. But I wasn't prepared for the sight on the other side of the ship. As I emerged out on the main deck, I was blown away. We had anchored near a picture-perfect tiny island where the waters were a crystal-clear, shimmering turquoise. Ludwig looked down from the upper deck and said this was our island for the day, Cocobandero.

A locker of snorkels and flippers was opened, after which the others donned them and dived in. I was a bit embarrassed to admit that I wasn't a strong swimmer and had never snorkelled before. But while clear waters were made for snorkelling, I floundered as soon as I jumped in and quickly retired to the beach instead to enjoy this paradise. Time passed slowly as I lay in the lapping waters. I was joined by two of the couples, of which both the girls, who were sisters, went topless. At first, they asked me whether I would be offended if they did, and I assured them that I had no issues as I recounted my time on Mexico's Zipolite nude beach. I was tempted to join them and shed my shorts, but we thought better of it since Ludwig had some local Kona people cleaning the barnacles off the ship and did not want to cause offence.

Elena and Hannah's boyfriends, Seth and Parker, who were cycling south were, in fact, sponsored by a fishing magazine. Cycling and fishing their way south, they had brought their equipment ashore and spent the day catching dinner for us. As per Rolli's judgement, their catches were impressive and our dinner was soon frying in the ship's galley. This journey was turning out to be the most unique experience of my life so far.

With this, the easy cruising portion of the voyage ended as it was time to cross the Caribbean Sea to Colombia. During dinner, Ludwig told us that the seas were very rough ahead with swells up to 7 m (23 ft), nearing the limit for a safe crossing. There was talk of turning back but all the non-travellers had flights booked out of Cartagena, so we had to get there.

As I was preparing greasy eggs the next morning, Ludwig announced that the weather had changed for the better and the swells were down to 3 m (10 ft). It would still make for a rough journey, though not a dangerous one. There was a sense of urgency as we prepared the ship for the rough crossing. Loose items were stashed away in lockers, cooking pots were secured on the stove with clamps, and everyone's luggage was safely packed under the bunks. The anchor winch roared into life and freed us from our island paradise. The day was clear and the winds were strong. Rolli unleashed the sails and under his direction, the strongest of us helped tie them down to best capture the wind. The diesel engine of the *Stahlratte* was singing its song as the wind against the sails stabilized us. Standing near the bow with the Irish biking couple, Martin and Nessa, it felt very liberating to have the fresh sea breeze in my face. And then, dolphins appeared.

A pod of ten porpoises in front of the ship played in the bow wave. Initially, I was worried because it seemed like the charging bow could ram into them. Just as lay people perceive leaning a motorcycle into a corner as dangerous, I was too quick in my assumption. These dolphins were expert swimmers and knew exactly the right speed to swim at to stay just in front of the ship. This was fun for them. Oh, how I wanted to join them.

By the afternoon, the swells in the open sea were quite pronounced and the *Stahlratte* pitched up and down rhythmically through 3 m (10 ft) high swells. They would ominously approach before lifting the prow and dropping it into the trough with a splash. Throughout this, all I was really worried about was the salt mist rusting sanDRina's steel chassis and brakes, even though we had wrapped her under a tarp before beginning the open sea crossing.

The constant swells made everyone seasick, including myself. This was my first time out on the open sea and I did not have sea legs. Some of the others started hurling over the edge of the ship and I followed suit. Perhaps greasy eggs were not the best breakfast for a day out on rough waters. I felt much better after emptying my guts but the queasiness did not abate, nor did my duties. I still had to work but couldn't be deep inside the kitchen, as losing sight of the horizon immediately made me queasy and wanting to hurl. Rolli excused me and prepared a simple rice and lentils meal. Hardly anyone ate. The mood of the ship had changed from the previous carnival. Everyone was sombre, off on their own getting through their sickness. People found spots all over the ship to sleep it off. It was better to be outside towards the aft of the ship and on the upper deck than inside, down or fore in the cabins. Keeping busy also helped but I couldn't do my job in the kitchen. Dinner was a light affair, just a salad and once again, it was hardly touched.

As everyone else retired to their beds for the rough night, Rolli went up to the helm to keep watch on the first shift. Martin and I joined him. The heavy mood left us with no need for any small talk. Surrounded by the dark sea, the ship shook violently in the heavy winds. Bracing ourselves against the railing, we quickly dived into deep conversations as we looked out beyond the ship's prow. In the course of which, one question stood out.

Rolli asked us both why we travel. I rattled off something along the lines of learning and meeting various people and seeing how we connect. Martin countered that he didn't need a reason to travel. It was his life. He was just 'being'. But we were intrigued by Rolli's story. He had grown closer to the two of us compared to the others, who he saw as tourists, and opened up to us. He had left Austria many years ago and travelled to India. He wasn't a typical backpacker and slept in public parks and accepted invitations from whoever offered. Then, he landed up in South America and somehow built a motorcycle using junk parts, travelling for five years around the continent riding it. Imagine the sight of a tall, muscular, blonde-haired biker on a Mad Max-style two-wheel contraption rolling through your town. But in reality, he was a gentle soul. He ended up getting stuck in Venezuela for a long time repairing his bike, and that's when Ludwig came across him. The

Stahlratte was in pretty poor shape back then and Ludwig enlisted Rolli to help him refurbish the ship and promised to take him to Asia when the ship left the Caribbean. That hadn't happened yet, but he was still enjoying the waters.

They asked me what my intended route was for South America and I said I was heading for the Amazon. Rolli had spent a considerable amount of time in the jungles there and told me to go slow when I entered the Amazon. He urged me to meet and spend time with whomever I came across in the jungle, for he had seen too many outsiders just enter to take from the forest. He wanted us to leave the locals with a positive impression of the outside world.

There is truth in the statement that travellers are ambassadors for their culture. Whether that be a regional, language or border-based one. It can even be a more abstract concept in today's world, with the urban–rural divide spilling over into all aspects of our lives. When a rural, poor person meets a traveller, for them, we represent the outside world. When some of those outsiders only come to pillage, it affects the rest of us when we visit. Rolli's point, that has proven true in so many of my own encounters, reflected the importance of meeting people and creating bonds for the next person who follows. Our conversations waxed and waned, but the constant swells eventually drove me to the relative comfort of my quarters and the chance to lie horizontal.

I awoke to the sound of the diesel engine cruising and wondered how many brain cells I had lost overnight to the engine fumes. I had got in some good sleep but felt queasy as I sat up and soon had to hurl. There was no shame as almost everyone on board was sick. Rolli and Ludwig, of course, were the exceptions. It was a solemn day as we just waited for the sight of land to signal the journey's end. By late afternoon, Martin spotted land and yelled, 'Land Ahoy!' This was an appropriate reaction as we were all indeed very excited to spot good old terra firma. Colombia was coming into view. Within a few hours, we were following a shipping lane that led into Cartagena's port. Ludwig had cranked up the engine, accelerating into the lane ahead of a container ship that threatened to keep us on the ship until the next morning. Whether we were in port or not, all we wanted was to feel steady land beneath our feet once again.

The *Stahlratte's* trusty, old, in-line six-engine delivered us ahead of the cargo ship and we soon docked in an area of the port for small ships and yachts. While all the passengers were stamped in and taken ashore, I would have to spend one more night aboard as customs was closed for the day. I was pleased to do so, despite my initial excitement to see land again. The extra night gave me precious moments of solitude and reflection to absorb my surroundings.

I was exhilarated to have made it to South America, that too by sea. I was on the shores of a new continent and it added some grandeur to the voyage that a considerable effort had to be endured just to arrive. Sitting on the deck that night, bathed in the port's lights, I couldn't help but smile.

The next morning, after milling about the ship and cleaning the deck, kitchen and cabins, Ludwig informed me that my temporary import papers were ready and it was time for me to proceed ashore. He thanked me for a job well done and I was grateful to him for taking me on. sanDRina was lowered into the dinghy and Rolli sat astride her as we motored up to the quay. Dressed in my black biking gear and riding a dinghy to a strange country made me feel like I was in a spy movie. I was smuggling in curry powder so I can argue that the premise worked. There was no crane and sanDRina was unceremoniously dragged onto the quay. It's a good thing she's no beauty queen with expensive parts to get scratched. We righted her up and after waiting for the petrol in the carburettor to realign itself with gravity, I fired her up and off we went. We had just crossed the Caribbean Sea and entered South America by water. I had a good feeling about the journey that lay ahead.

5

A FLAT WORLD

FERNANDO HAD INVITED me to stay as long as I wanted, but my visa for Colombia was only good for three weeks, all of which I could have spent in Cartagena itself. Bougainvillea hung delicately from wrought-iron balconies under which old ladies would sell their fried corn pancake 'arepas'. Sat on the northern shores of Colombia, this charming old town was an excellent gateway to the continent of South America.

It was here that Fernando, a successful businessman, had taken to motorcycling after the death of his wife as a form of self-therapy. He had bought a Suzuki V-Strom, a step up from sanDRina, and subsequently journeyed to Bolivia and back with a new partner. The trip had put him in touch with a compendium of fellow motorcycle travellers and as I was leaving his home, he gifted me all the SIM cards he had used during his trip. Loaded with the phone numbers of motorcyclists and mechanics along the way, this surrogate network was a blessing for my travels. I pulled myself away from Cartagena and hit the road heading south. From here,

I planned to meander around this vast continent and eventually touch the southern tip, Tierra del Fuego. The geographies ahead were tantalizing and intoxicating. The adventurer in me yearned for the next vista that patiently awaited me over the horizon. The Altiplano, the Amazon, Patagonia, all lay ahead. But first, I had to climb up the Andes.

This extensive mountain chain is South America's geological spine. In conjunction with North America's Rockies, it runs almost unbroken from the northern tip of Alaska to the southern tip of Argentina. From Cartagena's coastal dominion, I swiftly started gaining altitude. Outside Medellin, I pursued Colombia's major north–south highway plied by innumerable lengthy trailer trucks on its tight and twisting meander through the mountains. The prudent approach would have been to ride safely and exercise extreme caution on this dangerous stretch of the highway. But the racer in me saw the curvy road and twisted the throttle open. Switching between second and third gears, I used sanDRina's gorgeous torquey motor to power ahead of the trucks, enjoying the visceral grunt that a large single-piston motorcycle delivers. Hoping to make an exciting video, I captured my ride using the GoPro camera mounted on my helmet, darting in and out of the slumbering traffic as I wound my way uphill. The road was narrow and oncoming trucks would veer into my lane as we negotiated the tight bends. I was glad to be on a motorcycle as I only needed half a lane. In such situations, being in a car is dangerous, but fun on a motorcycle.

At the edge of Medellin, I met Jaime, who was riding a flashy new, bright green Kawasaki. Fernando had informed him that I was coming and Jaime planned a grand welcome as the head of the local chapter of the Touring Colombia motorcycle club. He was a graphic designer and questioned me about sanDRina's lack of stickers. With a large smile, he presented me with a Touring Colombia sticker, which I plastered on the left pannier. I had just enough time to unload sanDRina at Jaime's house before we set out to meet the local crew at a petrol station. It reminded me of weekend rides with friends back in the US. The petrol station was our hang-out spot. It's where we'd get our go-juice. As dusk set in, this group of eclectic bikers revved up and led me to a lookout point over Medellin. Stretching out in front of us down the long, narrow valley, I had a clear view of Colombia's second-largest city.

We ended the evening rally at a biker-themed café, munching on chicken sandwiches and fries. It was a rather surreal environment in which the well-known beauty of Medellin women became apparent to me. Most of them were girlfriends within my adopted group, yet some rode their own bikes. They all possessed a glowing, inherent grace and beauty. I later learned that plastic surgery is very popular in Colombia and neighbouring Venezuela. Regardless, the wide smiles and pronounced cheekbones brought out the natural beauty in these women. Their features were in sharp contrast to the men, who were comparatively average-looking. One can easily pass time over a beer pondering Colombia's evident gender 'imbalance'; a fate shared only by a few nations. That evening, I mused on stories about travellers who had reached Colombia and not ventured further because they had been trapped by the beauty of the women. The appeal was obvious, and if I stayed any longer, I figured that I might get caught up in it as well.

One evening in Medellin, I was invited to the birthday party of a group member. I cherished moments like these for the insight I gained into people's lives. Without such reciprocal experiences, crossing paths with others while travelling can leave you with little to no understanding of a person or a place. Owning a big motorcycle in Colombia puts you in the upper layers of society and we arrived at a poolside clubhouse burnished with glitzy birthday decorations for the man of the evening, Ricardo. There were about twenty people there, and by now, I was beginning to recognize many of them by name. After a delicious dinner of grilled meats and arepas, it was time for the birthday cake. The lights were dimmed and his mother brought out the cake. I was initially shocked to see a dazzling sparkler sticking out of the cake and smiled at how over-the-top this seemed, before realizing I could have easily been at a high-society birthday party in India. With the cake finished, it was time for dancing, something I had grown to miss terribly over the past few months on the road. The men quickly stepped out for smokes by the pool while the women cleared the tables and started dancing. In hopes of embarrassing me, Jaime's girlfriend dragged me onto the dance floor, thinking that I would be uncomfortable dancing like the other macho men. But the women were soon impressed and dancing with me as I kicked out my best moves, matching the beat and tempo of the Cumbia that was pumping out on the poolside dance floor. Covered in sweat, I stepped outside for a breather. Jaime expressed how surprised he was at my dancing prowess. I had to remind him with a smile that dancing is a huge part of Indian culture and something men often engage in.

As the party wound down, I reflected on how Colombia was one of the countries that I was slightly hesitant about when I was planning out the route of my trip back in Chicago. The cultural prejudice against Colombia is that it is a land filled with violent drug cartels that wreak havoc. That was definitely true when Pablo Escobar reigned supreme in Medellin, but it has been more than ten years since he was killed. Colombia has now become a relatively safe place for businesses to flourish. Along with following Colombian news, I kept up with blogs of other travellers passing through the country and learned that the international news media generally focus on sensational and negative news rather than the country's progress that might otherwise seem mundane. My experiences concurred and I wish I could have spent more time than the three weeks I was allotted by my visa.

After journeying through the rest of Colombia and relatively more-developed Ecuador, I was looking forward to spending time in the remote areas of northern Peru. Crossing the border into the land of the Incas, I came across a fork in the road. To the right lay the grand Pan-American Highway that went along the Pacific coast. I went left into the mountains.

For the past few days, I had been travelling in a convoy comprised of two other motorcycle travellers. I crossed paths with Anja and Holger, a German couple who had been on the road for three years in southern Ecuador, and since we were headed in the same direction, we decided to travel together for a bit. Anja, lithe and blonde with a deep laugh, was a modern dance teacher, and Holger, an eager, fit and short-haired man, was a high school teacher back in Germany. They had put their careers on hold so that they could live out their dream of riding around the world. Ten years in the planning, they were more than halfway through having already covered Asia and Australia.

They were travelling on two identical BMW F650 Dakar motorcycles. Holger said he would have preferred to travel on a more powerful motorcycle but since Anja was most comfortable on the F650, which allowed her to touch her feet to the ground while astride the bike, this was their chosen steed. Following advice that was common in the adventure motorcycling community, they had decided to get the exact same motorcycle to reduce the number of unique spares and tools that they carried.

We were still on the coastal plain with the dry Andes looming ahead when we realized that we wouldn't make our planned destination of Bagua Grande on the Amazonian side of the Andes. The sun was starting to lower behind the horizon and around one corner of this dry, mountainous landscape, lay the village of El Arenal. There were no hotels or signs of businesses except a lone provisions store that we stopped at. As we debated where best we should set up camp for the night, a young lady approached us with a group of children in tow. She seemed friendly, with a shy smile and a flowery yellow dress that had a few tears in it. I used my rudimentary Spanish and gestured a tent with my hands above my head and then moved them under my head like a pillow. She understood and waved us over, away from the road. Anja watched the bikes while Holger and I followed the lady surrounded by the group of inquisitive children. There were a few brick houses with tin roofing and dried branches set up as fencing. She led us to a small dirt field, that was probably used for football, and pointed at its expanse with a big smile, while a big tree at the edge of the field caught mine and Holger's attention. By then, the commotion in the village caused by our arrival had alerted the elders and a man from one of the nearby houses stuck his head out to see what was going on. I explained, growing confident in my Spanish, that we were just looking to camp for the night before heading to Bagua Grande the next day. He was all smiles and we were welcomed into the village.

Parking our bikes under the tree, we proceeded to set up camp. The kids and young adults were captivated by our tents; the children were crawling inside Holger and Anja's large tent with cries of excitement as soon as it was set up. I quickly zipped up my one-man tent as I didn't want anyone damaging it. Anja was having fun with the kids showing them all the stickers on her bike that had been accumulating from three years on the road.

The sun was just about to set and I quickly got out my camera and tripod and walked to the open field to capture the pink and golden sky. As I was clicking away, one of the boys from the group approached me. Clad in a worn-out Chicago Bears t-shirt, blue cotton pants and slippers, he had been quieter than the rest and seemed to be one of the eldest there. As he approached me, I gave him a smile and waved him over. I asked if he wanted to take a look through the viewfinder. He did, but it looked like he had something on his mind. He broke his silence and enquired if I would answer a few questions for him. What he asked stunned me.

'Is the world really flat?' Ignoring all the questions that suddenly flooded my mind regarding the state of education there, I was instead faced with the idea that this was a fundamentally deep question for a boy in rural Peru to pose to a stranger. Keen to answer his question as simply as possible, I explained, with

my ever-expanding Spanish vocabulary, that the earth is actually
a very large ball and if you start walking in one direction, after a
very long time, you will come back to the same point from the
opposite direction. He seemed to understand and I felt oddly
proud in being able to explain such a concept so quickly. But his
next question stopped me dead, the sunset view framed within my
camera suddenly forgotten.

'Is there a god?'

To this young boy, I was evidently someone who had the
answers, someone who knew the real world. The sincerity with
which he posed the question to a stranger indicated to me that he
must have had it on his mind for a while and was looking for an
answer. I was aware then that the only education in the village was
probably from missionaries. I recalled seeing a small church on
the way in, the only other identifiable building past the provisions
store.

I explained as best as I could that god was something that
humans are always in search of since we don't fully understand the
concept. My belief, I elucidated, is that god is in each and every one
of us. He nodded his head and seemed to understand, which made
me wonder if what I had said was prudent or not – religion remains
such a powerful social cohesion in rural, outlying communities
that providing alternatives to the area's adopted beliefs could have
caused conflict. To reaffirm this, I walked back to Holger and Anja
and told them about my conversation with the boy. They jokingly
told me we'd better pack up camp and leave for the local priest
could be coming for us. We laughed, but I still think of that boy's
future.

Later, over dinner, I asked Holger and Anja if being on the road
had changed them. After three years, they said that it hadn't, which
I found odd. Asking me the same, I said it had only been a few
months for me, but I felt I had changed in the few years leading
up to the start of my trip. Wanting to leave behind a steady, assured
life for long-term travel on a motorcycle makes one driven, even

stubborn, in pursuit of their dream. But then again, to really enjoy slow travel and its uncertainties, one must be patient and self-content. Earlier that evening, Holger had demonstrated how he managed to stay self-content on their long journey; he took a bath every night, no matter how. With a need to feel clean, he had stripped off his clothes and showered under a nearby hose after getting permission from the pipe's female owner. I was feeling grimy from the day's ride myself, but could not bring myself to strip naked and get that shower.

Breaking camp in the morning, we started our descent from the hills. Ahead lay the Amazonas state of Peru, the most western area of the Amazon basin. Roadsides were lined with paddy fields and palm trees. The air was humid and I was transported back to southern India and my parents' villages outside Chennai. After a quick snack in Bagua Grande, Holger and Anja continued on while I stayed to rest with my next CouchSurfing host. 'Julio', which was just a Spanish moniker, was actually an overseas Korean volunteer teaching computer skills at a local school. He had opened up his house to any travellers passing through this remote town. He had a decent command of English but his Spanish was better, so we communicated in that, which improved my fluency in Spanish.

Greeted by a lunch of chicken and beef with Korean noodles, I was put to work soon after. One of the conditions for my stay was that I would have to speak to his class, which I accepted whole-heartedly. We walked over to La Esperanza ('The Hope' in Spanish), which had a concrete courtyard filled with young kids playing during their afternoon recess. Surrounded by classrooms, Julio led me through the courtyard and to his computer class. He was studying to be a programmer back in South Korea and felt that he could share some of the joys of computing with these rural kids. The bell rang and the kids filed into the room, taking up their pre-assigned seats. Their eager faces encouraged me to share my story, but my Spanish was still very poor at that stage. I had been learning as much of it as I could with my language tapes and had plunged myself into situations where I had to speak more of it even though my proficiency was still basic. This wasn't an issue as I managed to entertain the kids for over an hour and explained that I was from India, which was on the other side of the world. They hadn't heard of India, but were familiar with China – several products available in town were imported from China – and I motioned to how India was next to China. To make a connection with them, I managed to convey that no matter how far apart our countries were, we were all very similar. This led to some head nods. Being brown, I felt like I could mingle with the indigenous population of Peru. If it wasn't for my attire, that comprised of a pair of cargo pants, a dry-fit t-shirt and Keen sandals, I might've passed off as a local.

By the end of the talk, the kids had become highly animated with roiling laughs from my antics, and in their fervor, they asked me to sing the national anthem of India. Tucked away deep in my memory, I managed to sing it briefly and then asked them to sing the Peruvian national anthem in return. Personally, I find nationalism to be a relic of the twentieth century and look forward to a world without political boundaries. Still, I knew that asking them to sing the national anthem would be a good move with the teachers, who were all very impressed with my talk.

At the end, after a group photo with all the kids, the teachers still at school wanted to have an informal talk with me and find out more about my journey. They were astounded by how someone from India had chosen to make a journey around South America and pass through their rural town. I was the first Indian they had ever met. Earlier, I had joked to the class about how Columbus thought he had landed in India when he reached the Americas and how all the indigenous people were subsequently called 'indianos' just to save him from embarrassment back home in Spain. That is before the politically correct term of 'indígena' (indigenous people) took over. The teachers wanted to treat me to dinner, so we went to a popular restaurant serving 'cuy', the highly-prized, roasted guinea-pig that is the Andes' equivalent to chicken. It was crispy and delicious, much like the dark meat in chicken. Being a fan of strange meats, I smiled when the cuy was served whole, head and feet intact, resembling a rat.

My plans were fluid and when Julio asked me to stay another night, I accepted. This would also give me time to take care of a niggling issue with sanDRina. She was blowing fuses regularly in some of the electrical accessories that I had wired up, such as power for my GPS unit and extra LED headlights. On the road, I would simply pop in new fuses, but I knew that I'd better tackle the issue before heading off into more remote areas. Working in Julio's small yard, I had sanDRina exposed down to her battery. With in-line fuses bought from the nearby hardware store, I managed to bypass the fuse box that I had originally installed in sanDRina. I realized that grime from the road was causing short circuits in the fuse box and a more reliable solution would be to put in individual in-line fuses that were sealed against the elements. This made the battery area messy with wires, but I labelled the function of each one with masking tape and brought some order to the chaos.

Julio was eager to take me on a tour of his town and I wondered just how much there was to see. We hopped in a mototaxi, which has the front half of a motorcycle welded to the rear of a tonga, resembling a tuk-tuk or auto rickshaw. First up was El Mirador, a viewpoint from a nearby hill that was up a very rocky, bouncy road. The view from up top was more interesting than I had expected. On my right, I was able to see the mountains I had ridden in from, and on the other side, the mountains that I would be riding into. After a quick stop for tender coconuts at the mototaxi driver's house, Julio took me to a spot where we had to leave behind the taxi and walk along the bunds of paddy fields. It felt a lot like Southeast Asia with rice fields surrounded by tall mountains. Our little hike led us to an expansive lake. It was very still and protected with tall reeds on its edges. Julio said he was training for a triathlon and he practised his swimming in that lake. He was certainly making the most of being posted in this remote part of northern Peru. After a night out with some other volunteers from Korea, it was time to hit the road the following morning.

Leaving behind the tropical paddy fields, I climbed the foothills of the barren Andes. In places, the well-tarmacked road was cut into the rocky face of the mountains and made for some dramatic riding. Such places would leave me in a dilemma, because the documenter in me wanted to stop and capture the twisting road in photographs, while the racer in me wanted to enjoy the sensation of leaning sanDRina into the corners. This road led me to the quaint village of Chachapoyas. It is a picturesque colonial village with a prominent church in its large plaza and is famed for the discovery of ancient mummies in a nearby cave. As I arrived in the open square, a busload of Western tourists disembarked and headed straight for the church. Not being one to spend time in churches and museums, I had a quick snack of boiled corn from a food cart and headed out. I was aiming for the ruins of Kuelap, perched up high in the mountains and said to rival Machu Picchu. During lunch in the next town over, I heard the rumble of two motorcycles and walked out to greet Holger and Anja. They were very cheery and excited to meet me again. They had spent two days in Chachapoyas, enjoying the charming village and Wi-Fi in their hotel. They were also heading to Kuelap so we grouped up once again.

A few kilometres later, the tarmac turned to hard-packed mud and up ahead loomed the high Andes. We had descended into a valley and the twisting river, along which we were riding, made for a pleasurable stretch of road that followed the flowing terrain. We reached the one-way 40 km (25 mile) turn-off for Kuelap and Holger stopped at the busy intersection to stock up on bottled mineral water. I didn't need this as I had my LifeSaver water-purifying bottle that could make clean water quickly from any water source. Even that remote bit of civilization was soon behind us and the road started to get gnarly. My instinct was to slow down when baseball-sized gravel rocks began challenging my balance. Just then, Holger went zooming past me, standing up on his footpegs, clearly having a much more comfortable ride. Though I admired his off-road skills, I didn't have the confidence to ride at that speed yet, given the kind of terrain we were on.

Trilling behind, I rounded a sharp hairpin bend along the precipitous cliff we were climbing up and saw Anja's bike with its front wheel punctured and removed. The sun was nearing its daily exit and we set about as a team to quickly fix the flat tyre. Holger was very fast in replacing the tube, and in that time, I had set up my small, electrical air compressor and we managed to inflate the tire in good time. Holger was beaming at the brilliance of using an air compressor instead of their handpump. He was determined to find one in the next major city.

At the end of the road, we reached a small clearing that was the parking lot and entrance to the archeological site of Kuelap. They were going to close the site in an hour, so we left our bikes immediately and hiked up in our motorcycle gear to enjoy the view in the golden light that bathed the sky. After twenty minutes of passing through brush and forest, we reached an impressive ridge that was topped with a massive, walled city. Not much remained of the city but its wall was formidable. It was at least 15 m (50 ft) high and encircled the summit. The wall was constructed with varying sizes of large stones that were cut precisely to accommodate the others. The earthen colour of the stones helped the wall to blend in with the surrounding rocky Andes. The only gap in the wall was a narrow opening that allowed inhabitants to monitor who entered their city. Kuelap dates back to pre-Incan times and to this day, not much is known of the people who built it.

More than the impressive ruins, I looked out across the mountainous terrain and was intrigued by the jagged sedimentary layers that lay exposed on a nearby mountainside. I could clearly see exactly where the land had kinked and pushed up the various layers of rock. This perspective gave me insight into the history of the land itself. The Andes form the boundary of two tectonic plates. As the South American plate pushes into the Pacific plate, the land buckles and up rises the Andes. I find the drama playing out in geologic time to be far more stimulating than that of our human time.

Before nightfall, we set up camp on the clearing at the site's entrance and it was finally time for me to fire up my camping stove for the first time on the trip. I had some leftover meat and fried potatoes from lunch, which I proceeded to mix with a can of chickpeas. I had been carrying this can since Panama, saving it for an emergency meal on the sea crossing to Colombia. It had been in my rations all this time and it was finally being put to use in Kuelap. It might have been a strange combination of food, but it was nutritious nonetheless, rich in carbohydrates and proteins, so what did my stomach care.

We were up at 3,050 m (10,000 ft) in the midst of the Peruvian winter and the temperature plunged with the sun. To combat the cold, I slept in most of the clothes I was carrying. Surprisingly, the night was comfortable and even toasty at times, in my compact one-man tent. Early the next morning, I set off before Holger and Anja woke up. I wanted to cover more ground that day whereas they wanted to spend time at the ruins. I didn't bother with goodbyes since we would probably see each other again on the road.

As I backtracked the 40 km (25 miles) to the main route south, I had a different experience than the previous day. I was on the same road but the scenery was much more dramatic. Perhaps it was just my state of mind as we might have been rushing on the way in, but now, at leisure, I was awestruck by the extreme cliffs I was riding along. There were drops of thousands of feet to the valley far below. The little single-lane road I was on humbly cut across the terrain. With greater confidence, I was now riding as one is supposed to in off-road conditions. I would stand on the footpegs, but judiciously slow down at every blind corner since I was unable to tell whether there would be oncoming traffic or not.

The route further south resembled the one to Kuelap. I set into a routine of riding along a river valley, ascending to a summit along sheer cliffs, then descending back down to another river, and so on. What a joyous routine. And there was hardly a soul around. My GoPro was recording all this as I enjoyed the playlists of enigmatic electronica music on my earphones. This is the kind of riding I had dreamed of when I was planning my trip; remote, hardy terrain with inspiring views extending to the horizon. The sense of freedom was immense. There was a lingering fear of the cliff edges and this made me focus more on my riding. My confidence mixed with the element of danger helped me enjoy the feeling of being at the edge.

While my right brain enjoyed the sensations of danger and freedom, my left brain was calculating where I would be spending the night. I had come down to another river valley and saw there was a police check post at the concrete bridge to the other side. There was about two hours of daylight left, and from my maps, I knew that the town of Celendin lay on the other side of the next summit. I could have camped at the bridge but decided to push ahead. The road up to the summit was filled with countless hairpin bends as I ascended from 853 m (2,800 ft) at the bridge to 3,108 m (10,200 ft). I was racing the sunset and started to look for houses to camp next to, as I felt I wouldn't make Celendin before dark. But I was already up around 3,000 m (9,843 ft) and knew it would make for another frigid night, so I picked up the pace. Gravel was getting flung under sanDRina's knobby tyres as I rounded the hairpin bends with more vigour. Such instances make me wonder which side of my brain is more dominant. The right side was enjoying the adrenalin and the left side was hoping to reach a warm bed for the night. Well, both sides worked together and I reached the summit in time to see a glowing sun on the other side.

Celendin was only about 10 km (6 miles) away and the sunlight would last long enough now for me to take it easy into town. And besides, I felt more comfortable charging up a hill rather than down it. It's about being in control of the danger. Going uphill and being racy on the throttle, I can instantly control my speed by relieving the accelerator, sometimes not even needing to touch the brake lever as the slowing engine acts as a brake. But in riding downhill, even with the throttle off, gravity pulls you and can require the use of brakes to control speed. If the braking is smooth and balanced between the front and the rear wheels, there should be no drama, but there is always the risk of too much braking, in which case the tyres will skid and lead to a fall. I arrived in Celendin safely and found a warm bed for the night. 70 km (44 miles) past Celendin, civilization was visible with the start of tarmac roads. I was on my way back to the Pacific coast. I had just crossed over the Andes, but this was an extensive mountain chain and I knew there would be more crossings ahead.

Before reaching the coast, I spent a night in the bustling town of Cajamarca. Owing to the fluid nature of the past few days, I was two days behind on my schedule. I had contacted a young German named Adam through CouchSurfing and he, soon after, spotted me in the large town square. He was out there for a volunteer programme and was staying in a farmhouse with other German students a few kilometres out of town. We spent the afternoon taking in the sites around town and munching on 'antiqucho', which are kebabs made of cow's heart. Not for the faint-hearted but right up my alley; I love strange meats. In the afternoon, we ran into Holger and Anja once again. Anja was excited about the farmhouse but Holger was in the mood for big town life with beer, after the two rough nights they'd had.

I followed Adam's directions to the farmhouse and wallowed in the twilight on the horizon on the ride over. The farmhouse was a patchwork of small buildings surrounded by expansive land, with mountains on one side and a river on the other. Earlier that day, I had told Adam about the curry I had made in San Cristobal, the prospect of which had him salivating. We couldn't find chicken easily and thus resolved to make a vegetable curry. After settling in at the farmhouse, Adam and his friends gathered in the kitchen as everyone was very curious as to how I would be making the curry.

It was important to be patient in caramelizing the onions before adding in the other ingredients, since it formed the base taste of the curry. I shared a little quip on how one needed to listen to the pot and judge the right temperature, based on the tone of the hissing noise. If the ratio of oil to water between the ingredients was correct, the hissing would be high, but if it was too dull, then the water was overpowering. They listened carefully and after we all agreed that the hissing was high, I added the chillies. I wasn't aware of how potent the local chillies were and putting three of them into the curry proved to be two too many.

It was an extremely spicy curry, even by Indian standards. A few of them were sad because they couldn't handle the spice and enjoy the curry. I had to become more careful of the chillies I would be coming across on my journey. I was intrigued by the fact that chillies had actually originated in Peru but are hardly used in their local cuisine nowadays. European tradesmen had brought chillies to India, where they are now deeply embedded in the cuisine that I had just brought back to Peru. Maybe the curry gods would be pleased with that.

A few weeks later, I found myself leaving Cusco after a wonderful few days in the old capital of the Incan world in southern Peru. Machu Picchu was everything people had said it was and much more, as I had found a non-touristed route to get to the famous Incan ruins. The road south out of Cusco flowed through the jagged terrain and just as I rode through a pothole, I heard a loud crunching noise from the rear of sanDRina. I pulled into a gas station and found that it was coming from the middle of the wheel, so I started removing the rear tyre. It's not an easy job on sanDRina as I can only lift her rear tyre off the ground once I have removed both her side panniers. With the tyre off, I saw the source of the crunching sounds. One of the rear wheel bearings had disintegrated. It was at the end of its life but had given no such indication. It had been only 24,135 km (15,000 miles) since the start of the trip and I had expected these bearings to last much longer, but perhaps they were under excessive load. I removed the broken bits from inside the bearing and reassembled the wheel. I needed to find a replacement as I wasn't carrying any spares with me. The gas station attendants, who had ambled over to watch my repair work, said that Cusco was the nearest place with shops selling bearings. I got on the road heading back to Cusco, but the loud crunching noise persisted and indicated that it was not safe to continue riding sanDRina. I needed to find a pickup truck to carry sanDRina to Cusco. I managed to pull over in the middle of the square of a small town that was bustling with activity. My map told me that this must be the town of Andhayahuallas (*and-a-wall-iyahs*).

Luckily, Lady Luck was watching over me because out of the blue, a white Toyota Land Cruiser pickup truck pulled into the square and I waved the driver down. A white man with a beaming smile and a cowboy hat asked if he could help in Spanish. I told him about my predicament and he suggested that we take the motorcycle to his house nearby for the night and then, we could head to Cusco the following day to get the bearings. We quickly got sanDRina onto the bed of the truck and headed to his house, a compound of old but well-maintained buildings. Helmut, who was in fact German, was about fifty years old and had come to the area in his early twenties from Germany to monitor development projects. He had decided to stay on since then and was now in the carpentry business. He lived alone and welcomed the company. We set about cooking in his kitchen, which was very inviting with rustic wood décor and exposed brick walls. Helmut's Spanish was stronger than his English so that's what we conversed in, and by now, I was able to hold a decent conversation.

The next morning, Helmut and I, along with Henry, one of his local carpenters who had a warm smile and shy demeanour, headed into Cusco in Helmut's second vehicle, an old-school Toyota FJ80 Land Cruiser jeep. It was a model I had not seen or been in since my childhood days in Zambia, and it was just as I had remembered; stiff, fun and bouncy. In Cusco, we found a bearing shop and procured what I needed. Before heading to lunch, I tagged along with Henry and Helmut as they attended to a job for a hotel wanting a skylight put in. Helmut took us for a traditional German lunch at a restaurant that Henry had built all the furniture for. It was amazing to look around the busy restaurant, knowing that I was dining with the man who had built its tables, chairs and even the staircase. Henry remained very humble and shared that he had learned the craft from Helmut, who had turned his woodworking passion into a business that trained locals to be highly skilled carpenters.

Back in Andhayahuallas, Henry and Helmut had some other work to attend to. Since I needed Henry's help to instal the bearings, I ambled about Helmut's house in the afternoon. I made myself endless cups of tea as I read about the journey ahead through Bolivia and the Brazilian Amazon, which I was still hoping to catch during its short, dry season in August. It was the middle of July and I wondered if I would still be able to get there before the rains.

I made myself lunch from leftovers in the fridge. There was a steel tin of curious-looking purple, wrinkled potatoes on the kitchen counter, and as I waited for my food to warm up, I took a bite of one. The taste was strong and unpleasant, and I realized they were fermented potatoes. Not thinking much of it, I continued with my lunch. In the evening, Helmut and I had a wide-ranging, engaging conversation at his dining table over dinner. He talked about his disdain for modern, Western life and how he wanted to preserve the colourful lives of indigenous people in the mountains, but also help give them a fighting chance in this changing world. He didn't have an internet connection nor an e-mail address, and instead, preferred to communicate in the old-school way of writing letters. He had lost touch with many friends this way but kept in touch with those that mattered the most.

In the middle of the night, I felt my stomach grumble unbearably and had to rush to the bathroom. The heavy wooden door to the bathroom swung open with ease in my hurry and I managed to relieve myself. Something was not right with my stomach. I went back to sleep, but had to wake up soon after and violently throw up into the toilet bowl. I saw the purple potato come up and knew then that I shouldn't have tried it.

In the morning, Helmut was concerned because I was very weak. I told him it was just a case of too foreign a food for my stomach and that I probably needed a day or two to get over it. He told me to stay as long as I needed to recover. He surmised that being on the road for so long had probably made my body weak and that I should rest up and regain my strength. I assured him that I had been in great health up until the previous night and it was just a case of an upset stomach. Through the day, my body won the battle with the strange new bacteria from the potatoes and by the evening, I was able to eat a proper meal. Helmut was very caring and insisted I eat in bed to avoid straining myself too much. The warm tomato soup with boiled eggs was very nourishing and just what I needed. He said that those potatoes were a kind of traditional food of the indigenous people that he worked with. He had a young teenage boy staying with him for help around the house, and they were his potatoes. They ferment them by burying them in the ground, after which a special bacterium grows on them that is considered a delicacy, in a manner similar to blue cheese. He would probably get an upset stomach from blue cheese.

By the next day, I was almost back to normal and Helmut took me to a fair in the town square. All his workers joined us and it was a jovial time with llamas on display and large glasses of pink 'chica', a local alcoholic brew made from corn, floating around freely. The food was typical of most fairs the world over; deep-fried meats and sweet breads. I'm usually a fan of eating all sorts of animal parts but wasn't too sure since I was still recovering from a stomach illness. My body took on the challenge and I relished the grilled intestines, deep-fried cuy and fried corn. Wandering around the grounds, I came across a beauty pageant of sorts for llamas. These strange-looking animals with thick necks and short snouts were being judged on which one had the best-groomed fur and best manners for a llama. Owners paraded their most-prized llamas, just like at a dog show, and a panel of judges decided on winners for various categories. Who knows, they might think that a dog show is weird and entertaining.

That evening, there was another event in town at the main church, which was 400 years old. The organ in the church had been restored and a grand ceremony had been planned. The restoration was supported by the French embassy in Lima and the ambassador was among those in attendance. The church was ornately decorated in frescoes depicting various biblical stories. The entrance had a very graphic depiction of hell, almost to the point of being grotesque. Contrastingly, the main sanctum was decorated with angels. I presumed the premise was that one needed to venture through dark times before reaching the sanctuary of heaven. I had found my heaven in untouched nature and longed to get back out there.

The next morning, Henry helped me instal the new bearings and I was ready to hit the road. Helmut asked me to stay longer but also recognized that I needed to get back on the ride. Andhayahuallas was a small pinprick on my map and it turned out to be a lively few days, all thanks to a faulty rear wheel bearing.

Just like Fernando back in Cartagena, Helmut had opened up his home to a stranger. I believe that these men had opened up their resources to others who had come before me and will continue to do so in the future. I noticed how much joy they took in being hosts. They were giving and in turn receiving value from being a benefactor. While some could say that I was thriving on other people's resources, I saw it as more of a give and take. Hyper-individualistic societies of the developed Western world have this notion that one should rely on their own resources. I myself love the concept of self-reliance and was practising it on this trip when not in urban areas, but I also saw the joy that these benefactors received from sharing with this traveller. I was taking from these hosts but was also giving in terms of allowing them to benefit someone in need; someone that they shared a kinship with. I looked ahead to other such interesting individuals that I might encounter on my journey.

6

INTO THE AMAZON

SANDRINA GAVE ME the bad news. I had just freed myself from a sandy embankment and she couldn't go faster than 32 kph (20 mph). We were at 3,660 m (12,008 ft) in remote southwestern Bolivia, riding the Altiplano, clutchless. I smiled. This, I mused, was part of the adventure I had signed up for.

I had a very small checklist for my journey through South America and one of the entries on it was to ride the Salar de Uyuni. It's a salt flat, the largest of its kind in the world, and one that is marooned high up in the Andes. I had been drawn to it since the time I had heard about it and seen pictures of it. Just the idea of it, serene yet almost apocalyptic, had piqued my curiosity. It *had* to be one of the strangest experiences a motorcyclist could hope to have on this planet. I had visions of standing atop my pegs, cruising above its blindingly white surface with my head held high and my eyes closed. It was a vision I could not shake. With that in mind, I left the buzz of La Paz after only a few days' stay at my friend Alfono's house.

Riding at such high altitudes, the cold pierced the thin air. It left me huddled with local residents over bowls of warm food when I reached Oruro at the end of the first day. But it was winter, after all. Here on the Altiplano, a flat, high plain sandwiched by the Andes, temperatures fluctuated from a high of 10°C (50°F) to a low of -20°C (-4°F). Oruro was the last big town in this remote corner of Bolivia and I was headed south to the vast expanse that lay ahead.

My early start revealed that the tarmac ended at the small, nondescript town of Huari. I topped up my Safari Aqualine tank to a full brim of 40 L (10.6 gal) of petrol. From there, I headed west to the town of Jirere with the intention of making a loop south and east through the Salar and exiting at the outpost of Uyuni. The route to Jirere was a soon-to-be commercial link between Bolivia and Chile's northern coast, but wasn't ready yet. The offered diversion was instead a loose, dusty and sandy route cut through the plain, parallel to the road.

At this point in the trip, despite the many miles sanDRina and I had put in together, my off-road skills were not up to par. I wasn't yet at the level where I could enjoy the front wheel wobbling or the slide of the rear tyre. Most of my miles had come from street riding, yet, I knew that the ultimate experience on an enduro (a large off-road motorcycle like sanDRina) was riding at high speed over an uneven surface and letting the bike dance under you. sanDRina wasn't dancing and I was getting tired. The sand was slowing me down and my minimal camping gear wasn't up to snuff for a night out in the Andean winter. As I mulled over these thoughts, I saw a local rider on a small Chinese motorcycle zip by on the barricaded tarmac section and I figured that if he could ride up there, so could I.

The tarmac section was separated from the diversion by a 1 m (3.3 ft) high loose, sandy embankment. I was riding parallel in the deep, sandy ruts, but soon spotted a path out. I built up some good revs and momentum, planted the front wheel where I was aiming and got over the initial small berm at the bottom of the embankment. But just as my front wheel made it over, my lower tool tube grounded on the berm. I cursed myself for the 'brilliant' idea of placing a large tool tube below my skid plate. I had just got it made in La Paz. I figured that carrying all my heavy tools, such as tyre irons and a bead breaker, as low as possible to the ground would help sanDRina's balance with a lower centre of gravity. However, any seasoned dirt-rider would know better than to do anything that would reduce the bike's ground clearance. I live and learn.

sanDRina was heavily loaded as I was carrying everything I thought I would need on the road for years to come. I was stuck on this berm with my bike at an incline and I couldn't get the side stand down as the sand was resting up against the bottom of the bike. I only had the throttle to free myself. But my rear tyre was now slightly lifted off the surface and it wasn't gripping, so with every turn of the wheel, it was digging itself a deeper hole. I was on a fairly fresh Metzeler Tourance tyre, which rides better on pavement than dirt. It was not the ideal tread to have for riding sandy inclines. I kept spinning the rear wheel and rocking the bike back and forth in hopes that it would catch enough grip to climb over the berm. Slowly, by increments, it did. I kept my elation in check and kept climbing the embankment. More throttle, more rear wheel slip, maintaining the balance, and I finally made it to the tarmac. I let my emotions flood out and as any motorcyclist would in this instance, I gave sanDRina more throttle. But she was spent and would not go faster than 32 kph (20 mph).

A sinking feeling, that I had done something terribly wrong to sanDRina, set in. Her engine case cover was burned hot to the touch and I knew at once that it was an issue with the clutch. I took stock of where I was. There was a village not too far ahead on a hill. Behind me was 10 km (6 miles) of sand and a further 160 km (100 miles) to Oruro. It was close to noon and I decided I had enough time to take a look at the engine and assess the severity of its damage.

I had taught myself not to panic in these situations, which is why I had all the necessary tools to allow me to make it through. For me, this included a full set of wrenches, music to keep my mood light, an attitude to never be too proud to ask for help and a network of contacts to call on for advice.

With my garage playlist on full volume, I began inspecting sanDRina's engine amidst one of the starkest landscapes I've ridden through. I had to drain the engine oil to access the clutch. However, since I wasn't carrying enough new oil, I had to drain and save the current engine oil so that I could put it back in when I was done, which is not the best practice but I had to make do. Giving the engine enough time to cool down, which didn't take too long in the chill air of the Altiplano, I drained the oil into thick zip-lock bags that I used for carrying nuts and dates. Once I had access to the clutch compartment, I realized that in slipping the clutch to free myself, I had completely fried one out of the eight clutch fibre plates of the clutch assembly. I was not carrying any spares. I had to regain compression on the remaining fibre plates for the clutch to engage. I tried fixing washers under the spring-loaded bolts of the clutch basket, but this did nothing and sanDRina stubbornly resisted anything past 32 kph (20 mph).

It was late in the afternoon and the chill was settling in. It was time to start thinking about shelter. Passing locals told me that the road was rife with banditry at night as cartels smuggled in old Toyotas past the porous border with Chile. Determined to avoid them, I removed the panniers to lessen the load and started pushing my sturdy lady up the hill to the village of Quillacas. I could only move a few feet at that altitude before I started gasping for breath. The sun was setting and the chill crept inexorably inward. Out of desperation, I started to drain the fuel tank in hopes of further lightening the load, but the trickle was no match for the remaining 34 L (9 gal). As other riders will attest, such situations put to test the bond between a rider and his motorcycle. Winded, with my sweat quickly turning cold against the freezing air, I started openly talking to sanDRina, telling her that I would get her up that hill even if it took all night.

As chance would have it, a local Quechua family of three were returning to the village on their bicycles after a day of herding llamas on the Altiplano, which I had seen from a distance earlier in the day. They stopped and offered to help. The tall, stocky daughter, who seemed to be in her twenties, had a tough build and helped me push sanDRina up the hill, while her father took my panniers on his bicycle. We made it to the village in a rapid half-hour. We didn't stop there as I had expected, but pushed on, quite literally, till we reached the mission of Santuario de Quillacas at the other end of the village. I thanked them profusely but was unable to give them any kind of payment for their assistance as they refused. Such acts never cease to reinforce my faith in the compassion of human beings, regardless of our cultural and geographic differences.

In the mission, I was delighted to find a safe place for sanDRina and a bed replete with warm blankets for 20 Bolivianos ($2.90), and they fed me for another 10. During dinner, I noticed their landline phone and asked if I could make a call to the United States. Who would I call in a situation like this? None other than my mechanic mentor, Gus Gans. He had rebuilt my engine and suspension in the southern suburbs of Chicago before I left and taught me through the whole process. Excited to hear from me, Gus soon got down to business when I explained my predicament. I was instructed to cut some metal discs and put them in the clutch stack to increase the compression. One $5 phone call and I was halfway out of this jam.

Gus had told me to use old coffee cans for the metal in such a situation, but there was nothing of the kind available at the mission or in the village. The next day, I put the ruined disc back in and decided to schlep it back to Oruro. With the washers in place as well, I could now go 40 kph (25 mph) and was ever so grateful to be riding on the flatlands of the Altiplano as any bit of incline greatly reduced my top speed. It took me the entire day to cover the 160 km (100 miles) to Oruro, where I arrived just as the shops were shutting down. It was relieving to be back in civilization, and early the following morning, I was at the mechanic's to help restore sanDRina. I traced the fibre disc and meticulously cut two steel discs from sheet metal with tin snips. Installed in the clutch, sanDRina happily gripped tight and surged through the gears to 100 kph (62 miles). I was ecstatic beyond measure.

With my spirits rolling in the right direction, I headed out on the highway and rode the last 225 km (140 miles) to La Paz, straight without a break and eager to get back to the comfort of Alfonso's home. Roaring up the steep inclines of La Paz, sanDRina's clutch gripped confidently, which encouraged me on the prospects for the trip ahead.

Alfonso did not let me berate myself too much for not being able to ride on the Salar and quickly set about finding me some replacement parts. The next morning, we found clutch discs from another motorcycle that matched the dimensions of sanDRina's at a local shop, enough to equip me till I got to the big cities of Brazil.

Whereas riding on the Salar was a major goal of mine, there was something even greater I had been planning this entire time, so abandoning the Salar for now wasn't too big a loss. Most of the overland journeys across South America conform to a north–south route along the Andes. It's a fantastic route. It covers most of the continent and puts the most dramatic sceneries and cultures on display, from Colombia to Argentina. But there is a large part of South America that this trail doesn't pass through. I had read about a legendary road that cuts across the whole of the Amazon rainforest – the TransAmazonica Highway. It is almost mythical – not in terms of its existence, but because many travellers believe the road is incomplete and rendered impassable by being in complete disrepair. I was beyond intrigued. I wanted to venture out there and find out for myself. My reason for leaving Chicago in the cold of March was so that I could cross the Amazon in August, the driest month of the year in the rainforest and the safest time to make the crossing solo.

I spent a few days at Alfonso's getting ready, getting psyched about crossing the Amazon. It was not just another leg of the journey but a massive commitment. In my mind, once I would depart La Paz, the only way out was 5,000 km (3,107 miles) ahead, on the Atlantic coast of Brazil. The Amazon is a very remote part of the planet. There isn't as much information on crossing it as there is on riding down the Andes. Very few travellers have made the journey. I had come across a bicyclist's decade-old travelogue and read it in detail, trying to learn the names of the towns and villages so that I could create a geographical map in my mind. He mentioned having camped all through the jungle and advised carrying a machete for the animals, vines or just safety in general. I had been against carrying any sort of weapon with me besides my Leatherman multi-tool that had a sizeable flip knife in it. But this was the Amazon. Maybe I would come across jaguars or pythons. Alfonso laughed at my new fear but eventually caved and took me to a market where I bought a fifteen-inch machete for $3.

At the market, we also bought supplies for a chicken curry. I had made my curry for Alfonso and his family during my previous stay and the word had spread by now. Gonzalo, another motorcycle rider in La Paz, was eager to try the 'famous' chicken curry, and as we walked into the upscale apartment in a quiet, leafy part of La Paz, I went straight to the kitchen. Gonzalo's wife, Maria, tall and fair with tired eyes, was inviting yet skeptical as to what the boys were up to in her kitchen. She was peering over my shoulder as the onions, garlic and ginger fried in the oil, warning me that they were getting overcooked. I understood her concern. Kitchens and cooking, no matter how sociable, are also very personal. But I assured her I knew what I was doing, and she backed down with a wry, yet-to-be-convinced smile. This changed as soon as lunch was served.

Her face lit up on the first mouthful with the new flavours she was experiencing. The boys were undoubtedly impressed with the food, but I was most satisfied when she complimented the complex flavours, noting the initial spice and velvet finish. To the playful chagrin of her husband, she even expressed amazement at the idea of a man cooking such a complex and well-tasting meal. I sensed a marked difference in how Maria was treating me during the meal than before while I was cooking it. Now, she was intrigued by my travels and upbringing in Zambia and India. Perhaps she was just being a polite host, but there was a warmth emanating from her that was absent earlier. I suspected that the curry had something to do with it. Her astounded facial expression on that first bite revealed to me that she had just experienced a eudaimonic moment.

Eudaimonia, found at the intersection of what's true, good and beautiful, is an oft-forgotten philosophy from Socrates's time. I had begun dabbling in this concept in the lead-up to my trip and it grew to become the purpose of why I decided to finally go all in and commit to this journey. I wasn't making this trip to feel happy; that was too fleeting of an emotional state. I wanted to seek a deeper contentment with life. I wanted to experience more moments that were true, good and beautiful at once. When I came across the concept of eudaimonia a few years earlier and read that more than happiness, if people aimed for eudaimonia, they might actually be more content with their lives, I realized I had found my life pursuit.

True, good and beautiful are all subjective terms, and thus, cannot be defined easily. This leaves room for varying interpretations. But any moment that is true, good and beautiful is often quite easy to detect. It could be a child laughing, a cat stretching or meeting an old friend after a long time. I was exploring that very idea, curious as to whether tasting my chicken curry could create a eudaimonic moment. It might seem bold of me to state that, but the more I cooked this curry, the more it was evident that the people I was with would change their relationships with me after the curry. Why was that? Perhaps seeing a bald Indian motorcyclist cook a curry from scratch in front of you, being a true moment, and having that curry taste favourably, being good, would bring about smiles, which was beautiful, would make you realize that something interesting just happened. This was primarily why I would whole-heartedly agree to slave away for at least two hours by the stove when someone would ask me to cook my curry, just so that I could see if my hypothesis about creating eudaimonia through curry had some merit to it or not. If not, and if I was simply reading too deep into things, then at least we had a tasty meal.

The next day, I bid farewell to my hosts and headed north out of La Paz. I was well acclimatized to La Paz's extreme altitude by now and climbed higher still to reach La Cumbre pass at 4,651 m (15,260 ft) that separates Bolivia into its two distinct halves. On the west side of the pass lay the dry, barren and cold Altiplano, extending at altitude to Chile, and on the east side, the land dropped immediately to the Amazon basin. The weather also changed instantly as soon as I crossed the pass. A dense fog set in, reducing my visibility to a few metres ahead. The road was winding but this was a new, wide and well-made concrete highway. In years past, the only routes down this side of the Andes were narrow, single-lane mud roads cut into the steep mountainsides. They still existed and Alfonso had taken me for a ride one day on the infamous 'Death Road.' It was the old road out of La Paz down the east side of the Andes, and was called so because of the high number of fatalities on the road with buses and trucks slipping over the edge. It had been sunny when we rode on it and I had wondered what the scare was all about. Yes, there were no guard rails and the drop-offs into the ravines were precipitous, but now, in the dense fog, I could see and feel the danger. In such conditions, the Death Road would be unforgiving. A miscalculation of its blind corners could easily lead to an immediate and fatal plunge. I had never been more thankful for a new road.

There were many tunnels on this new road and I stopped in one of them to put on my rain gear as the fog was seeping through my mesh jacket and pants. Just as I exited the tunnel back into the blinding white haze, I came upon a very slow-moving, dilapidated dumper truck. The driver was being extremely cautious on the winding downhill road, probably due to his poor, aged brakes. I was frustrated as I couldn't find a way past. The fog was too thick to judge oncoming traffic on his left and I found myself braking too abruptly whenever he would slow down unexpectedly. The absence of any working rear brake lights also made it tough to judge braking distances. There was a 1 m (3.3 ft) wide shoulder on his right and I decided to pass him.

As soon as I touched the shoulder, it was too late. The surface was slick as slime and sanDRina's front wheel tucked in and we fell on the concrete road. It happened all too suddenly. The truck was still moving and I stared fixated at the rear wheel as it rolled just inches past my head. sanDRina's windshield was not so lucky as the rear wheel of the truck rolled over it, destroying it. Alerted by my crash, the truck immediately stopped and the driver and his assistant jumped down, worried that I might have added to Bolivia's road death statistics. Bruised, I felt like cursing at them for going so slow which is what forced me to overtake them, but I didn't. Really, I couldn't. My own lack of patience was to blame. After ensuring that I was okay, they helped lift sanDRina and then continued on as traffic was building up behind us. I took a breather and assessed the situation. My helmet had not touched the ground because my left shoulder took most of the impact. With the foam impact-absorbing armour in my riding jacket, my shoulder was spared a serious injury. It was a scary moment to see the massive rear wheel of the truck lumbering right by my face. I cursed at myself for the poor decision and then laughed it off. I guess I had managed to experience the Death Road without actually dying.

With my head cleared and sanDRina not damaged beyond a broken windshield, we continued down the steep, declining road. At the town of Coroico, I turned north to head into a wet and green mountainous terrain called the Yungas. The Yungas is a transitionary region between the high and dry Altiplano and the flat savannah region, called the Pampas, that borders the Amazon. The wide, concrete road had ended and now we were back to the older single-lane gravel track cut into the mountainside. It made for beautiful riding accompanied by the sun's rays that penetrated through gaps in the clouds and dissipating fog.

In Bolivia, just as in all the Americas, traffic drives on the right. So I was a little perplexed when a white Toyota Corolla wagon, Bolivia's de facto taxi vehicle, came rushing towards me on my side of the road, honking and flashing its lights. I managed to pull to the left on the narrow, muddy road and gestured with a raised fist at his recklessness. A little while later, another oncoming Corolla drove past on my side of the road. And then, I saw it as two trucks up ahead carefully passed each other around a sharp bend. Considering how steep a drop there was to the left, it made sense for drivers to actually be on the outside of their lanes. This way, they could lean out of the window and judge precisely how close to the edge their tyres could be in order to let the oncoming vehicle pass. This helped me understand the rules of the road and I subsequently fell in line.

The mist finally subsided as I pulled into the town of Carnavi, a seemingly remote outpost on the map but, in fact, a thriving jungle town. It was connected to the outside world by only one narrow and winding muddy road that I had just come down on. The air was no longer thin and rakish. We had dropped 3,050 m (10,007 ft) from La Paz and the air now hung heavy, filling my lungs with every breath.

Contrary to the sandy plains of the Altiplano, the earth was once again a rich red loam, a layer of which coated sanDRina's radiator. Luckily, I was able to clean the mud from sanDRina in order to keep her radiator functioning properly; courtesy of the local 'car wash', which was basically some hoses pumping water out of the nearby river.

I set out the next day on a road thick and slick with clay. The road had absorbed all the fog's moisture and sanDRina's tyres were soon caked in thick mud. It robbed me of grip and made for slow going, restricting me to first gear only. sanDRina, being air-cooled, was not getting enough air blowing across her engine. Having planned for such situations, I had installed an engine temperature sensor that gave me a digital readout on the Vapor dash computer mounted on my handlebar. With the current engine settings, 132°C (270°F) was a good temperature for the engine to be at and it would not have been a problem even if it went up to 150°C (302°F). Chugging along in the mud in first gear, the engine temperature would soar to 166°C (331°F). I had read on online forums that 182°C (360°F) was dangerous for the engine and thus, at 166°C (331°F), I would cut off the engine and wait for the temperature to drop to around 150°C (302°F) before resuming. Within a few minutes, the temperature would reach 166°C (331°F), necessitating another short break. During these repeated five to ten-minute stops, I would sit and listen to my music with my eyes closed. It was an exercise in discipline and patience. I had only covered 50 km (31 miles) in four hours. There was no point in complaining – I had already accepted that this would be an arduous crossing.

By the afternoon, as I moved towards the eastern end of the Yungas, I could see the vast savannahs, the Pampas, spread out as far as the eye could see, beyond which lay the Amazon. Exiting the foothills of the Andes had finally brought me to the plains. The road ahead lay before me wide and covered in deep sand, extending all the way to the horizon. By the end of the afternoon, I had arrived in Rurrenabanque, called 'Rurre' for short. It was the largest town between La Paz and the border with Brazil. Located on the banks of the Beni River, its economy is supported by a popular tourist trade with backpackers who come there looking to experience the Pampas and river life.

I had not fuelled up sanDRina's massive fuel tank since La Paz and when the petrol station attendant said that they did not have any petrol, I figured I would head to the next town, 25 km (15 miles) away and fuel up there. But 10 km (6 miles) past Rurre, I hit my reserve fuel limit. I found that strange. It had been only about 440 km (273 miles) since La Paz and my outsized fuel tank was supposed to give me a range of 600 km (373 miles) to 700 km (435 miles). But all the first-gear slow riding had eaten into my fuel efficiency and I was now in need of petrol. I turned back for Rurre. At the edge of town, I stopped by a mototaxi stand, which was a taxi service on two wheels, run by a group of young Bolivians. The word was that the petrol tanker trucks had not arrived from La Paz for a few days. These were the same kind of trucks that I was passing on the way there. I checked in to a hotel and the proprietor told me that the scarcity of petrol was common in Rurre, which had in turn given way to a thriving black market. He said the trucks would most likely arrive the next day.

The following morning, there was a buzz about the petrol tankers arriving and I rushed out of town to the petrol station only to be told that it was a rumour and that the trucks would not be arriving that day. I had just spent a bit more of my reserve fuel on a wasteful run. Back in town, I committed to patiently waiting for the petrol tankers and made use of the downtime. I washed my grimy underlayers and did some other housekeeping tasks, such as reorganizing my toiletry bag and cleaning my helmet, before relishing the day off from the rough riding.

Two days later, just as I was considering buying petrol on the black market, at three times the nationally-fixed price, from a tour company that had large reserves for their operations, the mototaxi driver I was using for the past few days told me that the petrol trucks had arrived. I questioned whether it was true or not, but then saw a scramble across town as everyone on cheap, Chinese scooters and motorcycles were rushing out of town towards the posto (petrol station). I also joined in and soon after, found myself waiting in a long line. There were three orderly lines, one for motorcycles, one for cars and one for people with jerrycans. The trucks had still not arrived, but everyone there was eager with anticipation. A few of the mototaxi drivers had congregated around sanDRina and were checking out all her modifications. They confirmed that the trucks had indeed reached the plains and would be there shortly.

The scene was characterized by excitement and when the three tanker trucks pulled in, a chorus of cheers broke out amongst the crowd. People who had been waiting under trees to avoid the sun rushed back to their vehicles. Unfortunately, there was only one pump at this station and the attendant dutifully alternated from filling a motorcycle to a car to a jerrycan. The mototaxi drivers raised their voices saying that they outnumbered the rest and should thus get priority. I was witnessing the power of protest in this country that has empowered its majority indigenous population, having recently elected an indigenous peasant to be their president. But the attendant, a representative of the government, was adamant in following the rules. He pleaded with the people to come back later in the day as there was now enough petrol for everyone but there was no way anyone there was willing to take the chance.

Two hours later, it was finally my turn and people gathered around once again as sanDRina swallowed copious amounts of fuel into her cavernous tank. Most regular motorcycles, such as the ones the mototaxi drivers had, have fuel tanks of about 11 L (3 gal). I had 39 L (10.3 gal) put into the 40 L (10.6 gal) tank on sanDRina. They were all amazed and curious as to how far I could ride with that much fuel. It really wasn't as far as they might have imagined since their fuel efficiency was a lot higher than sanDRina's. However, her large single-pistoned engine gave me a lot of torque to carry a heavy load across tough terrain.

Fuelled up to the brim, I packed up and hit the road right away. It was already 3 p.m. and I wasn't sure how far I would reach, but

I was done being stuck in a town. I wanted to be out there, out in the Pampas. The road and the dust-covered shrubbery soon shooting by brought out a smile in me and I sped on towards the impending dusk.

As the day neared its end an hour later, I greeted a lady and a small child waving to me from the side of the road as I rode past. I realized that it was probably safer for me to camp next to their house than head further along and get caught in the darkness on this remote road. Hauling a quick U-turn, I asked in my best Spanish if I could pitch my tent next to their home for the night. They welcomed me in.

Their property was a few metres in from the road and fenced off with barbed wire to keep their cattle out. Their house was simple and thatched with an outdoor kitchen area. I set up my one-man tent there and took a bath next to their outhouse. It felt refreshing to clean off the grime and be at peace out on the Pampas. They were preparing their dinner and not wanting to impinge on their resources, I took out my camping stove and pot set. But the lady said that I was welcome to eat with them. I could have refused and eaten my own food, but I accepted her offer out of respect more than in hopes of conserving my own resources. It was a kind and powerful gesture, the kind of selfless act that reinforced my faith in humanity. They were clearly poor with limited resources, but the one thing they could offer me was food. As social beings, there comes a certain sense of fulfilment in giving and being able to benefit someone else's situation. I accepted the bowl of rice and mashed potatoes she offered me and ate with them in silence. After dinner, the old man there, who was presumably the lady's father, sat staring into the fire where the meal had been prepared. She brought him tea and he welcomed me to join him. It was a warm evening and the fire created a sense of bonding. With his tea consumed, we bid each other goodnight and by 8 p.m., they were done for the day, as was I.

Further along the road the next morning, I came across a shortcut off to the right. It looked smoother than the jarring, rocky surface of the highway through the Pampas that I was bouncing along on. I took it. It was a joyous few hundred metres. The pedestrian path, no more than half a metre wide, provided relief from the morning of riding in deep sand that was punctuated with sections of large, loose gravel. But it ended all too soon. The path rejoined the road at a deep and sandy section and just as I turned sanDRina's front wheel towards it, the sand gave way and the wheel tucked in. We fell slowly to the right and the right pannier came to rest on the sand berm on the edge of the road. It was more of a lie-down than an accident. Either way, I couldn't put her upright. She was too top-heavy, loaded with water, fuel and all my other gear. I struggled for a few minutes in the scorching sun, but then decided to wait for someone to come by on that lonely road. Fifteen minutes later, a man on a small, local motorcycle rode by. I waved to him frantically to stop and at first, he rode by, leaving me in despair. But a few metres on, he stopped and came back to help. It seemed like he didn't really want to help but found it tough to leave someone stranded on a remote road. With a quick shove, we righted sanDRina and he rushed off. I thought I had learned from my attempt to visit the Salar not to get caught up in shortcuts but the temptation was too strong.

Back on the sandy highway, I saw a dust cloud slowly coming towards me. It wasn't a truck, as it would have approached me much quicker. I saw the shapes of legs and horns poking through the leading edge of the cloud, after which the herd became more visible. An enormous number of hefty cattle were lumbering towards me, spread out across the road from shoulder to shoulder. They looked well fed and I wondered how they avoided poking each other with such massive, outstretched horns in the scramble of the herd. I was soon amongst them and the mind-numbing straightness of the road was replaced with me zigzagging around the cattle. Emerging from the other end, I found myself in the billowing dust cloud that was left in their wake. With dust in my teeth, my left brain questioned why we were even out there before the answer came from the right – the Amazon up ahead.

The deep sand faded and the road turned into a rumble of corrugations. The harder surface was a welcomed change but the corrugations created another kind of discomfort. The vibration from riding in and out of each one was too severe and I was worried about the damage being done to sanDRina's chassis. If I was an expert off-road rider, I would zoom by at a high speed and stay at the top of each bump, but my confidence had ebbed after my recent falls and I had resorted to riding in and out of each bump in first gear. It made for slow going but it gave me time to absorb my surroundings. The dry shrubbery had now been replaced by taller trees, some of them blooming with pink flowers, and the dark, red loam was an improvement from the browns of the sand and dust from before.

In the late afternoon, I passed the first proper ranch house since leaving Rurre and waved at the owners who were standing by the gate. I pulled up, and sure enough, they welcomed me for the night. The farm owner, Frederico, was a very congenial person and told me to make myself at home, but I knew better than to get too comfortable, so I set up my tent in their front yard. Frederico's estate was a stark contrast to my previous night's stay. There were many buildings and large sheds with ploughing equipment and tractors inside. The bathing room was large and well lit, and I managed to wash my baselayers that had captured all the dust that passed through my mesh riding gear.

Dinner was served in a thatched kitchen area where they were frying catfish. I learned from Frederico, whose fair complexion was in contrast to the farm workers, that the government had convinced him to come there by offering him land at a very low price. But not much could grow in that dusty, dry landscape, which was otherwise smothered in rain. The clay surface was very hard to cultivate because it would turn to dust during the dry season.

Instead, he got into catfish farming, which explained the bounty of fish at dinner. All his workers were eating with him and he seemed to be an equitable employer. After dinner, we relaxed in the central pavilion. I lay in a hammock while his family spoke in a hushed and relaxed tone from reclining chairs. I soon fell asleep in the comfort of the hammock. I woke up a little later to see that the kerosene lamp had been put out and everyone was asleep by 8 p.m. I lumbered into my tent for the night, wondering where the next day would take me.

There are only a few small towns in this remote northern part of Bolivia, some of which have strange names. 'Australia' was no more than a few buildings next to a bridge named Yata, where I purchased a few litres of petrol from a jerrycan before heading out of town. Most towns there were in shambles. I scoffed at hotel signs, preferring to stay out in the Pampas in my tent than a dingy hotel. The land was open out here. While I knew I was tied to the road and everything that lay on either end of it, signs of our concrete civilization were far away in this place. This realization remained a constant throughout my journey. Not everyone has to love where they come from. We do not choose where we are born but we can choose where we live. I wish to live out there; not next to the dusty road, but away from the commotion of modern life. Don't get me wrong, I have been an engineer and I have enjoyed the commotion, the energy of being around interesting people, the roar of an engine and the adrenalin of speed, but its opposite – which I was surrounded by – is also worth cherishing.

At about 200 km (124 miles) from my previous night's stay, the invitation to my next campsite came from a group of friendly villagers sitting on benches by the roadside. They beckoned for me to camp next to the benches in an opening between some trees. It felt too close to the main road but I knew that there would not be much traffic, so safety was not an issue. With the children shooing away piglets from a shady spot beneath a big tree, I threw my one-man tent in the air and it popped open, much to everyone's amazement. I hammered in the pegs for the rain cover, although in this situation, it would be protecting me from dust. After blowing up my thin air mattress and setting up my light sleeping bag, home for the night was ready. The adults were quite impressed, as were the piglets that came back and went to sleep right next to my tent. Oh well, on that night, I was to sleep with the pigs.

Next up, it was time for my ablution, which wasn't a spiritual cleanse, unless grime is considered to be evil. There was a lady washing clothes next to a concrete well and I asked her where I could bathe. Right there would be fine, she responded. It was just a few metres from the road but there was no one else around and the kids had dispersed, so I proceeded to strip down to my boxers. Growing up in India, I had seen people bathing in public while leaving their underwear on and found it strange, then and now, to take a bath with clothes on. When I saw that she wasn't the least bothered with my state of undress, I went ahead and stripped naked. I poured water over my body from the bucket she had hauled up for me. I had Holger to thank for showing me that it was perfectly normal, at least in rural parts of South America, to strip naked if it was to bathe yourself. This whole continent is quite conservative since Roman Catholicism is the major line of faith, but that is primarily in the urban areas. In rural areas, privacy is a luxury that not many can afford, and people go about their business without putting much thought into coming across as prudish. I soaped up my loofah, scrubbed off the grime and rinsed myself. Towelled and dressed, I dwelled on the fact that we are all naked under our clothes.

A young man, who was present when I had arrived, invited me for dinner and I gladly accepted. Accompanied by children from the village, we walked to his home. We arrived at a modest, two-room thatched house. It was dark without electricity and I was greeted warmly by the man's young wife, who offered me a bowl with boiled cassava and deep-fried pork that was kept in a glass jar on their table. Looking at their belongings inside, I could tell the family didn't own much and realized that even the fried pork must be a prized resource. Despite their insistence, I ate just two pieces because I didn't want to consume too much of their precious resource, filling myself up on cassava instead. It's like potato but stringy, with a strong earthy flavour. I was once again humbled by the display of how people with so little were willing to share so much of what they had. They didn't talk much so we ate in silence. After dinner, I played with the kids for a while outside, bid everyone goodnight and proceeded to walk back to my tent in the dark. I wondered if any wild animals would surprise me and thought about my machete. But it was clear from my journey so far that there were no wild animals anywhere near signs of civilization in Bolivia.

Back on the road the next morning, I had the last stretch of 175 km (108 miles) of the Bolivian Pampas to cover till Riberalta. The corrugations and deep sand had made my ride in the past few days monotonous and slow-paced. My mind would have been fatigued were it not for the audiobooks I was listening to on my iPod. I had amassed a large collection of non-fiction audiobooks, and during my short journeys around the US, I had discovered that listening to them on boring stretches helped me stay alert. Following a narrative kept my mind stimulated and alleviated the fatigue.

On this particular day, I was listening to the Dalai Lama's book, *The Universe in a Nutshell*. I was pleased to learn that the Dalai Lama was updating Buddhist philosophies with the discoveries of physics. Richard Gere narrated the book and talked about Life Conferences that the Dalai Lama organized in his Dharamshala home in India. He would invite eminent philosophers and qualified scientists to educate him and help integrate the teachings of science with the world of spirituality. In my previous years of travel, I had discovered that my soul was most content when surrounded by the grandeur of nature and playing in it, such as skiing in the Canadian Rockies, or riding through the Bolivian Pampas. I yearned for that vast expanse of space and pursued it.

A signboard, the first one I had seen since leaving La Paz, informed me that Riberalta was straight ahead. The landscape had slowly changed over the past few days from the brown swathes of the Pampas to the distinct red ground and green trees of the rainforest. The trees were taller and as I approached civilization, there was a smoky haze on the horizon from the burning of the forest. All too quickly, I was on a tarred road and surrounded by traffic of mototaxis and other vehicles.

Riberalta was the largest town in northern Bolivia, and I had arranged to meet a CouchSurfing host here. We had got in touch while I was in La Paz and he had warned me about the arduous journey of the Pampas. A black Troller jeep (from Brazil), with tinted windows and large, studded off-road tyres, pulled up to the café I was waiting at and Rodrigo came out with a large smile. He was happy to see me and greeted me with a warm bear hug, surprised that I had actually made the journey.

Surrounded by a high wall with barbed wire, his suburban house was in stark contrast to my roadside tent stays. Soon, we left for a scrumptious meal at what I thought was an upscale restaurant; depends on how impressed you are by steak on a stick. It was served with a yoghurt rice, similar to curd rice, which is a comfort food for this south Indian. I ate heartily and savoured my first proper meal in quite a few days. Sitting at the confluence of the Rio Beni and Rio Madre de Dios rivers, we chatted over dinner and watched the nightlife unfold in the remote city.

Rordrigo was from the second city of Bolivia, Santa Cruz, and was involved with the Brazil nut trade. He explained that it was a highly prized nut for its many applications, and strangely enough, could only be harvested from wild trees. The flowers would not pollinate in plantations, because if they did, vast swathes of the jungle would be cleared to make way for Brazil nut plantations. It seemed like nature had developed a self-preservation mechanism against exploitation. Rodrigo only flew in and out of Riberalta and thus, could not imagine what the road journey was like from La Paz.

That night, I had a few drinks with Rodrigo and his friends, who drank glasses of the intensely flavoured local liquor made from the caju (or cashew) fruit, just like the cashew feni liquor of Goa in India.

I spent the next morning working on sanDRina, since I had only a short day's ride to the Brazilian border. A nearby welder fixed up my left highway footpeg that had broken off in the fall past La Paz. There was no way to replace sanDRina's windshield here, and it didn't really matter since I was relishing the extra air-cooling in the warm weather. A crack had emerged in my pannier frame due to the vibrations of the corrugations, and this needed to be welded. Hence, I repositioned some heavy items from the side panniers to be placed behind me on the seat. With sanDRina riding with better balance, we quickly covered the 90 km (56 miles) on the wide, well-maintained dirt road to Guayaramerin.

The small border town sat on the banks of the wide Rio Mamoré, with Guajara-Mirim of Brazil on the opposite side. I had to cross the river in order to continue my journey, but there was no bridge or working vehicle ferry in sight. All the other border crossings so far in South America had been by land on the Pan-American Highway. There was no highway in sight at this remote outpost.

The town was abuzz with trading stores selling all sorts of items from toys to clothes to appliances. I had to process sanDRina's checkout from the Bolivian customs office, but it happened to be closed for a leisurely afternoon siesta. The immigration office was open, but I wanted to ensure sanDRina was checked out properly first. While lunching on rice and fried beef at a nearby shack, I learnt who all the stores were meant for. A boatload of passengers had just arrived from Brazil and they seemed more affluent than the Bolivians with their fashionable clothes. A buying frenzy ensued as they proceeded en masse to the shops along the road that lead from the passenger port. Within an hour, they were all back on the next boat, loaded with items purchased for a lower price, presumably imported from China. In exchange, I saw imported Brazilian cars and jeeps plying the few streets in town. I was compelled to figure out how to make the river crossing with sanDRina. There was a large vehicle ferry chained to the docks but I was informed that it sailed only once a week when there were enough cars to fill up the ferry. I didn't have that much time. Next to the ferry, I saw dugout canoes emptying their cargo, either from Brazil or further along the river. I approached the boatmen to enquire if they would take sanDRina and I across to Guajara-Mirim.

A rotund Bolivian boatman said it would cost 70 Bolivianos ($10) for the crossing. It seemed too much for me; I offered 40 Bolivianos. He joked openly to the other boatmen there about my low offer and while most of them ignored him, a young Brazilian boatman came up and said he would take me over for 40 Bolivianos, which produced a scoff from the others. My first impression of Brazil was a positive one. He had just unloaded his cargo and I realized that he would be heading back with an empty boat, which is probably why he accepted the low offer. I told him to wait till I could get processed out and he told me to hurry since the customs and immigration offices on the other side would be closing within the next few hours.

While waiting for the customs officer to return, another friendly-looking, lissom Brazilian man approached me and struck up a conversation. I had been listening to my Portuguese language tapes and started practising immediately with him, but we soon switched to Spanish. He was in the internet business from across the river and was in town to instal connections for a few businesses. He explained how the town we were in, even though it was in Bolivia, was connected to the outside world through Brazil rather than its own country. This was because of how far it was from La Paz and other major cities of Bolivia. He also told me there was a big street party happening in Guajara-Mirim that night and he offered to take me around. I had planned on leaving the city to camp out somewhere in the wild, but it seemed like a good offer. We made plans to meet at 5 p.m. at the customs office on the other side.

The customs officer, who was sporting a bulging belly under his uniform, stroked his few hairs as he looked over sanDRina's temporary import permit, issued three weeks prior at Lago Titicaca where I had crossed from Peru into Bolivia. He said it was a very rare occurrence for him to meet a foreigner who was travelling overland with a vehicle, especially a motorcycle. He invited me to join him for a coffee, which I would have gladly accepted but I was more eager to get across to Brazil and process myself in before the customs office closed there. With sanDRina's exit processed and an exit stamp in my passport, I proceeded down to the docks and motioned over to the young Brazilian boatman.

The boatman positioned his long and narrow canoe with the stern against the shallow bank, removing his long propeller shaft to make way for sanDRina to get on board. I remembered my short canoe trip in Panama before boarding the *Stahlratte*. We employed the same tactics here. The panniers were removed and two other boatmen helped us get sanDRina's front wheel onto the boat first. With me on board and steadying the front, the rear wheel was heaved on subsequently. Two planks were placed under the engine to steady sanDRina and I sat astride to further balance her. We pushed off as the outboard motor fired up. I saw that the propellers were spinning just below the surface of the water, which the boatman explained was because of the shallow waters. There were sandbars just below the water that shifted with the seasons, and inexperienced boatmen would get stuck if they couldn't read the surface waters properly.

The fifteen-minute crossing gave me time to absorb the experience. I was crossing from Bolivia to Brazil, across a tributary of the Amazon, in a remote place not frequented by outsiders. As we approached the other side, I saw large boathouses moored along the shore and imagined what a journey down the river would be like. With the canoe secure on the bank, we proceeded to offload sanDRina. The bank was steeper on this side, which made it a big challenge, so we asked a neighbouring boatman to help us. sanDRina's rear tyre was lifted over the brow and then, to my horror, she started to tip over and almost fell into the water. I called out for more assistance and a lady nearby jumped in to help. We got sanDRina's front tyre onshore, and with the kickstand down and steady, we all had a little laugh about the mishap. I thanked the lady and she went on her way, but the other boatman asked for 10 Bolivianos for his help and walked away with a snicker.

The bank was covered in loose sand, so I revved the engine and had to slip the clutch to climb up to the pavement. I hoped that the clutch plates didn't get damaged again. The formalities on the Brazilian side were more complicated than in Bolivia. I was waiting in the passenger terminal before being told to go to customs a few blocks away first. With sanDRina in the gated customs compound, I found the customs office a few blocks away. There, I was told I actually first had to process my immigration at the Federal Police office a few more blocks away. It reminded me of the runaround people speak of in India. Walking around a Brazilian river town before being properly processed into the country was a strange experience for someone with an Indian passport. I was already enjoying the relaxed feel of Brazil. I received a ninety-day stamp in my passport, and back at the customs office, I was sought out and greeted by the head officer who had heard a foreigner was there. Jovial and polite, he offered me some cake from an ongoing birthday party at the office, and helped to quickly process sanDRina's temporary import permit. We got into a conversation about India and he asked me a few questions about my home country in English. He was curious as to how so many people lived so densely together and did not fight all the time. I responded that there was indeed unrest in various parts of India from the past till the present, and found it interesting that he thought otherwise.

It was past 5 p.m. and I couldn't find the Brazilian man who had offered to show me around town. I rode out of the customs compound and it was dark by then. I tried to follow a policy of not entering a new country at dark, but somehow, it felt quite safe there. I was aware of the crime in large Brazilian cities, such as Rio de Janeiro and São Paulo, but way out there in the Amazon, it felt safe. The first small hotel I came upon was fully booked, and because I was tired from the long day, I asked if I could just camp somewhere in the area. They invited me to pitch my tent in their garden, and that too, for free. Each positive experience in Brazil was helping me build a very friendly impression of the country. They even let me shower and use their cold drinking water cooler at no cost. With my tent set up next to their large satellite TV dish, I walked into town to get some local currency from the ATM. The streets were paved and separated by flowers and trees. The step up in development from Bolivia was immediately evident. I treated myself to a chocolate ice cream bar and had a comfortable night's sleep in the garden.

In the morning, there was a bit of excitement about as I packed up my tent. I walked over to the where the proprietor's family stayed and saw a river turtle, about two feet in diameter, placed in a large bucket of water. A knife was being sharpened and the family invited me to stay for lunch. I was interested but had a long journey ahead. I stayed to watch, however, as their teenage son proceeded to take the turtle out of the water and slit its neck, followed by squeals from his sister. She couldn't bear the sight but admitted that she was looking forward to the feast. It might seem cruel to kill a large animal for food but the river most likely provided plenty of food for its inhabitants. No doubt, there must be some over-exploitation happening, but a sustainable harvest of animals was not at odds with nature's balance of one animal eating another.

Filling up my water bottles with cool water for the day, I offered to pay something for using their services but they refused to accept. Embracing the warm Brazilian welcome, I hit the sealed road north out of Guajara-Mirim. The development of the roads with proper tarmac and regularly spaced distance boards confirmed that Brazil is much more advanced than Bolivia. But I was looking forward to leaving these tarmac roads and highway signs behind. The jungle was pushed back a hundred metres or so from the main road and I wanted to get closer to it.

Highway BR-425 took me north along the eastern bank of Rio Mamoré, that merged into Rio Madeira at the confluence with Rio Madre de Dios. The route joined Highway BR-364 and took me into the large Amazonian city of Porto Velho. I had expected to spend the night there, but I reached much sooner than expected. It was only early in the afternoon. I had made excellent time on the smooth, paved highway and decided to push on. Crossing Rio Madeira, I joined the fabled BR-319 that I had read so much about. Thus far, it was a proper highway, but I knew that further north, it reduced down to a seldom-used mud track. It was known to carry travellers to the city of Manaus on the Amazon River, which then provided an exit to the Atlantic Ocean. Near the town of Humaita, I turned on to the road that I had come to ride, BR-230, the legendary TransAmazonica.

This road is mythical in the adventure riding community and as I later found out, even amongst the locals. It was built in the 1970s by the then military government of Brazil to bring development from the Atlantic coast deep into the vast Amazon region. The construction was treacherous as a rainforest is no easy place to clear a path and then keep it clear. The initial plan was to pave the whole stretch from west to east, but thankfully to adventurers, it is yet to be done. Being out of the way, in terms of typical overland travel routes, few travellers have ventured on the TransAmazonica, and those that have, regale stories of the utmost difficulty in traversing this route. It is an unpaved road through not just any rainforest, but the Amazon rainforest, which means the road surface is primarily clay. When clay gets wet, as it does in such a setting, it becomes slick as snot. The few photos I could find on the internet of this road all showed vehicles mired in mud, slipping on the clay and being broken down by the treacherous road conditions. I was terrified when I first saw those photos and decided not to make the journey. But then, I started reading about climate change and the important role the Amazon rainforest plays in our global climate. It is common knowledge that deforestation is rife in the Amazon and that made me angry. If I could document my journey across this precious treasure of the world, perhaps it would help raise awareness, and besides, the challenge of the impassable route was perversely alluring.

In my research, I'd realized that the local climate of the regions I would be travelling through would have a major impact on whether I would enjoy it or be miserable getting caught in the wrong season. I had created a heat map by plotting the areas I planned to travel through against the average rainfall expected there over the course of a year. The heat map came alive as my route moved south through Central America and around South America. Months with very little rainfall were marked in shades of orange to signify dry seasons, and months with very heavy rainfall were marked in blue, the darkest shade for the heaviest rainfall. Globs of blue appeared on my heat map. It was evident that Central America experiences its heaviest rainfall in the middle of the year, which coincides with their hurricane season. A little rainfall never hurt a motorcycle traveller, but the hurricanes of Central America were known to create landslides capable of destroying the few roads there. The heat map also revealed that it rains eleven months of the year in the Amazon, being the heaviest around the beginning of the year. Of course, it was quite intense during the other months as well since it was a rainforest. For me to safely cross the TransAmazonica, and that too, solo, I would have to be there in August. That was the only month with no predicted rainfall. With 27,546 km (17,120 miles) and ten countries under my belt, and after quite a few major mechanical breakdowns, I had somehow managed to stay on schedule and arrive here in the middle of August. I was quite proud of my planning and the discipline that had brought me to this special leg of the journey. After this, the climate wouldn't play a major part in my trip around South America, with the exception of my attempt to reach Ushuaia in the brief summer at the end of the year.

Back to the TransAmazonica. Just saying its name had got me hyped over the past few months. What was more worrying than the road conditions was whether the road was actually connected all the way through or not. I had read that the road was punctuated by numerous small, wooden bridges and due to the lack of traffic, they weren't really maintained. Photos of the TransAmazonica showed broken bridges and many in a decrepit state. I wondered what I would do if I journeyed halfway along the TransAmazonica and then came across a gap in the road that I couldn't cross. Simple, I would have to turn back and change my route. There was only one way to find out, and just like that, I was committed.

As I approached Humaita, the westernmost start of the TransAmazonica, I pulled into the large posto at the edge of town. It had been a long day from Guajara-Mirim, 540 km (336 miles) away. I appreciated the change in pace and road conditions. The smooth tarmac had made for quick work in covering large distances.

The posto was oddly modern with multiple fuel-filling islands and a large convenience store. Trucks with trailers filled the large, clay-covered parking lot, and I saw dormitories in the back along with showers and toilets that were free to use. There was also a free, chilled drinking water station. After filling up sanDRina's fuel tank, I was offered a shot of coffee from a thermos. What fantastic service. I asked the friendly, moustached attendant where I could camp safely for the night and he said right next to the main building was a good spot. I didn't want to be so visible to everyone and suggested camping behind the main building. But he warned me of the dangers of the dark and suggested I camp in a place where the attendants could keep an eye on me through the night for my safety.

Just as I finished a refreshingly cool shower and unpacked my stove to prepare dinner, I heard the distinctive rumble of large motorcycles. I saw that three BMW GS motorcycles had pulled in. I approached them in my shorts and t-shirt and thought they might think I was a local. I said hello and pointed to sanDRina and my tent and they recognized me. They had buzzed by me two days prior in Bolivia and were thrilled to meet another motorcycle traveller.

Franco, his father and his friend were from Cordoba in Argentina and were on a two-month trip heading north on BR-319 to Manaus, then into Venezuela, then down the Andes and back home. He thought I was crazy for attempting the TransAmazonica, which brought some laughs from all the riders. We were all crazies but we understood each other. They also thought I was crazy for camping at a petrol station and warned me of the danger. They zoomed off instead to find a hotel.

I had pitched my tent under the awning of the outdoor café and kept sanDRina close to the tent. To protect sanDRina from unsolicited attention, I always kept her covered at night with a thin bike cover I was carrying. My one-man tent didn't offer much space inside, so I kept my riding pants, boots and helmet on the seat, under the bike cover. I kept my riding jacket under my legs to provide some cushion since my compact air mattress only came down to my knees. This set up worked well in terms of stowing my gear for the night and providing me with good comfort in the cramped tent. By this point, I was sleeping with my right hand on the machete rolled up in my thermal top so that I wouldn't hurt myself at night. I tied a laptop security cable connecting the bike cover and the tent's rain cover, rationalizing that if someone tried to lift the cover, it would rattle the tent and I would spring out wielding the machete. I wondered if that plan would ever work, but thinking through the process had, at the very least, heightened my awareness.

I had an extra spring in my step the next morning as I was eager for the journey ahead. The pavement ended in Humaita and there was a ferry back across Rio Madeira, which was very wide; a kilometre or so to the opposite bank. The ferries were free as they were considered a part of the road. The simple, flat ferry was large enough to hold a few trucks, and I recognized one of them – a purple semi-truck and its occupants, a young couple. They had stopped next to me the previous day at the entrance to the state of Amazonas to take some fun photos with the highway sign. I approached them and we chatted a bit. I gathered that they were from the state of Santa Catarina in the southeast of Brazil, and they were on duty to pick up timber from the jungle town of Apui, 402 km (250 miles) along the TransAmazonica. When I told them I was planning on riding the whole length of the road, they said that the road became very rough after Apui. In spite of all the warnings coming from different sources, I was still undeterred. I was going to find out for myself.

On the other side, it started to feel more like I was actually on the TransAmazonica. The dusty, dried-up, clay road was wide with tall, thick vegetation bordering its length. I was ecstatic at finally riding in the Amazon rainforest, and best of all, it wasn't raining. The road was extremely bumpy with massive potholes covered over in talc-like dust that made for slow going. I had got ahead of the semi-truck, but kept taking breaks to stay hydrated and relish the sensation of being in the Amazon. I would quickly get going again, though when I saw the semi-truck catching up. It would come lumbering around a corner with an enormous wake of dust, obscuring the entire road behind it. There were a few oncoming vehicles, and whenever a truck approached, I had to take a quick look at the road ahead and then be prepared for the dust-out, similar to a white-out in snow. My visibility would be reduced to

just a couple of feet until I would emerge from the other end of the
dust cloud. I could have stopped, but then, it would take longer for
the dust cloud to pass me and I would also be running the risk of
being driven into from behind. It dawned on me that even in the
dry season, there were dangers of riding on the TransAmazonica,
but luckily, traffic was sparse.

I cherished the feeling of solitude and being so far away from
civilization. I felt happier whenever the jungle would be right
by the roadside, but for most of the day, it would be at least a
hundred metres or so away from the road. Farms lined the road
and barbed-wire fences demarcated property in this wild region.
I was pleasantly surprised to see that the Amazon was not a flat
plain, as one might imagine while seeing satellite pictures, but is
instead quite hilly. The deforestation would run up the sides of the
hills, creating bowls of bald land and leaving a tuft of jungle on top
of the hills. This 'islandization' of the jungle was not good for the
fauna still living there. Their habitat was vastly reduced and their
food resources were diminished. It's as if the ranchers felt like they
were doing at least some good in leaving the disconnected areas
untouched by their bulldozers. It saddened me to see such rife,
brutal deforestation.

At 180 km (112 miles) from Humaita, I came across the first
village, aptly called '180 km'. It consisted of a posto and a few
buildings that advertised rooms for the night, surrounded by
run-down, single-storey wooden houses. The posto attendant
confirmed that I could indeed camp there and I proceeded to pitch
my tent next to the truckers who were already parked up for the
night. Once again, there were free services to use. I showered,
washed my baselayers and prepared dinner in the small kitchenette.

For some reason, I thought lentils would be an appropriate
choice of food to carry in my rations. I had bought some in La Paz
along with quinoa, not realizing that both take an extremely long
time to cook without the use of a pressure cooker. Growing up in
India, lentils provided the proteins in my diet and I was keen to

carry some with me into the jungle. In my provisions, I had some pasta, rice, packets of tomato puree and two cans of mackerel. I figured I would use the fish when the camping was rough and if there was no time to prepare a meal. But now, with access to a kitchenette, I set about preparing my dal and quinoa dinner. The truckers gathered around to see what strange food I was eating. They, on the other hand, had filled their bellies with some grilled meat at a nearby shack.

My Spartan diet continued the next morning with oats for breakfast, along with a sesame seed drink that Alfonso had given me. He said it provided lots of strength and was a hearty morning food. sanDRina got filled up and the attendants even oiled her chain while I enjoyed a cup of coffee from their thermos. I had not enjoyed this level of service from such a remote petrol station before. My admiration for good-natured Brazilians was only increasing with each interaction.

Leaving the outpost, the road was in a better condition and I was making good time, feeling inspired by the enigmatic landscape. I would crest a hill and see green tops heading into the distance. There was a purple hue hugging the ground from the constant burning of the forest, as though it were a sadness that hung in the air. The putrid smell of freshly burned trees was a constant reminder of the negative side of global models of development that are currently in practice.

By the early afternoon, I had reached Apui, and the town felt quite modern with paved roads separated by flowered medians and rows of well-kept shops. There was even an internet café. I was in expedition mode and didn't care much for the internet then, but I managed to get a post out to the people following my journey, saying that all was well but that the real rough part was coming up. I wondered where the internet connection came from in this remote outpost. It was remarkable to see that no matter how far away from civilization one might be, Facebook and Gmail were just around the corner. The young men running the café expressed shock when I told them I was heading to São Luis on the Atlantic coast. They said the road was not connected due to broken bridges and that I wouldn't be able to do it. It was becoming increasingly apparent that this road was mythical even to the people living along it.

There was a crack in sanDRina's overloaded pannier frame again and I got it welded up at a Honda showroom; this had become a maintenance ritual in the past few days. Afterwards, I hit the trail in search of a place to camp for the night. The town was too civilized, even vanilla, for my taste, after so many months on the road, and I wanted to be away from it all. About 20 km (12 miles) from town, I came across a couple waving to me from the front porch of their 'fazenda' (farmhouse). I turned in and said in the best Portuguese that I could muster that I was travelling from India and heading across the TransAmazonica. I went on to ask if I could set up my tent near their property for the night. Jose, the ranch owner, said that I most definitely could and even permitted me to take a shower, which brought a smile to my face. I align myself with cultures that consider a shower at the end of the day to be a basic necessity, which I presume is the case in most places with hot weather. There was something about the openness among the Brazilians I had come across so far that I found very comforting.

Jose's ranch was quite expansive and I set up my tent next to a large shed filled with tractors and farm equipment. Nearby, however, stood a large corral in which a herd of horses milled about, for whom the rolling land had been cleared to make pasture. After a refreshing shower, Jose invited me to chat on the porch, as dinner was prepared. He was quite a learned man and asked me many questions about India that ranged from the current situation in Kashmir to our electoral process and why we don't eat beef. I assured him that I did eat beef and many people in India did too, but that many sections of our society are morally against it, which is why the general image of India in other countries is that we are all vegetarians. This was my fourth night in Brazil and I was having a conversation in Portuguese, and that too not on simple topics. The language tapes I had listened to were paying off. Of course, it wasn't the best Portuguese and I only managed to get the gist of the conversation, but that was enough to communicate. Considering how I had managed to get by in Spanish, I hoped the switch to Portuguese would be quick.

When I asked Jose where he was originally from, he said the south of Brazil. The government had incentivized people to migrate into the Amazon years ago, along the TransAmazonica, and had given them land on the cheap. Cleared rainforest land is not good for growing crops in the long term due to the high acidity of the soil, but it is good as pastureland and serves Brazil's beef industry well. I mentioned how I was studying for a master's degree and learning about how economic development was driving climate change around the world. He jumped in and said that the Brazilian government was being pressured by the global community to do something about the high rate of deforestation in the Amazon. As a result, they had recently changed several policies and were trying to convince people living in the Amazon not to cut down the rainforest and to let it grow back instead. For a businessman who had invested capital in equipment and the land, I could see how frustrating this pivot in policy was for him. I knew that people like Jose were not to solely blame for deforestation. The burden lies more on our markets and consumers who demand cheap products immediately. But that is a complicated argument where many factors must be taken into account before we can determine what the right thing to do is. And with that, the right thing to do was eat.

There was a large spread of food at the dining table, set in an open corridor between the main house and the kitchen. Jose's titillating young partner, dressed in short shorts and a revealing top, invited me to sit in the middle of the table so I could be close to all the food. I smiled and helped myself to some rice, grilled vegetables, beef, salad and farina, which is made from tapioca powder and adds a crunch to the food – it is considered a staple table condiment in Brazil. With a belly full of scrumptious food, I slipped off to sleep against the quiet neighing of the horses.

Jose had warned me that a few bridges up ahead were not in the best condition and that trucks were advised to not make the journey, but that I should be fine on a motorcycle. sanDRina was much heavier than most of the motorcycles I had seen in the towns so far, but that wasn't going to stop me. A few kilometres from his ranch, I came across the largest wooden bridge I had seen on the TransAmazonica thus far. It spanned 100 m (330 ft) across a small river. It was constructed with planks going across the bridge with two sets of planks going along the bridge for reinforcement, which is what the tyre tracks of a truck would ride on. The challenge on a motorcycle was picking which set of planks to cross on. It's not a good idea to ride in the middle since that is the weak point of the bridge. This particular bridge was in pretty good shape with only a few planks missing, but I had already come across a few that I crossed in a hurry before my fear of falling through took over.

With the rolling land, there was an endless number of hills to crest and trough. But the challenge with the troughs was that most of them had a small stream running through them, necessitating a wooden bridge. The tyres of larger vehicles had dug out the mud at the start and end of the wooden bridge, requiring me to slow down almost to a stop to get over the bump before crossing over. These features of the wooden bridges broke my pace but allowed me to slow down and choose which set of planks to ride across on. Some would have nails erupting from the planks, which I would only see with a metre or so to go, forcing me to navigate quickly around without slipping off the planks. Once on the other side, I would charge up the steep hill, riding the large roar from sanDRina's engine.

The riding was tremendous and I was standing on sanDRina's footpegs for long stretches and dancing with her along the bumps and curves of the TransAmazonica. I smiled the most when the forest cover was dense and right up to the roadside, and felt heavy and sad when the jungle was pushed back by clearing, which was unfortunately more common.

At the small village of Sucunduri, I saw petrol for sale in used two-litre Coca-Cola bottles and bought a few to top up sanDRina. I had enough fuel to reach the next town, but I had learned that it was better to be safe than sorry with fuel out there. Just past the village was a river crossing, but the ferry was on the other side. I had not passed a single vehicle all day and hoped the ferry wouldn't wait for enough vehicles before making the crossing. I shouted and waved at the boatman and finally roused him out of his shed. He got into the small boat next to the large vehicle ferry and fired up his outboard motor that pushed the ferry across the river. I quickly embarked and was happily surprised when he turned his boat around to push the ferry back the other way at once. The whole ferry was just for sanDRina and me.

I had seen recently-burnt forest land all along the ride so far, but an hour later, I came across my first actively-burning forest fire. The land clearing was underway. I could see the destruction already caused by the flames near the road and they were beginning to lap up against another row of tall trees. I had to stop. It was too disheartening. I looked at a nearby stream in hopes of dousing out the fire but I knew that was futile. This was a massive fire, most likely deliberately started to clear forest land. The tree crowns were over 60 m (197 ft) above the ground and the unwieldy fire was rapidly lapping at them. I felt partly responsible for this. I was part of the civilized world that demanded products at the lowest price possible. That simple involvement leads to virgin rainforest being burnt down. I thought about the vast number of plant and animal species being destroyed, many of which might have still been unknown to humans. How foolish we are to not realize that the economic benefits from a forest are much higher if it is left intact as opposed to being razed to the ground for other purposes. Forests clean the air, help regulate the climate, harbour vast numbers of plants and animals that might hold the key to solving various diseases and other problems we face, yet the incentive to burn them down is greater. Future generations will see our current civilization as barbaric, similar to how we see our ancestors. In terms of distance, I was so far removed from the civilization that was in demand for that land, but standing next to this fire, I felt its tendrils reaching out and consuming the rainforest. Just around the corner, I saw a herd of cattle in the middle of the rainforest. It was more than evident what the land was being cleared for.

Riding along the TransAmazonica reveals the true brutality of deforestation. Along many stretches of the road, untouched rainforest stood on one side with newly burnt and cleared land on the other. This contrast, separated by the man-made road, enraged me. I decided then that after my journey, I would try and make a difference in bettering the environment, probably not for our generation – for that, we are already too late – but for future generations. There are many people who understand the value in preserving the land, and I was hopeful that once enough of us come to the same realization, we can make a change for the better.

I had to remember to stay sharp while brooding over these thoughts, as the TransAmazonica along this stretch was gnarly at times. The road would go straight up and straight down a hillside, instead of zigzagging its way along the contours. I had asked Jose about this and he said that the heavy rains during most of the year caused the water running down the road to create ruts and deep channels across the zigzagging road, making for an even more difficult crossing. The roads would run along the same path the water would take, and hence, the ruts were cut along the road. This was still challenging because I had to ride on the plateaus of these steep ruts while charging up or down the hillsides, but they did not hinder my progress. Instead, they made the ride more fun as my off-roading skills were improving dramatically and I was starting to enjoy the feeling of dancing with sanDRina when the road surface was loose or bumpy.

It was late in the afternoon and I crested one last hill. It had been a long 250 km (155 miles) from Jose's fazenda. The jungle cleared and I saw a palm tree cluster ahead that looked out of place amidst the jungle trees. I pulled into the long driveway of a fazenda amongst the palm trees and parked sanDRina under one of the trees near what looked like the main house, its walls made of white plaster with large glass windows. Only the lights in a nearby house were on, which I assumed was the servant's quarters since it was made of wooden planks. The latest Brazilian funk was playing on a radio and there was a harsh glow from the incandescent bulb out front.

I called out for someone but no one came. After a few minutes, I went around the back and saw that the back door was also open but no one was home. I gathered that whoever was living there had just stepped out briefly and would be back soon. I had not yet been invited to stay, so I politely sat on the porch of the main house with most of my motorcycle gear still on. After a day of being exposed to the dust of the TransAmazonica, my sweat-wicking baselayers were horrid and I needed to take a bath. I waited.

The sun was starting to set and it had been over an hour with no sign of the owners returning. The music and lights indicated that they would be back at any moment. But I was getting restless. I want to strip off my sweaty gear and get clean for the evening. I was smiling at the thought of taking a bath under the garden tap a few metres from the house. Why was I hesitating? I had taken enough baths in public places. Even though this was someone's private home, I gave in.

I took out my loofah and bath gel from my toiletry kit in the right pannier. I stripped and walked over to the tap just in my boxers. I looked out to the street and saw some vehicle lights going by as dusk had set in and wondered how I would know if the owners were returning. Not caring about it at that moment, I stepped out of my boxers and crouched under the tap. It was revitalizing. The cool water was my reward for slogging it out through the sand and heat of the TransAmazonica. I stood up and started soaping myself with the loofah, but just as I finished lathering up my whole body, a headlight turned into the driveway and towards the house.

Still covered in soap, I hastily yanked up my boxers as a young couple on a small motorcycle pulled up. I waved to them as they stopped, and with a sheepish smile, explained that I was a traveller and hoping to stay for the night. Explaining how the dirty road had pushed me into taking desperate measures, I apologized for my actions. They didn't even blink an eyelid. I was laughing inside at the situation. The young man told me that I was welcome to stay the night and to join them for dinner after I had finished my bath. With that, they rode over to the second house from where the music was coming.

I felt silly for not having waited for just a few more minutes, but was also relieved that they didn't care about seeing a nearly naked stranger covered in soap in their garden. Maybe Brazilians have an understanding of how important a bath is at the end of the day since it is always so humid and hot. This was my kind of place. I enjoyed getting dirty during the day, but it was satisfying to be clean by the end of it. They seemed to understand that in Brazil. In most parts of India, as soon as one comes home, they take a bath either for physical cleansing or spiritual ablutions. More than anything else, it helps the mind separate two different aspects of the day. The moment after a bath is characterized by a feeling of being fresh and resetting the body.

I stepped out of my now soaked boxers and got back under the tap and finished off. It wasn't the most comfortable shower and I had to be aware not to knock my head against the low tap. I dressed in my usual cargo pants and t-shirt and walked into their house. They served me 'arroz com fejao' (rice with Brazilian black beans) and when they didn't join me for dinner but served me instead, I realized that they were the house help. The young man explained that the owner was in Itaituba, a major town further ahead, and only came out there occasionally. I presumed that this was a second house in the jungle for them. The young couple probably catered to other random visitors as theirs was the first house after a long stretch across the TransAmazonica. After dinner, I excused myself for the night and went to bed in my tent with a smile.

The next morning, I turned off the main road to head to the small town of Jacareacanga to fuel up. The attendant told me it was 400 km (249 miles) to the next petrol station in Itaituba and that on my large motorcycle, I would reach there in about six hours. The local minibus drivers plying the route between the towns there drove with excessive speed as if they were in a hare race, and I figured that it was their standard for how anyone should drive. I was on a more leisurely track. I was planning to reach Itaituba in two days. There wasn't much to the town besides the posto and a few buildings on the banks of Rio Tapajos, a major tributary flowing north to the Amazon River. I was far removed from the current popular trends, lost in my own world out in the Amazon, but Justin Beiber's latest hit song was still blasting from a radio at a nearby shack. In reality, there was no escape from our globalized civilization. It is all pervasive, for good or worse.

Backtracking to the main route and heading north, I noticed on my GPS that the route was now following Rio Tapajos. I didn't really need a GPS for directions as there was only one road. It was more useful for marking waypoints for other travellers and to see the average speed I was managing to help determine where I would reach by the end of the day.

This section of the route had the steepest hills with the expected bridge at every trough. The road got narrower and it felt satisfying to be riding through a proper jungle with trees leaning overhead. Straight sections of the road were a rare sight as the road curved left and right and up and down. I stopped at many places to admire the grandness of the Amazon and the super tall trees that were next to the road. Some of them had to be over 75 m (246 ft) tall, of which only a few metres must have grown in my lifetime.

About halfway to Itaituba, with the sun below the tree crowns, I came across a lone, wooden hut in a clearing where a man was sipping on a cup with a metal straw. Once again, my evening routine played out. I pulled up and asked him if I could stay for the night and he welcomed me. His name was Sebastian. He was also from the south of Brazil, which explained the 'yerba maté' gourd and metal straw in his hand. It's a tea that's sipped through a metal straw in Argentina, Uruguay, Paraguay and also southern Brazil. After offering me a freshly-made maté, we sat at his outdoor table and he recanted how he too had moved out there with government incentives to cultivate the land. I revealed my story and he found it interesting that an engineer would give it all up to travel, considering engineers to be the more sane members of society.

I asked Sebastian if I could take a bath and he told me to get my bathing accessories and follow him. We walked for about fifteen minutes into the jungle, past his farm and a grove of fruit trees that he was cultivating. Soon after, we came across a small clearing where a stream of cool, crystal-clear water was collecting in a pool. Sebastian told me to go ahead with my bath and he proceeded to sit down at the bank of the stream. He was watching me. I proceeded to strip and went about my bath. The fact that I was naked in front of another man whom I had just met deep in the Amazon was not something to ignore. Once again, when beyond the niceties of Western culture, clothing really did not matter. Washing in the thick of the jungle surrounded by bird calls was undeniably liberating. We walked back to his little hut as I wondered why he had sat there looking at me while I bathed. But I knew that Brazil was more open than most cultures and nudity was really nothing special.

His hut was stocked with tinned food from Itaituba and we had a simple meal of rice with beans and meat. When it came to sleep, he offered me a spare hammock, but I would not have been comfortable sleeping like that and set up my air mattress and sleeping bag on the raised wooden floor of the hut. He warned me of bugs that could crawl over me, which was why he slept in a hammock, so I put a t-shirt over my face and fell asleep.

In the morning, the trees just a few metres behind his house were engulfed in a thick jungle fog. It felt eerie, but the fog soon burnt off as the sun started to rise. Just north of Sebastian's place, I entered the official Parque Nacional da Amazonia, the only protected area in this whole massive jungle, but that too appeared to be just a park on paper with no real fences. The only difference about riding through the actual park was that I didn't see any burning tress, so perhaps there was some kind of enforcement there after all.

At times, the road would follow close enough to Rio Tapajos that I could take in the sight of the large, snaking Amazonian river. Near Itaituba, the river became so large that it resembled a lake. I wondered what the Amazon River, much further north than where I was, would look like in places where it was said to be kilometres wide. Reaching Itaituba, I felt a sense of triumph. I had just traversed one of the most remote roads in the world and came out unscathed. From here on east, the TransAmazonica was more developed and busy but still a challenge at times, as it was unpaved and under construction in many places. It was another 1,000 km (621 mi) to Maraba, where the dirt road ended and from where I turned north for São Luis.

Just 135 km (84 miles) from São Luis, I had a tyre puncture. It was, of course, a nail, not a thorn or splinter. Its uninvited intrusion was as good as any reminder of my impending return to civilization. I set about fixing it on the roadside, but the puncture had damaged the heavy-duty tyre tube in such a manner that I couldn't fix it. Like an angel appearing in the time of need, a lady riding a Honda Bros motorcycle, a very popular bike in Brazil, stopped by. After I explained my situation to her, she offered to take my tube to the nearest 'borracharia' (tyre repair shop) to get it hot-vulcanized, a method of tyre tube repair that I could not do with my portable tools. She was back in fifteen minutes and did not accept any money for the repair job. I thanked her and she zoomed off. The contrast and seemingly conjoined nature of fortune and misfortune in the Amazon stays with me to this day. So it was that after a minor delay, I rolled into the seaside city of São Luis and rejoiced in the accomplishment of having crossed the entire immense TransAmazonica Highway.

At my destination, I was to see an old childhood friend from my schooling days in south India. And so when I knocked on the door of his fourth-floor apartment, Kavin greeted me with an enormous bear hug. We had not seen each other in many years and he was currently spending a year in São Luis doing research for a PhD in history. I sat myself down with a heavy sigh in the chair in his small apartment and just smiled in silence. I had been on the road for about six months now and had not interacted with anyone who knew my past. I had to introduce myself to everyone I came across and that became my routine. But sitting there in front of Kavin, it was a relief to be known and just be me. This was someone who knew where I came from, who knew my parents and my home town. He was a connection to my past. It had been only six months of separation from the life I knew but it felt like an eternity. From La Paz to São Luis, the 5,000 km (3,107 miles) journey was an epic ride and it was time to hang up my helmet for a well-deserved break.

7

CHASING CHE

AFTER TWO MONTHS of travelling through the more developed parts of Brazil and northern Argentina, I was ready to head back to more remote places. I checked out of Argentina at the small border post of Aguas Blancas and across the bridge over Rio Bermejo, I realized that I might have been the first Indian to enter Bolivia through that border. The rotund, balding immigration officer in the border office leafed slowly and deliberately through the regulatory tome he had plucked from the sagging shelves behind his desk, examining the pages for rules on allowing Indians to enter. I assured him that India and Bolivia had excellent relations and jabbed at my new Bolivian visa that I had acquired only a few weeks before in Buenos Aires.

I was back in Bolivia to see parts of this geologic marvel of a country that I had missed on my first sweep south five months ago. I was on a tight schedule then, after my clutch incident, but I finally had enough time to savour the rest of the country. I was relieved to be back in a lesser-developed area after the expenses from the past two months; my meagre budget would go further here. The Andean nation of Bolivia is not as poor as much of the international media coverage would have one believe, but neither is it as rich as some of its neighbours. It simply keeps chugging along to its own beat and I craved more time there.

With a stamp gracelessly inked in my passport, I headed to the southeastern city of Santa Cruz, where I was greeted by the resplendent, white colonial buildings of the central plaza, flanking rows of palm trees. This low-lying part of Bolivia had been in the news lately after discoveries of large natural gas reserves were made nearby, and this, along with other factors, was fuelling local demands for autonomy. In turn, it was being stoked by the more right-leaning local political sentiments that were in contrast with the current president Evo Morales's government in La Paz and the Andean side of Bolivia.

Following an introduction from Alfonso in La Paz, I met with Oscar and his son Miguel. Gearheads of the 4x4 kind, they rallied with a Land Rover and were active in the local off-road community. They were also kind enough to put me up for a few days, during which I basked in the splendour of Santa Cruz and prepared sanDRina for the rough challenge ahead. New tyres were mounted, a new chain attached and the boys helped me make a windshield to replace the one that I had broken on that foggy road out of La Paz a few months prior. It felt fitting to have this done in Bolivia. Using a flame torch to heat up and shape the thick Lexan plastic sheet, we soon had a windshield just like the one I had made back in Chicago. Thus, with sanDRina prepped and primed and my own belly replenished with meat and beer, the Andes beckoned once more.

I bid farewell to the boys and left Santa Cruz behind in the eastern flank of the Andes and headed for the lush foothills. With the mountainous terrain quickly building, the twisting road to the small town of Vallegrande was a joy to ride as it had been newly paved, but the boys had warned me of the dirt roads ahead at higher altitudes. There were dark, ominous rain clouds looming in the distance and it seemed as though the roads there were in the process of being churned to mud.

Vallegrande is an inconspicuous town, famed only for one event – the death of Che Guevara. Parking up for the night at a small hotel in the central plaza, I joined a Colombian couple for a local excursion marking the events around Che's death. Our guide, Mauricio, from the 'museo municipal' (local museum) took us first to the town hospital, Nuestra Señora de Malta, where Che's corpse was brought to display to the world. A giant mural with the face and beard that grace millions of t-shirts around the world greeted us. For me, the visit was something of a pilgrimage. By no means a revolutionary, I was instead inspired by Che's own epic motorcycle journey around Latin America.

Che, an Argentine doctor, felt that revolution was the only answer to the poverty he witnessed in his travels around the continent. One of his journeys was on an old Norton 500 motorcycle in 1951, a story that was captured ever so exquisitely in the book and movie *The Motorcycle Diaries*. My decision to ride a motorcycle through South America inevitably led non-motorcyclists to ask whether I had seen the movie. As most other motorcyclists on a long trip, I had seen it probably a hundred times by then. The story was captivating and its musical score gave way to vivid imagery of the grandness of travelling in far-off lands atop a motorcycle. It had played a significant role in getting me to start my own journey and my experiences thus far, in the first few months, were constantly reassuring me of my decision. But back to Che's story.

After assisting and becoming a central force in the Cuban revolution, Che sought to assist similar causes around the world. But much to his vexation, he did not find willing revolutionaries. After an unsuccessful attempt to assist the revolution in the Congo during the late 70s, he felt Bolivia was ripe to ignite the uprising that had yet to happen around Latin America. He chose the remote mountainous area near the town of Camiri in southeast Bolivia to train a guerrilla force to fight the Bolivian Army. Many factors worked against him – he underestimated the revolutionary desire of the local people, who were poor but not particularly discontent, and the strength of the Bolivian Army turned out to be greater than expected as the CIA was assisting them. After being wounded in battle and encircled in a canyon, Che surrendered, only to be executed as ordered by the Bolivian president who feared a lengthy trial. That all happened in La Higuera, a small village about 125 km (78 miles) away, but the body was flown to Vallegrande where the world's press was invited to witness the death of Che.

Our guide took us to the small open cement shed in which Che's body was displayed. Every inch of the three walls was inscribed with messages of solidarity by countless visitors. It was undeniably a hallowed place for anyone with a rebellious tinge to them, and others on our tour entered in near reverential silence. I had seen photos of this little building in documentaries and magazines and felt a connection with it myself as I entered. His body had been placed across two shallow laundry basins in the centre, after which photos were taken to prove to the world that he had indeed been killed. They showed him off like a wild animal that had just been slaughtered. Their conduct backfired spectacularly. Che instantly became a martyr for revolutionary causes around the world and generations of rebels. He became a symbol of counterculture across time and societies. Albeit with some irony, his image has become a popular brand in the past few decades, emblazoned on t-shirts, flags and caps for many who didnt even know anything about Che, except that he had fought the system. Fans and followers have visited this little laundry house over four decades since his death to communicate their support and worship. His famous slogan, 'hasta la victoria siempre' (until victory, always) was spray-painted in large red letters across the back wall.

In exploring Bolivia during my time there, this slogan kept coming up again and again. This obviously didn't take shape in the violent overthrow of the system that Che had denounced but in the socialist and progressive policies that the government has embraced in minority rights, healthcare, climate change and perspectives on the structure of the global economy. Bolivia remains a small player in the global scheme of things, but this has also allowed it to experiment with less-frequented policies. Time will tell, but it might very well pay off for this Andean nation.

Our next stop on the tour was a cemetery for the other guerrillas that fought and died alongside Che. I lingered around a small stone slab memorial to Tania, an ex-Stasi (East German secret service) agent who was placed in Bolivia to assist Che. She was also purported to have worked for the KGB and inadvertently led the Bolivian authorities to Che's whereabouts. Che was instrumental in developing the Soviet-Cuban relationship, and with the US embargoes in place, Soviet assistance was an economic lifeline to Cuba. Che was also behind the plan that brought the Soviet nuclear missiles onto Cuban soil, which almost led to a nuclear war in 1962. He saw the backing down of the USSR in that situation as a betrayal to the Cuban cause, and thereafter, dismissed the Soviet Union as much as he did the US. He was also getting friendlier with Chinese communism, much to the irritation of Castro and the USSR. All these events suggest that perhaps the Soviet Union also wanted him brought down.

From the shed, we were taken to the newly constructed Mausoleo del Che. After showing off Che's corpse to the world, the Bolivian government added to the story by hiding his body and not telling anyone where it was. They feared that his grave would become a pilgrimage site, which is exactly what happened, but about thirty years later. In 1995, a retired general revealed that the bodies were hastily buried near the airstrip in Vallegrande and a search was carried out for the corpses. They were found two years later and the remains were taken to Cuba to be given proper honours. This mausoleum was built on top of the graves.

The return of Che's body to Cuba was a boon to Fidel Castro, who, at the time, needed something to keep up the revolutionary spirit on home turf. Cuba had benefited enormously from Guevara's influence. Castro admired Che's intellect as he made literacy a top priority, due to which the country greatly benefits to this day, but they also disagreed on many things during their partnership, including Che's dogmatism and strict ideological adherence.

In the centre of the mausoleum was an open pit with seven stone slabs in the earth, representing the bodies that were discovered there, thirty years after their hasty disposal. I posed for a solemn photo with the slab that read, 'Ernesto Guevara de la Serna, Che, Argentino, Cubano, 09-10-67'. Che put the word of revolutionaries into action and met his expected fate, although much sooner than anyone thought. His influence is evident to this day because he was not simply a thug touting Marxist principles but in fact a profound intellectual who was fighting for all humans to have control over what they were entitled to. Instead of aimlessly raising questions regarding the purpose of life, he went and stood up for what he felt was in everybody's best interests. History will, no doubt, look at such figures and their ideals as being ahead of their time, but actually, the progressive thinkers of every era are the ones who create the stories that are later told in history.

Adorning the walls of the mausoleum were various photographs depicting the lighter side of Che's life. I smiled when I saw one of him and Granado, his travel partner on the motorcycle trip, on the raft that was made by lepers in Peru. It was named the Mambo-Tango since Che wasn't a good dancer and couldn't discern between the sounds of tango and mambo.

At the end of the tour, Mauricio, in a spontaneous act I had come to love and expect in South America, invited us to a street party in the evening. That night, we joined the throngs of Vallegrande on the streets, as musicians strummed out Andino wino music that didn't sound very pleasant to my ears with its characteristic croaking and nasaly tone. Evident from the large bulges on either side of the musicians' mouths, I could tell they were chewing on huge wads of coca leaves, keeping them buzzed through their gig. I made a note to purchase a large bag for the arduous journey ahead. Surrounded by the vibrant crowds awash with the beat of the music, we kept the chilly mountain night air away with large swigs of the staple drink of the local people, chicha cochabambina, a fermented corn beverage that tasted like diluted beer.

From Vallegrande, there are self-guided tours covering Che's last days in the surrounding hills. Even if it wasn't for his story, the route provided a terrific ride with twisty tracks going up and over the ridges, exposing expansive panoramas. Luckily, the rains from the previous day hadn't made the dirt roads impassable. Passing the sign 'Ruta del Che', I knew I was on the right track. I crossed one last summit and the temperatures rose as I dropped in elevation to La Higuera, the small, remote village that played witness to the death of Che Guevara. A large bust stands outside the village schoolhouse where the captured Che was shot and killed. An inscription under the bust reads, 'Tu ejemplo alumbra un nuevo amanecer'. It translates to, 'Your example lights the way to a new dawn'. Che's vision of the future has yet to play out but his legend will live on for centuries to come. And to illustrate how commercial his image has become, there was a hotel in his name, serving tea and coffee right next to the larger-than-life statue of him. Paying my last respects, I hit the trail and headed for the main attraction of Bolivia.

A few days and a thousand kilometres later, as I was cresting a hill, I was brought to an abrupt halt by the landscape before me, a kaleidoscope of colours. There were distinct bands of red, yellow, maroon and grey rocks across the barren land that contrasted against a magnificent blue sky flecked with bright, white clouds. The altitude was extreme at 4,300 m (14,108 ft). The road from Atocha, a small hamlet in a valley along the dry riverbed I was following, was akin to riding through an art gallery of rocks. There were lone pillars of stone, dramatic colour changes in the exposed sediments, and canyons of dry rocks that towered over me. This was the road to Uyuni and the start of the Salar de Uyuni.

After being forced to abandon it the first time, I was getting a second chance to ride the Salar ahead. I had seen photos from other travellers of this psychedelic landscape north of Atocha, none of which compared to actually witnessing it in person. The vastness of the earth and the absence of civilization, bar the dirt road that snaked apologetically through the landscape, was striking. A deep calm and feeling of contentment washed through me as I sat atop sanDRina and soaked in the stunning vista. I was stocked up on food, water and petrol, and was planning to be away from it all for the next few days. From Uyuni, a scrappy frontier town existing on the southeastern edge of the Salar, I turned left onto the largest salt pan in the world.

The blinding white salt surface of the Salar de Uyuni raced ahead of me all the way to the horizon, discernible only by the abrupt interruption of the crystal blue sky. I was overjoyed. I had read and dreamed about this place for years. The numbers were mind-boggling. This is a 10,582 sq km (4,086 sq mile), flat, dry salt lake at 3,656 m (11,955 ft) that doesn't vary by more than a metre across its whole surface. Due to its near-uniform geological flatness and high reflectivity (being white), the Salar has been used for many decades to calibrate the altimeters of earth-observing satellites. It's also an easy place to get lost.

Getting started on the route into the Salar was tricky because of the innumerable tracks heading in various directions from the main road. After some trial and error, I found the right one leading me deeper into the middle of the Salar. With the obvious absence of landmarks, I was depending solely on my GPS and had no backup. I had to move a certain distance to calculate if I was heading in the right direction on the GPS. In this vast uniform landscape, I could ride in whichever direction I wanted, but with the rainy season already underway, I was warned by other travellers to stay on the established hardened tracks. This was not the kind of landscape in which I wanted to get stranded. As if to prove my point, I passed a sinkhole in the salt crust, an 'Ojo de la Sal' or 'Eye of the Salt'. This was not solid ground that I was riding on. The crust of the Salar varies wildly in thickness from about a few centimetres to a few metres, covering a lake of brine about 20 m (66 ft) deep. I had no intention of dying pickled.

The brine is a solution containing large amounts of different salts ranging from sodium, potassium, lithium and magnesium. Of those, lithium has the most economic value. Bolivia harbours about 50 per cent of the known reserves on this planet and most of those are under the Salar de Uyuni. This rare substance is already in very high demand because lithium batteries power almost all electronic devices today. The demand for lithium is set to skyrocket with the increase in electric vehicles, which is why foreign companies are already trying to establish means by which they can go about extracting it. However, Bolivia's leftist leader, Evo Morales, is taking a cautionary approach to ensure that the local population and Bolivia itself benefits directly from these new developments.

Riding on the Salar was the strangest experience I'd had on a motorcycle. The surface was rock hard, similar to concrete but covered in a crusty layer of salt. On well-used paths across the Salar, the loose granules were pushed aside making for a high-speed, smooth riding surface, but when I veered off the path, the loose salt was gravelly and kicked up a salt storm in my wake. I was the only one on the Salar at the time and thus, it was very still all around; no smell, no sound. If other vehicles were around, they would've roughed up the surface, kicking up a salty dust. Even though I had on dark sunglasses under my tinted helmet visor to combat the blinding white surface, my pupils were still constricted.

A truly special place on our planet, I hope it doesn't change much when lithium mining picks up and the brine is drained, although it would be highly unlikely for that to happen. The flatness has been attributed to its annual flooding, which levels out any changes in the malleable topography. During the rainy season, Lake Titicaca to the north overflows into Lake Poopó, which overflows into the salars of Coipasa and Uyuni when it is full. It's not advisable to ride a motorcycle through a salt lake because of all the rust it could lead to, but the experience of riding over the giant mirrored surface is said to be bewildering.

I was happy to be there when the Salar was still dry, enjoying the results of the flooding. The annual flooding leaves behind pentagonal and hexagonal patterns in the rough crust, an odd feature of shallow flooding found the world over. With these patterns buzzing underneath me, it was undeniably the most stunning and hypnotic road I had ever been on.

With no visual cues on the horizon, sanDRina and I accelerated to 100 kph (62 mph). I stood up on the footpegs with my face in the wind and closed my eyes. With the exception of sanDRina's steady, powerful, single-piston pulse, I could hear nothing but the wind. I wanted to see how long I could ride with my eyes closed. Thirty seconds, sixty seconds, two minutes! When I opened them again to the blinding white landscape, nothing had changed. The world was flat, the sky was blue and standing aloft, I was flying on this plain alone. What a stupefying experience.

Two hours later, a blip finally appeared on the horizon. It was my destination for the night. Although I drove doggedly toward Isla Incahuasi, the island of rock stubbornly refused to grow until I was almost atop it, due to the lack of reference points in my horizon. This island in a sea of salt is actually the tip of an old volcano, which was engulfed when the Salar formed about 12,000 years ago. The whole area is actually a part of the Altiplano, the low-relief, high-altitude plateau sandwiched between the two primary ridges of the Andes – the Cordillera Occidental to the west and the Cordillera Oriental to the east, making it the widest part of the Andes mountain range.

Theories suggest that when the Andes rose (due to tectonic deformation), prior weaknesses in the earth's crust contributed largely to the formation of the Altiplano. It was in this original state that a massive contiguous lake called Ballivián formed. In slowly drying up, it left behind Lake Titicaca in the north, Lake Poopó further south near Oruro and the two salt lakes of Coipasa and Uyuni. Salt lakes form in these environments because the rainwater does not escape to the sea. This was an endorheic zone where minerals washed down from the mountains, collected as salt in these lakes, and their concentrations slowly built up over the ages into the salars of today. Salar de Coipasa is a smaller salt lake to the north of Salar de Uyuni.

I reached Isla Incahuasi and as the sun began to fade, I set about taking some fun photographs, playing with perspective and the lack of visual references. Aligning sanDRina closer to the camera, I set the self-timer on and ran behind her so as to appear like a small figure standing on her seat. It took a few tries to get it right, but the final photo made sprinting across the salt flats in the dying heat of the day worth it. For another, I positioned sanDRina much further behind me as I lay on my stomach with my lips puckered, making it appear as though I was kissing a toy motorcycle. Say what you will about how travelling alone for too long can change you; I was having fun in nature's playground.

This old volcano, being at the centre of the Salar, was the prime destination for visitors and it was dotted with Land Cruisers and other tourists taking similar photos. To my disappointment, it resembled a parking lot when I first got there, with a vast number of jeeps serving the tourist trade, but as the sun dipped, the area began to empty. The island itself was a protected area and stepping foot on it cost B15 ($2). This allowed me to hike to the top for a good view and gave me access to bathrooms and a freshwater supply. There were also a few hotel rooms, but I was camping out.

Adjacent to stone picnic benches on the edge of the island, I was setting up my tent when a Japanese bicycle traveller stopped by. Yoshi was cycling around the world and was heading east, having just come down from Vancouver. It was reassuring to meet someone crazier than me. We decided to join camps for the night and proceeded to hike to the top of the island; its unique setting growing with every step. We passed fossilized corrals and giant cacti, some of which were quite large with sprouting flowers. This corral is a Pleistocene-era relic from the days when the volcano was engulfed by ancient lakes. From the top, we could see the growing shadow of the island towards the east, where the full moon was rising over the track from Uyuni. Towards the north, we saw the tracks heading to Jirere, the town I had sought to reach on my first attempt to ride the Salar, as well as a track to the active Volcan Tunupa, a prominent feature on the horizon. The volcano has importance in local Aymara legends. It is said that the spirit of Volcan Tunupa cried when her lover ran away and the resulting tears mixed with milk and created the Salar. The Aymaras prefer for it to be called the Salar de Tunupa rather than Uyuni, which isn't even on the Salar.

I sat on the edge of a large rock and reflected on being at peace in this strange land as the sun dipped below the horizon. With that, hollowing winds swept in and the temperature plummeted. It was quite comfortable to be on the Salar during the day, but at night, it is a hazardous place for humans. We got back to our tents, and strangely enough, we saw two llamas. The island caretaker told me that they were residents of the island but I was still curious as to what they were doing in the middle of a salt desert on an island of cacti; I guess anything they wanted. They were running around and playing on the Salar like it was their backyard, and just then, the sky turned purple for a brief moment with two llamas dancing on the salt. I didn't have a camera at hand to capture the moment, but it has stayed with me through the years.

I prepared for the impending chilly night. It was summer now in the Southern Hemisphere, but I was still expecting it to get very cold at this altitude, dropping way below freezing. I put my thin, silk sleeping bag liner inside my summer sleeping bag, and put that inside another newly acquired, down-filled sleeping bag. In addition, I wore all my cold weather gear, including woollen socks, a neck gaitor and a fleece beanie. Honestly, there is nothing intimidating about the cold so long as you're prepared for it.

Yoshi and I prepared our dinners on our respective camping stoves and we both had ramen noodles with canned tuna. Not only was it easily available, but it was also quick and hearty – the perfect food for long-distance travellers. We sat on the benches and ate hastily as the cold wind was quickly sucking the warmth from our bodies. Afterwards, we tucked in for the night and I sealed my tent's top cover to the ground with rocks to cut off the draft.

Around midnight, the howling wind suddenly stopped. I stepped outside to relieve myself and was stunned at the sight enveloping me. I was hoping to time my trip to the Salar with a new moon for the expected super clear night skies at this altitude. However, I was two weeks out of sync with our lunar neighbour and would have a bright moon for the next few nights. And what a display it was putting on. The entire Salar was lit up in the moonlight and in the absence of the wind, it was extremely still. Nothing moved, not a single rustle. I had a tinny sensation as my ears adjusted to the deafening silence. It felt as though I was on hallowed ground. Nature was stupefying me with her brilliance. I was able to capture an extended exposure photograph on my old Konica Minolta SLR camera as sanDRina and my tent were adequately exposed in the natural light.

The night was cold but I was pleased that my sleeping arrangement proved sufficient for the harsh environment. I was up before sunrise and hiked back to the top of the island with the winds howling around me once again. There were a few people there who had stayed in the hotel rooms, and we gathered at a flat spot on the top, looking east. The darkness of the night slowly peeled back for the sun's return. At daybreak, the winds quickly died down as though they were bowing down to the mighty power of the sun.

Back at camp, with the sun in full force, Yoshi and I packed up and went our separate ways. He was heading to Uyuni and onwards to Potosi. Before embarking on his travels, he told me he had worked at a Toyota factory back in his home city of Nagoya, and was actually a motorcyclist more than a bicyclist. He said he was a member of various motorcycle clubs and had built a café racer from an old Yamaha RD400. He had actually wanted to travel by motorcycle, but his worries about finding enough spare parts and the overall cost of maintaining a motorcycle led him down the minimalist path of pedal power. Surprisingly, he said he didn't enjoy pedalling for so many days in a row, and I chuckled as I reminded him of the three years that lay ahead for him. You can only second-guess yourself so much. I saw the appeal of travelling by bicycle, not burning any fossil fuels, but one obviously needs a lot more time to cover the same distance. I could tell that Yoshi was pleased to see an old Japanese motorcycle going so strong because he kept probing me about the maintenance I had done on sanDRina on my journey. By the end of our parting conversation, I felt like I had, to a certain degree, reignited a spark of desire in him to come back to the motorcyclist world.

He had given me his diary to write something in for him to read later, but forgot to take it back before leaving. Soon after realizing this, I went after him. I was impressed to see that he had covered 7 km (4 miles) in thirty minutes. It was a strange experience to be searching for a moving object on the horizon of the blinding landscape. He was on a parallel track and as I veered towards him, I could see his wheels turning but it didn't appear as though he was moving. He was jubilant to have his diary back as he had captured in it all his thoughts from his travels till then. I myself had a diary and took extra care of it as I chronicled my journey.

I turned south and looked for the exit from the Salar that all the tracks heading south pointed towards. Taking frequent breaks to enjoy the visual sensation of the Salar for a final few moments, I gave thanks for being fortunate enough to experience this surreal playground. The knobby off-road tyres I mounted in Sucre just a few days before were not of much use on a hard surface, but it would be much needed in the terrain coming up. I reached the southern edge of the Salar and joined the hardened-mud main road heading to the remote town of San Juan.

The tourist attraction of the Salar de Uyuni was done with and it was time to get down to some serious business and begin the infamous Lagunas Route. I would be riding through remote southwestern Bolivia across a lone, sandy, rutted, high-altitude track heading to San Pedro de Atacama across the border in Chile. I was dreaming of and simultaneously dreading this route for the longest time. It is supposedly challenging even to the best off-road riders and I knew my skill level wasn't up to par, but I was still throwing myself in on the belief that I could make it through.

The hard mud road gave way to washboard-like corrugations, shaking sanDRina and me to the core. I put an abrupt stop to the complaining and simply told myself to enjoy whatever kind of track I came across in the next 500 km (310 miles) to San Pedro de Atacama.

The landscape ahead was mountainous, dry and cold. There were a few unwelcoming shrubs near the track punctuating this high-altitude desert covered in loose sand. And just then, I saw a few guanacos flit across the track. These sturdy antelopes were eking out an existence in this inhospitable landscape. It was comforting to see another sign of life as civilization was far removed from there. To add to the strangeness of the experience, I passed by a basketball court as the route went through a small, lifeless village. I had seen a number of these basketball courts on the Atocha to Uyuni stretch, and remembered seeing signs for USAID and EU donor organizations. In the desert, external aid agencies felt basketball courts would be considered development. Perhaps they felt it would give the inhabitants a sense of progress, but I wondered if they bothered to ask the inhabitants what kind of progress they would like to see instead of having it brought in from the outside.

As I continued, the track improved in sporadic bursts, but the corrugations were ever present and the surface lay consistently covered in loose sand. I was tracking a storm that was brewing towards the east and hoped that Yoshi wouldn't be affected. The route followed what appeared to be a coastline of a now dry lake and then turned into a valley. I had GPS waypoints from other travellers, but it was relieving to see a worn signboard for San Juan as the GPS was only capable of drawing a straight vector between my current position and the marked destination. The route went through deep, loose sand just before getting to San Juan. By the time I arrived, my energy was completely sapped after bouncing in and out of deep corrugations and ploughing through the sand all afternoon.

The streets of San Juan were empty and appeared lifeless. I pulled up to a shop that had a Coca-Cola sign painted out front. Nothing else seemed to be open in this frigid, remote outpost. A young boy was kicking a ball around and he passed it to me. We volleyed for a few minutes before his father opened up the store for me. He was known to be the last reliable source of petrol on that route until the crossing into Chile. He was selling it for B6 ($0.88) per litre, much more than the nationally-fixed price of petrol, but I wasn't going to complain if it permitted me to fuel up for the rough route ahead.

Too tired to camp, I opted for the only lodging available in town, a salt hotel for B30 ($4.38). The beds and all the furniture were constructed from blocks of salt and I was impressed with the cleanliness of the place. It was circular with rooms on the perimeter and the sandy-floored courtyard made for a hushed setting. It felt luxurious compared to the places I had stayed at the previous few nights for just a few Bolivianos. Hotels along this route were mainly set up to provide lodging for the Land Cruiser tour groups, so food wasn't provided as the tour groups carry their own food as was I. Given the scarcity of water there, a cold shower cost another B8 ($1.17), which I decided to pass on.

The next morning, the track disappeared soon after leaving town, but it hardly mattered. Being on the track wasn't important as long as I was headed in the general direction of my next waypoint, Laguna Cañapa. The GPS showed that it was beyond the mountain range in front of me, so I knew beforehand that I would be crossing the range at some point. I duly pointed sanDRina towards it and soon found myself on the Salar de Chiguana. There was a train track across this salar and a short freight train chugged past under the view of the lumbering Volcan Coyumichi, the tallest peak atop the range. A Land Cruiser passed me and headed straight for the tracks, proceeding to climb the embankment and cross the tracks. I followed suit. I wasn't sure if there was a proper vehicle crossing further along but that only added to the adventure.

Crossing train tracks on a fully-loaded motorcycle is quite a challenge. First, I had to climb the steep embankment and then get over the two smooth iron tracks. I couldn't attack it head on and instead, resorted to climbing up alongside the tracks. By laying a few gravel stones next to each track to act as a small ramp, I crossed over and then got down the other side. As I made the crossing, I didn't really consider what would happen if I fell on the tracks. I assumed that there was probably only one or two trains cutting across this landscape from southern Bolivia to Chile, so if I had fallen, I would probably have enough time to yank sanDRina out of the way.

On the other side, I felt inspired and stood on the footpegs as I twisted sanDRina's throttle. I felt full of life. I was riding on another salt lake heading towards a giant volcano. This salar was muddy and brown compared to the previous one, as the rains brought out the dirt in the salt. There were many salars in the area like the one at hand, but all much smaller than the expanse of the Salar de Uyuni. With volcanic peaks all around, I stood still for a while under the nearby conical Volcan Luxsar's gaze and gained an appreciation for why these landforms were worshipped in ancient times. Their destructive power, however, still commands respect to this day.

Reaching the end of the salar, the route started climbing up the flanks of Volcan Coyumichi. The surface was covered in loose sand as the constant winds battered the bare rocks. Besides the individual overlanders, the only other vehicles were from the numerous tour groups that plied the route. Being a gearhead, it was satisfying to see trusty old Toyota Land Cruisers being used in such tough terrain, as their marketed image in the US is that of a luxury SUV. I got passed by around thirty jeeps over the next few days, which made it feel like a busy road at times. Some were nice and stopped to make sure everything was okay and asked if I had enough water. Others were rude, storming past on the single-lane track without giving much clearance. Their fast speed, which was probably intended to thrill their tourist occupants and help stick to their respective schedules, was the primary reason for such deep corrugations along the whole route.

I reached the summit of the broad V-shaped pass and took a break. The peak of Volcan Coyumichi rose to my left with other volcanic peaks scattered out to my front and right. The elevation had rapidly climbed from around 3,650 m (11,976 ft) on the salars up to 4,300 m (14,108 ft). I had read that the elevation would remain such and go even higher till the exit to Chile.

Looking back at the expanse of the salars down below, I opened up my bag of dried coca leaves and stuffed a handful in my mouth. They were slightly bitter and astringent. I moved the wad of leaves to the right side of my mouth and let my saliva soak through and soften them. After about ten minutes, I took a piece of 'lejia', a stick of ash made from quinoa plants that I had bought with the coca leaves in Atocha, and pushed that into the wad of leaves in my mouth. There was an immediate release of flavour; the cocaine alkaloids from the coca leaves. It is hard to describe but it was a pleasing taste, even though I was doing it more for the effect than the flavour. Coca leaves are known to be effective against altitude sickness and also curb fatigue, hunger and thirst. It provides the base from which cocaine is made, but in its natural state, the concentration of the alkaloids was very mild and didn't even produce a buzz, let alone a high. Besides my right cheek going numb for a few minutes, there was no discernable effect. I hoped that the medicinal benefits would help me through the next few days of the high-altitude terrain. Unlike the musicians in Vallegrande, who kept a wad in their mouths for hours on end, I spat them out after about half an hour. This was because my tight-fitting helmet left no room for the lump in my cheeks.

My GPS indicated that the destination for the night, Laguna Cañapa, was 22 km (14 miles) away as the crow flies, but was over 30 km (19 miles) away taking into account the rugged landscape. As I descended down the other side of the pass, I realized I was on a shortcut from Salar de Chiguana over the Coyumichi pass as I had joined a much larger track, resembling a highway in these parts. The highway headed back to Uyuni and was the way to enter the Lagunas Route in the rainy season when the salars would be flooded. I took a turn to the right and smiled at being back on a smaller track. With Volcan Inti Pasto on the left and Volcan Callejon on the right, I had entered the 'Valle de los Volcanes' (valley of the volcanoes). Dormant peaks, all part of a massive range, stretched out in front of me in two rows. Some were covered in snow, others were bare to the harsh sun. The air was brilliantly clear at this altitude. With most of us living near sea level, we've gotten used to a haze in the skies (either from pollution or just water vapour from the seas) and the clarity of the high-altitude sky was stunning for this low-dweller.

I came across a few muddy puddles and saw stormy clouds up ahead. After all, it was the rainy season in this high-altitude desert. I turned a corner and Laguna Cañapa spread out across the horizon. It was to be the first of many magical lagoons on the aptly named Lagunas Route. Snow-capped volcanoes surrounded the lake and as a bonus, so did hundreds of flamingos. There were about three different types of flamingos in the lagoon – grey, orange and pink ones – and most of them had their heads to the water, constantly feeding on the algae and crustaceans that thrived in the salty lagoon. Having stopped to gaze at this sight, I bounced about on the large, soft and green balls of moss that lay at the edge of the lagoon. It was an intriguing place to camp, at 4,150 m (13,616 ft), next to a salt lagoon and under a snow-capped volcano. All the hardships of the route were worth the experience.

I had arrived by early afternoon, and upon seeing the rain front moving swiftly in my direction, I decided to take it easy and break for the night there. The weather would probably be better in the morning. I set up my shelter and got the cover on sanDRina just as the first few drops fell. I tucked in to escape the cold and the wind, lying down to relax by listening to an audiobook by Arthur C. Clarke. It was his first novel, *The City and the Stars*, and its futuristic setting of a global desert landscape seemed quite appropriate. In a few hours, the rain clouds had passed, leaving behind the cold winds.

Back out for sunset, I was captivated by the changing colours in front of me in this striking landscape. The hues of brown and green turned a brilliant orange as the sun dipped down behind the volcanoes. I was the only human being for miles around in this remote mountain landscape, and instead of feeling lonely, I felt content and one with nature. I was a part of nature, so this was very much my home. Right there. Yes, I was fragile and needed shelter, clothes, water and food, but I envied the flamingos that were designed for what humans find to be an inhospitable environment. Being comfortable in a remote setting helped cultivate the idea that nature isn't just a force we're meant to survive against, but it serves as the very essence of our existence. I was thankful for not being in a situation where I would be rushed off in a jeep after taking the obligatory photo. Instead, I was able to travel at my own pace and nurture my thoughts and feelings as they would be influenced by the grand setting.

Finding an abandoned rock and mud structure nearby, I used it as a shield to escape from the wind and get some water boiling to cook ramen. With the noodles ready, I settled into my tent as I continued to prepare dinner. I had bought a can of tuna in Santa Cruz and didn't think twice before piercing its top. The pressure difference between the point of purchase at 400 m (1,312 ft) and consumption at 4,150 m (13,616 ft) resulted in a small abrupt geyser of tuna juice that now coated my sleeping bag and other pieces of gear. What to do, I thought? Oh well, I dumped it on the ramen noodles and enjoyed my meal, hiding from the wind.

Up at the crack of dawn, I noticed a layer of frost on my tent and sanDRina's bike cover. It had been a cold night, but my tent and multiple layers of clothing had kept me warm. The full moon was just about setting as the sun's rays shimmered across the lagoon. It felt serene. There wasn't much movement among the flamingos, but then I saw one of them getting ready for flight and captured the moment with my camera. A flamingo taking flight was at the same time elegant and clumsy, but it soon climbed into the air. Having watched this flamingo flit over to another area of the lagoon, I packed up camp and got back on the trail that followed the perimeter of the lagoon.

Crossing a few ridges, I came across two smaller lagoons with their own colonies of flamingos. Nearby, there was a faded concrete signboard with the official name of the route, 'Ruta de la Joyas Alto Andinas' (Route of the Jewels in the High Andes), but in the overlanders community, it's simply referred to as the Lagunas Route.

Laguna Honda (with no reference to the motorcycle manufacturer) was the smallest lagoon on the route and its edges were lit up in a white band as the salt layer was exposed to the sun. I had read that the salt in the lagoons, which here was primarily potassium chloride, fed the algae and they in turn fed the flamingos. How interesting that salt in itself could be a food source.

Leaving the lagoons behind, I was faced with a red, barren desert covered entirely in large sand grains. It extended till the horizon with volcanic cones of various sizes all over the area. There was no road there but I could see the track that was most commonly used by the other jeeps. There were two tyre tracks cutting across the sand leaving a series of large corrugations in their wake. It was a challenge deciding which surface to ride on. The loose sand surface didn't provide enough traction at the slow speed I was going at and the large corrugations rattled sanDRina and me to the core. At least, I could make steady progress on the corrugations by slowly going up and over each bump and so that's where I stayed, but always with envy of how flat and smooth the sand appeared. If only I had a lighter bike and was confident enough to ride blazingly fast, then this surface wouldn't be a problem. But alas, I chugged along slowly.

The strong winds were constantly blowing, to which a constant dance of dust funnels across the desert attested. These little tornadoes appeared to connect the sky to the land as they stretched from the white, fluffy clouds down to the red desert. Some even crossed right over us, engulfing sanDRina and me in a storm of sand grains for several seconds. I had my goggles and a neck gaitor fixed firmly around my eyes and mouth respectively, but could still taste the sand after each dusting.

Besides the few volcanic peaks in the distance, the land was flat, making this big sky country. And at this altitude, the horizon appeared closer to the ground, giving the sky a larger portion of my vision. I felt small and insignificant, yet content and safe.

The jeeps made tracks wherever they wanted and I just picked one that was heading in the general direction of the vector on my GPS. The tracks all pointed up a mountainside and I gained even more elevation as I inched towards the upcoming pass. Expecting to cross a summit, I was surprised to see a very high-altitude plateau extending to the horizon ahead of me. I was up at around 4,650 m (15,256 ft). I was astonished at the very thought that I was riding a motorcycle at altitudes higher than most mountain peaks in the US, where I would have to take a ski lift to reach a height of only 3,660 m (12,008 ft).

I was well prepared to spend time at this altitude, slowly taking my time to get adjusted on the way there from the plains of Santa Cruz. I was also taking an altitude sickness pill to make sure any signs of acute mountain sickness were kept at bay in that harsh environment. Along with the pills, my constant chewing of coca leaves kept my fatigue under control and probably contributed to my quick adjustment to the high altitude.

The sun was out in force and whenever I stopped for a break, I quickly donned my hat because even though it was cold, the ultraviolet rays are very harsh at such altitudes and I would feel the burning on my exposed scalp. All day long, the only colours I saw were the browns and reds of the earth juxtaposed with the blue and intermittent white of the sky. Not a single green plant in sight. There were the occasional brown shrubs scattered about and it seemed like a difficult place to survive in general. I couldn't understand how vicuñas, an antelope that I saw roaming the desert in the distance, could eat enough to thrive in this inhospitable environment. I was constantly amazed by the endurance living beings develop just to exist.

In what really felt like the middle of nowhere, there was a welcome sign to the 'Reserva Nacional de Fauna Andina Eduardo Avaroa', a national wildlife refuge. Some of the tracks were graded within the reserve and that provided a relief for my aching shoulders, as the deep sand made for tiring riding.

A little up ahead, a strange rock formation was jutting out of the ground. This was the famous 'Arbol de Piedra' (Tree of Stone). I'd seen many photos of it from other travellers and dreamed of one day getting there. And this was it. This rock, hewn by the sand-filled wind, resembled a misshapen tree. Supported by a stoutly trunk of white rock, a large bulbous mass of even more white rock sat atop, resembling a solid mass of branches that leaned precariously to one side. 3 m (10 ft) in height and width both, it stood out from its surroundings – a lone wind-carved boulder in a sea of sand. The last sentinel of some lost edifice. The same sands that had carved this rock now assaulted me relentlessly. As I arrived, two park employees sprang up and offered to take my picture. I felt sorry that they had to hang around there and just wait to take pictures for the occasional tourists passing through.

From the Arbol de Peidra, it was only 15 km (9 miles) to Laguna Colorado, my destination for the night. However, this route was covered in the deepest sand that I encountered on the route so far. I knew the techniques to apply while riding in deep sand – lots of speed to get the tyres up and surfing across the sand. But the equally strong, less glamorous brother of speed is braking, with a high chance of dropping the bike if the rider is inexperienced in such conditions. I could not drop the bike on this route because I knew I wouldn't be able to pick her up. So I resorted to slowly ploughing my way through the sand with my feet down to provide support. It was not ideal. It was monotonous, tiring and took me two and a half hours to ride those 15 km (9 miles), but it got the job done. The deep ruts carved through the sand by jeeps provided me with intermittent relief. They made a firm base on which sanDRina could accelerate, but were flanked by one-foot-high ridges of sand that could easily snag and flip me to the sides, so I had to ride slow and steady even in these channels.

Strangely, I spotted a traffic sign, the first since Uyuni, requesting all traffic to head straight and make a right at the orange sand mountain up ahead. I could see Laguna Colorado to my right and just to spite the sign-makers, I took the diagonal shortcut. It was either deep sand and washboard on the main route or deep sand and rocks on the shortcut. It probably wasn't any faster in the end, but at least the rocks added some variety to the image of sand that was by now burned onto my retinas.

As I rode over the small ridge of rocks, I saw the track split in two directions. The option was either to go straight and join the main route that I knew was laden with heavy corrugations, or continue in the deep sand and rocks. Just as I got to the fork, constantly negotiating the sand with the handlebar sawing back and forth, I ended up on the route of more rocks. It wasn't a conscious decision. The momentum influenced me. The handlebar sawed to the right just as I reached the fork and the decision was made for me. I had learned that fighting the sand was a losing battle with gravity and that I'd better just follow where the sand wanted to take me and sanDRina.

Eventually, I had to join the deep sand and huge corrugations of the main road. The diminishing daylight was evident as the sand berms on the edge of the route were so large that they cast their shadows into the troughs of the corrugations. I tried to improve things by dropping the air pressure in sanDRina's tyres down to 8 psi in the front and 15 in the back. Normal pressures on tarmac roads were 30 and 35, respectively. The reduced air slightly flattened the tyre, increasing the footprint across the sand and allowed me to float a little better across the loose sand. The deep sand was wearing me out and I took frequent breaks to relieve the tension in my shoulders. The road got better as Laguna Colorado came into sight, but I had to restrain my right wrist to keep the throttle steady to ensure a safe arrival. I finally reached a lifted gate and high-fived myself for making it safely to Laguna Colorado.

The route from there passed through the gated portion of the national reserve, which ran from Laguna Colorado to Laguna Verde near the Chilean border to the south, and required an entrance payment of B150 ($21). There were a few buildings making up Camp Ende on the western side of the large lagoon, the largest along the route. The camp was well established with residents all through the year and I managed to get some indoor lodging for B30 ($4.38). I came out just in time to catch the remarkable colours in the sky that the setting sun was painting. The clouds were lit up in soft glows of orange and pink that reflected this colour across the lagoon and surrounding hills. It was quite a majestic sight and a fitting reward for the gruelling ride I had just completed.

They didn't serve food at the basic hotel I was staying at, but as I had experienced earlier on the ride, some Land Cruiser crews felt sympathetic towards lone bikers on the Lagunas Route and shared their food. They probably understood how tough the ride was and knew we couldn't carry much food with us. The staff of the tour group staying at my basic hotel offered me some leftover dinner of fried chicken and rice with a hearty vegetable soup, which was a feast to me after the epic ride I had been on.

Rested, I hiked up a small hill to get a view of Laguna Colorado in the morning. It spread out across the entire valley in front of me and was steely blue with patches of salt visible in the low water levels. Flamingos were feeding with their heads to the water while others stood still in what seemed like a meditative state of contemplation.

The route leading away from Laguna Colorado, much to my relief, was not as sandy as the previous day's ride. It was hard-packed with rocks that made for quicker riding. The route now joined a well-graded path, which I learned was maintained by a Chilean company extracting boric acid nearby. This helped in reminding me that I was soon to approach an international border. The customs office on the Bolivian side was off the main route by a few kilometres. There was a large overhead metal sign from the Bolivian customs, making it known that they take border security and customs very seriously. The terrain was still the same Martian red as the previous day, but the route was better managed, allowing me to enjoy the landscape without any hardships. Following a street sign in the middle of the desert, I reached Apacheta, a small gathering of concrete buildings that formed the customs compound. It felt like the end of the earth as it stood poised on a cliff. This was probably the highest customs office in the world with the elevation registering at 5,020 m (16,470 ft). But no one was around. I waited patiently in the chilling winds for twenty minutes and when no one turned up, I left to get back on the trail. I wondered if there would be any consequences for not checking sanDRina out of Bolivia. I wasn't planning on coming back any time soon, so I took the risk.

Back on the trail, I came across an area covered in geysers and fumaroles – fountains of hot mud. The earth was alive beneath my feet and it was spewing up hot sulphuric gases. The acid had discoloured the surrounding rocks, making them a pale yellow against the surrounding red sand. The deformed land was also a welcomed change to the general flatness that I had been seeing for the last few days. It was exciting to see how this whole area of geysers was open with no restrictions anywhere. I could get as close as I wanted to a geyser or bubbling mud pool, but of course if anything untoward were to happen, there would be no help nearby. An individual's sense of responsibility and execution of common sense prevails in such cases.

I carefully stepped my way around the geysers, wondering where all the energy was coming from. I got back on the track and soon found myself at the hot springs of Salar de Chalviri. It was on the other side of a ridge from the geysers and I figured that the same underlying magma was heating the water there. I set up camp next to the lone guest house at the hot springs and quickly hopped inside the adjoining hot water pool constructed over a hot spring. It was a fantastic reward for the tough riding of the Lagunas Route. At 4,420 m (14,502 ft), the air above the water was chilled, but I kept pouring warm water over my head. I took in the mountainous landscape and breathed relief as the salts in the hot water soothed my aching muscles. I sat there for about two hours through sunset, observing flamingos and other wildlife pass by. It was the perfect end to the epic adventure of the past few days.

In the morning, I was woken up by hordes of Land Cruisers emptying foreign tourists for a sunrise dip. How lucky I was to have enjoyed the place by myself the night before. I filled up my hydration bladder from a freshwater spring next to the guest house and hit the trail for the border. The route passed through a valley called the 'Desierto de Dali' and the vivid colouring of the mountains was indeed very similar to Salvador Dali's psychedelic painting style. The route was still sandy and corrugated but much better maintained than further north. I finally arrived at the last jewel in this desert, Laguna Verde, covered in green algae. A guard at the southern gate to the reserve offered to take my picture; it must've been customary for overlanders to do so after successfully making it across the Ruta de la Joyas Alto Andinas. I stood with my arms outstretched in joy with a large smile under my helmet for the photo.

From there, it was a short climb up a mountainside to the Bolivian post at the border at 4,500 m (14,765 ft). I didn't tell the officers in the lone shack about the customs office being closed the previous day because they probably would have made me go back. With an exit stamp in my passport, the gate across the track was lifted open. It seemed strange to pass through a gate in the otherwise open landscape.

I bid goodbye to Bolivia for the second time. Many travellers had told me that it was the highlight of their trip and I finally understood why. I figured it was going to be hard to be impressed by any landscape after Bolivia, but Patagonia deserved a chance at least.

8

PATAGONIAN SOLITUDE

IT WAS A crisp, clear morning in the high Andean town of San Antonio de los Cobres. I rolled sanDRina out of the hotel lobby after saying goodbye to Mario, the guest house owner. A genial man with a lop of grey in his groomed hair, I could tell that he was fairly in touch with urban life in that he wore slacks, unlike most of the locals in the area. Based on his fair skin, I assumed that he belonged to the majority of Argentines of European descent. The previous night, as I was walking around town sourcing provisions for the trip ahead, I noticed the people were primarily indigenous, resembling Bolivians more than the Europeanized image of Argentines. In this remote corner of northwest Argentina, I was off-the-beaten-path where adventure usually looms. 'Adventure' in the sense that things don't always go according to plan and you're faced with challenges. My life for the past few months had been filled with small and grand adventures since leaving Chicago on my trusty stead, sanDRina. This motorcycle and all it carried summed up my worldly possessions, and as long as she was rubber-side down and rolling, my journey was smooth.

sanDRina fired up with ease despite the thin air and we headed south. The tar road ended at the edge of town and we were back on gravel. I had entered Argentina the day before from a brief visit to Chile and started on my trip down Ruta 40, the legendary road that runs the length of this extensive country. Running along the gorgeous landscape of the mighty Andes and Patagonia, it spans almost 5,000 km (3,107 miles) from the border with Bolivia to its southern end near Ushuaia. Its reputation for being a gnarly and difficult journey that separated the amateurs from advanced motorcyclists was slowly coming to an end as the majority of the route had been paved. Part of the reason I started my trip sooner rather than later in my life was to sojourn in remote places that were arduous to reach on rough roads before they were made more accessible.

A few kilometres out of town, I reached a fork in the road. If I went left, I would be taken on a new paved road, skipping a high mountain pass through which the old Ruta 40 passed. I had just finished the extremely tough Lagunas Route and successfully come out the other end unscathed, so I didn't think twice. I turned right and started the climb to Abra del Acay, the highest point along Ruta 40.

The blue skies and puffy white clouds invited me to relish being in the wilderness and I frequently stopped to capture the landscape in photos. At one point, I drew to a halt next to a road marker that said I had another 4,626 km (2,875 miles) to go until I reached the end of Ruta 40. Such signs with large distances always reassured me that I was on the right path of this journey. I wanted to go far, in whichever direction, and so long as I was on the road and riding, I was at peace. It was a feeling I had developed back in Chicago after completing one of my training trips to Alaska. Large distances felt comforting. Hence, I opened the throttle on sanDRina and started on the rough road that led into a protected nature reserve. I passed a huge sign that listed the various dangers I could potentially be facing – the risk of falling rocks and dips on a twisting, narrow and inclining road. It did not mention, however, that there would probably be no traffic and no humans around for the next 100 km (62 miles).

I lowered the air pressure in sanDRina's tyres to better grip the loose surface and stood on the footpegs to let her dance over the uneven road. With a smile on my face, I revelled in the joys of how wonderful a compromise the Suzuki DR650 was for a motorcycle. sanDRina could cruise along on a paved highway and then thrive even when it would end, all while carrying a full load.

The road climbed upwards and the air grew thinner with each hairpin turn. For a relatively unused road, the hard-packed dirt and gravel surface was surprisingly in decent shape. But the hairpin turns were loose and sandy, pulverized by tyres struggling for grip. By then, I had enough experience to not be fazed by such road conditions.

Standing on the footpegs with my wrists loose, I made a wide right-hand hairpin turn by swinging as far left as I could and then leaned right. No brakes are needed when going uphill, just a slight deceleration on the throttle while approaching the turn, after which one must lean in and accelerate when the turn's exit comes around. Easy. I was enjoying myself with my Andean playlist on shuffle and just for a second, took my attention away from the riding.

I approached the next turn, a left-hand hairpin turn. It was sandier than the previous ones and just thinking about that caused me to pay less attention to how I was heading into the turn. Instead of swinging out to the right to get as wide a turn as possible, I found myself in the middle of the lane, staring wide-eyed at the sand and the cliff beyond it. I realized I wasn't going to make the turn. I came down from standing on the pegs and hoped I could get my left leg on the ground to catch sanDRina before she fell over. It was too late. The front tyre skidded in the sand and sanDRina was down. It was a slow-speed drop and with my left foot already going for the ground, I was left standing while sanDRina decided it was time for a nap. I immediately turned off the engine and shut off the fuel taps. Based on a similar incident that I had previously experienced in Montana, I knew that my adrenalin rush just after such an event would be very high and attempted to lift sanDRina back onto her wheels right away. It was a no go. She was much heavier than the time in Montana and was leaning against the slope, which made the lifting force too great.

It was time to calm down and take stock of the situation. I'd mentally prepared myself for the tough hour or two ahead of me. I had learned from previous travels that it helps not to panic at such times and instead be grateful. I smiled at my usual thought of positive reinforcement, 'at least it's not raining.' And if it was raining and I was in a similar situation, I'd probably say to myself, 'at least it's not snowing,' and hopefully, I would never be riding in the snow. This kept my mood stable and I was able to take a second to acknowledge how lucky I was to not have been injured or in any kind of danger. If sanDRina had skidded over the cliff and left me hanging on some rocks, I would've probably still started with the 'not raining' line. Fear and panic are the mind's worst enemies when things go wrong.

Dusting off the fine, sandy dust that covered my pants, I reminded myself that adventure was all about coming across hurdles and finding a way forward. I removed my helmet and heavy Kevlar jacket, and donned my sun hat. I was at 4,815 m (15,800 ft) and whilst I'd become acclimatized to the high altitudes of the Andes, I knew overexertion in the thin air would exacerbate my situation. I moved slowly.

Capturing my folly, I took a few photos of sanDRina on the ground and thought about what a stunning location she had picked to have her nap. We were above the tree line and all I could see were small, dry shrubs among the rocky surface of the steadily sloping mountain face and the blue sky above. I would be enjoying the view more if sanDRina was standing upright. Before trying to lift her again, I waited for about fifteen minutes to see if any other vehicles would come by and lend me a hand in picking her up. Nope. Not a single engine in earshot.

I hadn't passed another vehicle all morning and accepted that I was on a path only used by those seeking to pursue the road less travelled. It was up to me to get sanDRina back on her wheels. Seeing how she had fallen downslope, I spun her around so that she was now lying upslope. I remembered the technique of lifting a motorcycle from a Horizons Unlimited Travellers Meeting workshop, where you stand with your back against the bike and lift it up. That didn't work as my feet kept slipping in the sand. She was too heavy. I had to lighten the load if I was going to be able to lift her and I set about unloading about 80 kg (176 lbs) of kit.

I removed the spare set of tyres, emptied everything from my two side panniers and large top box. It looked like I was having a yard sale on Ruta 40 with my gloves, jacket, stove and laptop in one pile, tools and spares in the other; everything I owned for a life on the road was sitting in the dust. But that didn't matter. The most important thing was to get sanDRina back on her wheels.

With sanDRina much lighter, I put my back against her, grabbed the handlebar with one hand and the pannier frame with the other and heaved. A flood of emotions welled up as she rose and stood on her tyres. I punched my left fist in the air and yelled out, 'I will survive!' I was careful about not pushing her over on the other side in my jubilation, and quickly got her side stand down.

This was exactly what I had signed up for when I started my journey. It was another hurdle conquered. I wanted to face life and all its random occurrences, allowing it to let me grow. Having all of it centred on a motorcycle and set in beautiful locations just made my experiences that much richer.

Now that sanDRina was pointing downhill, I had to ride down until I could turn around at a wider spot since the road was only about 2 m (7 ft) wide where I was. After packing her up, which took over an hour, I came back to the same hairpin, where the nicely graded sand now resembled a battle scene, and took the proper line through the turn. When a situation bites me, confronting and successfully surmounting it was essential in removing any doubts from my mind with regards to my ability. This was no more important on this journey than anywhere else in life. A year and a half ago, I had torn the anterior cruciate ligament (ACL) in my right knee during a ski trip in the Rockies, and I had to get reconstruction surgery as a result. I went through physical therapy and then promptly went back and skied the next winter; albeit with more caution. This approach helped me make the decision to go on this journey. I had experienced tough situations and come out the other end without any long-term scarring, so I knew I would survive and perhaps even thrive.

Safely motoring along, I once again took in the landscape. Descending on the other side of the pass, I had a gorgeous view of the barren Andes, its sedimentary layers painted in shades of red and brown. Down in the river valley, two young boys herding goats told me that a good place to camp would be past the town of Cachi, where it was less rocky. Topping up with petrol and fresh water in town, I continued along the dirt road of Ruta 40, which was now narrower and lined thickly with trees.

A half-hour out of town, I came across an elegant yet faded and deserted-looking farmhouse. I walked through the gate and met with an old lady who lived at a small house in the back. Soon enough, I had my invitation to camp. The lady explained that the owners were away in the large city of Salta and rarely came anymore. Currently in a state of neglect, I could tell the house used to be grand, because its veranda was lined with arched columns and terracotta tiles.

The large front yard was covered with tall eucalyptus trees and I chose the one with the most leaf cover to set up camp under. Even though I hadn't requested it, the old lady sauntered over with a 5 L (1.3 gal) jug of fresh water. I proceeded to take a bath with just

2 L (0.5 gal) and kept the rest for cooking and cleaning. Bathing with two litres is not as satisfying as standing under a shower and letting over sixty litres wash over you, but it gets the job done with a bit of practice. Stripped down, I would dip the loofah in water and run it over my skin. A small amount of soap can go a long way with a loofah; it is enough to clear the dust and dead skin cells off with just a tiny amount well applied. I would then wash the soap off with another rinsed loofa. An evening bath would always leave me feeling comforted and a little civilized.

Feeling fresh in the cool of dusk, I gathered up firewood from the yard, strewn with branches and twigs, and got a roaring fire going before darkness set in. Rather than cooking directly on the fire, which would cover my sole cooking pot in soot, I fired up my camping stove and made a simple meal of pasta with tomato sauce and soya chunks. Sitting on a log, staring into the fire, I felt content and at home. The fire was a new and satisfying addition to my camping. All my previous camps to date were based primarily around shelter and safety; I'd felt as though a fire would make my presence too conspicuous. However, I knew from other travellers that Argentina was a safe country with an established camping culture. I was soon reassured of that when a pickup truck drove past and the men in the back waved with big smiles at seeing me next to the campfire.

Having been at a high altitude over the past few days and always dressing accordingly, it was a relief to feel the warmth of the fire. The altitude was around 2,100 m (6,890 ft), and coming down from 4,300 m (14,108 ft), shorts and a t-shirt were enough to feel comfortable. The fire had all my attention. I watched how the flames danced and the fire crackled when I threw in pine cones. It was my entertainment. My solace. This is where I belonged. I felt a deep connection and satisfaction with what I was doing with my life. Feeling secure by the fire, I voiced the thoughts in my head. There was no one around, so I felt compelled to speak out loud. I spoke to the fire and the dancing flames.

I raised a wide range of questions. Why was there so much dissatisfaction and negativity in the world? What was the purpose of living? Was there a greater purpose to living than to simply be content? This thought in particular lingered as I stoked the fire. I had already been on the treadmill of our global economy. I had studied intensely and then worked intensely, all to continue paying bills. It was an intensity that now seemed pointless to me. Granted, it had funded my current experience, but I was now on my own treadmill. In the morning, I would get on sanDRina and get back on the road. There was no grind and no judgement. I could even sit next to a fire and talk to myself. This life was of my own choosing.

With dinner done, I stoked the fire for another hour before spreading out the large pieces of wood and turning it down. There was no wind, so the risk of the fire spreading at night was low and the ambers were left glowing as I tucked in for the night.

Over the next few days, Ruta 40 took me south, past the city of Mendoza and into Patagonia, the vast territory of land covering the bottom third of South America. Only recently settled by modern civilization, its vastness is still its trademark impression. Having Antarctica close by kept the year-round temperatures cooler than similar latitudes in the Northern Hemisphere. The unbroken chain of the Andes all the way to Tierra del Fuego created two distinct Patagonias – the wet and green mountainous side in Chile, and the dry and flat side in the eastern rain shadow of Argentina.

In northern Patagonia, both sides of the Andes are blessed with lush temperate forests and glacial run-off lakes. Its popularity with international and local travellers makes it a highly touristic region, but still worthy of a visit. That being said, all the major attractions in Patagonia could be considered touristy, but that does not diminish the feeling of awe that it inspires. It's still one of the most remote places to travel in the world.

Before getting to the Lakes District of northern Patagonia, I had a vast swathe of barren land to cover. Ruta 40 was paved in and

I let my eyes wander in this big sky country. The land here was defined by a series of steppes; windswept plateaus devoid of much of anything. I tracked storms moving across the horizon as I rode onward, their power and vastness emphasized by the bleak stage on which they now performed. Nature was putting on a grand show in this remote land. Storms or no storms, this part of the southern summer was the best time to visit. But Patagonia is rather unusual. Strong winds and storms are common throughout the year; it was just a little less cold now than a few months before.

I stopped at a mile marker south of Chos Malal, indicating that 2,300 km (1,430 miles) were left to the end of the road in Tierra del Fuego. The land was naturally devoid of any flora taller than shrubs and the only trees were those around farmhouses. Sheep, introduced from the Falkland Islands, were the mainstay of 'estancias' (ranches) that span all of Patagonia. The ribbon of tarmac in front of me snaked all the way till the clouds at the horizon. Gazing at the cotton clouds as I rode down this empty road, I saw shapes of dogs, dragons and even a Suzuki DR650. This expanse was not discomforting. I felt part of it, however small, and glided on toward the horizon.

All of a sudden, the landscape changed into forests of evergreens. I had arrived in the Lakes District. I passed the first town of Junin de Los Andes and found a lovely campsite in San Martín de Los Andes. The mountain town with timber log buildings resembled the ones I had passed in Montana. Having eaten bare essential meals over the past few days, I splurged at the grocery store. I prepared an elaborate meal of polenta with chickpeas and red bell peppers on my stove as I sat next to a roaring fire.

From San Martín, the scenic 'Ruta de los Siete Lagos' (Seven Lakes Route) meandered through Parque Nacional Lanín. Its fame has grown over the years and the road was crowded with enthusiastic hikers, bicyclists and cars. Regardless of the crowds, the scenery was stunning and it was an enchanting feeling to be so close to deep blue lakes.

When I stopped to take in the view of a waterfall on Rio Hermoso, a large group of cyclists joined me. Argentines are very friendly people and this group of friends from Buenos Aires, who were on a multi-day cycling trip, chatted me up with questions about India and the trip down the Americas. Like most others, they were surprised to see an Indian making this trip and complimented me on my Spanish. By now, I had picked up on the variation of the language that was spoken in Argentina, using more swishing sounds compared to the staccato Spanish of Peru and Colombia.

Back on the road, I was distracted by the scenery but had to stay focused on the sharp bends. It was a pleasure to ride on a well-maintained road that was wide and protected with a guard rail. There were sharp mountain peaks jutting out from the crystal blue waters and I took my time with frequent breaks to soak it all up.

South of the town of El Bolson, I camped on the shores of Lago Puelo. I knew these waters were fed by glaciers and thus would be freezing cold but the absolute purity of it drew me in. I put on my swim trunks and waded into the lake. I had to wade in about 30 m (100 ft) until I could fully submerge myself in the glacial run-off. It was chilling to the bone but deeply refreshing. No one else there was splashing in the water, which caught the attention of some teenage kids who looked on in amusement at this bald, brown man throwing cold lake water over himself.

I felt a deep connection with this lake, as I did with much of Argentina and Patagonia as well. Its rawness and beauty spoke deeply to my core. I felt more in touch with myself when exposed to these elements. The cold was soon overcome and the energy from it seemed to refresh my soul. As I emerged and dried off with the winds across the lake blowing swiftly, I could not help but let out a deep sigh of satisfaction.

The next day, after about 250 km (155 miles), I bid adieu to the Argentine Patagonia for the Chilean side. As I drove past the gate, an enormous sign welcomed me to Chile. The remote border at the Rio Grande crossing took me into the small town of

Futaleufú, marking the northern entrance to the famed Carretera Austral, which translates to 'Southern Highway'. After a night on the shores of Rio Futaleufú, I turned south onto a dirt track that is treasured in the adventure motorcycling community. It was hard to reach, but those that did were rewarded with a lone dirt road cutting through a verdant land covered with tall trees and crystal blue lakes. This was one of the truly great destination roads in the world, famed for its remoteness and unending natural beauty.

In southern Chile, the Andes butt up against the Pacific with fjords defining the coastline. These numerous inlets with steep sides created by glaciers make it very challenging to connect this sparsely-populated region to the rest of the country by road. Thus, in many places, water becomes the only means of connection. It was possible to get to the Carretera Austral with a limited ferry service from Puerto Montt, the last city in contiguous Chile. But I was told by other travellers that this was not a dependable option, so the overland route from Argentina through Futaleufú was the best way to access this gem of a road.

Small isolated communities existed there long before there were any established connections via land, as they were seafaring people. During Chile's last military dictatorship, General Augusto Pinochet decided to forge a road through the wilderness in order to better integrate these isolated communities with the rest of Chile. Almost twenty years after and the project has yet to be completed. With the connection to Puerto Montt being the hardest to surmount, overland access is primarily possible by crossing from Argentina. The Carretera Austral was built during the 1980s by the Cuerpo Militar del Trabajo (Chile's Army Corps of Engineers) and it was only since 1988 that travellers had been coming through it on their own vehicles. Prior to that, visitors and locals would have to come via sea and navigate the numerous fjords scattered across the coastal landscape.

I was extremely satisfied to be in a place where deep, blue lakes and snow-capped mountains were a common sight. Some might have found it to be boring after the first few grand vistas, but for me, the rapture was unending. That whole area of southern Chile was under the Patagonia Ice Sheet during the last ice age. It ended there about 17,500 years ago and the lakes are all that have been left of the ice sheet, along with two huge ice fields up in the mountains. Apparently, the melting of this ice sheet alone raised global sea levels by 1.2 m (4 ft). It has been predicted that if we reach a tipping point in the current warming of the planet that triggers the Greenland Ice Sheet to melt, sea levels will rise by 7.0 m (23 ft) in just one century.

The road was straight and devoid of any traffic. It cut straight ahead to the horizon that was bordered with steep, snow-capped mountains. I would reach the summit of one ridge only to be presented with another road, straighter than the one before, heading to the next ridge. This was a true pleasure to ride. There were a few twists and turns, but I wasn't complaining about the straight sections. Instead, I let my mind roam free in this vast arena.

Early into the ride, I started seeing signs of an ongoing local conflict. The Chilean government wanted to build five large dams for hydroelectric power on two major rivers in Patagonia. Owned by Spanish and Italian companies, the project came to be known as HidroAysén. However, the locals, along with several environmental groups the world over, were fiercely against it. I came across a billboard sign next to a newly constructed cement bridge that was spray-painted with 'No represas, Fuera HidroAysén' (No dams, get out HidroAysén). These billboards were erected in remote areas where projects to improve infrastructure had been recently completed. They were put up to show the local people how the government was bettering their situation. The people had felt neglected by the rest of Chile for so long, and all of a sudden, the government wanted to show them that they were bringing progress to the region. It was amusing to see a brand new concrete intersection in the middle of nowhere, followed by a huge billboard with the photo of the intersection and a message reading, 'Look at how we're progressing Chile – by the ministry of public works.'

The road was lined with tall evergreens and I felt as though our civilization was imposing on this land of thick forest. The carpet of green was a treat for my eyes and I found comfort in knowing that there were many places on our planet that had not yet been razed to the ground for the sake of development.

Initially, I was planning to spend the night near La Junta, the first major settlement on the route. My plans changed when a couple, travelling on a new Honda TransAlp motorcycle, approached me at the petrol station at the turn-off to the town. Francisco and Liz greeted me warmly and told me about a hanging glacier that we could camp at a bit further south. Making a note of it on my map, we set off together. The road was covered in loose rocks and I had lowered sanDRina's tyre pressures to make the ride more enjoyable on the rough surface. Francisco told me that it was the couple's first big motorcycle trip, which I could tell in seeing that they were riding extremely slowly on the loose, rocky surface.

We stopped a little further down the road so I could put in my wind-liners as the temperatures dipped with the dying sun. I asked Francisco if he knew about lowering tyre pressures for riding on dirt roads. Having only ridden on paved roads before this trip, he'd never needed to modify tyre pressures. I explained how the lower tyre pressure would lead to more stability on loose surfaces, giving him more confidence on gravel roads. But they were extremely particular as a couple with regards to playing by the rules and feared that lowering the air pressure might lead to a puncture. I had to assure them that I would pump their tyres back up if they weren't comfortable, before they allowed me to slightly lower their tyre pressures. Back on the road, they both gave enthusiastic thumbs-ups as I passed them. When we pulled up past the small fishing village of Puyuhuapi, Francisco was beaming with glee at having cracked gravel roads. It seemed as though I had an off-roading disciple and he insisted that I continue to share my motorcycling wisdom with them.

It was quite late in the day but the bonus of riding near dusk was the magical light. It was the height of the southern summer and the sun was setting later into the evening the further south I went. The sunlight hidden behind the clouds cast a warm glow over the Puyuhuapi fjord as the Carretera Austral skirted along the ocean waters.

We found the turn-off for Parque Nacional Queulat, and since we entered the park quite late, we didn't have to pay any entrance fees, which was a relief in expensive Chile. We set up camp and shared stories of our travels. Francisco and Liz were from Santiago and had been bitten by the long-term travel bug. They were currently on a three-week trip to test the waters and learn about long distance motorcycling, before setting off on their dream ride to Alaska soon after. I quipped about how my test trip had been to Alaska so that I could fulfil my dream of riding in Patagonia. Francisco mined me for all sorts of information about necessary tools, how to carry food and figuring out the route. I remembered doing the same with other travellers when I was in the initial stages of adventure motorcycling, and it felt good to pass on my knowledge.

The next morning, we set off for a two-hour hike to get a view of the glacier. The trail went through wet forests, full of lively plants that were growing with vigour. The huge-leafed Nalca plant was typical of the region and Francisco said that its stalk was a delicacy, having a similar taste to rhubarb. We passed a weeping wall with water soaking down the rock face, allowing a carpet of moss to flourish. And finally, we reached the view point. Ahead of us lay a narrow valley and across it, we saw a small glimpse of blue ice from the Ventisquero Colgante, the hanging glacier. The chill of the night still had clouds hanging low that obscured most of the glacier so we waited for the sun to work its magic. The glacier was constantly melting and there was a huge waterfall on the left side coming down from it. It was transporting age-old locked-up fresh water down the mountains and eroding the land in the process. The waterfalls had a height of around 500 m (1,640 ft), and in our time there, we saw new waterfalls form and disappear. It was exciting to see nature work in its own rhythm.

After giving it an hour, the clouds lifted and revealed Ventisquero Colgante in all its majesty. It was a sight to behold. A river of ice hanging in a high valley with the ice so free of impurities that it was vivid blue. There were frequent loud cracks that reverberated through the valley as the glacier slowly retreated back to its mother, an ice field in the mountains.

Francisco and Liz would be moving at a slower pace, so I bid them goodbye and set off on the route south. Between Puyuhuapi and the turn-off to Puerto Cisnes, the route got extremely twisted as it climbed up and over a mountain ridge that extended to the sea. I gained elevation quickly through continuous hairpin turns, which I welcomed after the long, straight sections of the road in the north. Reaching the pass, I could see an ice field beyond the snow peaks extending all around me. The effect of glaciers on the land was unmistakable with the large U-shaped valley in front of me that was carved by the ebb and flow of icy rivers. It's hard to imagine its process given that it occurred over a period of time much greater than an individual's few decades on this planet. When my awareness of geologic time was realized, after having read the works of science communicators such as Carl Sagan, I started appreciating the dramatic geologic events that are ongoing on our planet irrespective of our human civilization. With all the talk of saving the planet from climate change, it's become quite evident that it's not the planet that needs to be saved, but us. Our extinction will just be another footnote in this world's evolution.

Descending down the other side, it was hard to pay attention to the road as new snow peaks came into view. I would stare at them, searching to see if they were revealed to be part of yet another mountain glacier or not. I came to a fork and turned right towards the fishing community of Puerto Cisnes.

As I sat at the mouth of the Cisnes River, I thought about how this little seaport had only recently been connected by land to the other communes in Chile's Patagonia. The sea was the lifeline of this community. I rode into town and saw large fishing boats moored at the docks. There wasn't much activity happening, and the run-down wooden-plank buildings harked back to more glorious days. I had read that the youth were not interested in staying in the fishing business, and instead went outside the isolated community to study and work in the tourism sector. It's hardly a unique story in today's world but seemed all the more poignant there where the outside world had only just arrived.

I rode around the large bay to a public park nestled against the coast. The tide was slowly ebbing and pulling back to leave fishing boats beached in the shallow water. I stopped by a few picnic tables and barbeque stands that looked like they had not been used in some time. The park felt oddly abandoned. With the wind blowing in from the water, creating a choppy surface and biting at me, I found a nook amongst a grove of poplar trees to set up home for the night. I pulled sanDRina in behind the trees and she blended into the background with her drab olive paint job. I had that exact reasoning in mind when I had decided to paint her and my helmet this colour and my theory was finally starting to show results.

There were branches lying in the woods nearby and I gathered enough for the evening's fire. To have some more substantial firewood, I hacked at a fallen birch tree with my machete. I had been carrying it since my first visit to Bolivia, but quite honestly, this was the first time I had put it to real use. I had never really chopped wood before but my recollection of cutting V-shaped notches by alternating my blows against the wood soon delivered enough logs for a long fire. Gathering up some kindling, mostly from hacking at the trunk, I laid the foundations of a fire in a teepee shape in a clearing that had been used for a fire previously. Soon,

I had a roaring fire going, much to my satisfaction. No matter the progress of our civilization, being able to set your own fire remains a visceral emotion and no more so than when being camped out in the wild.

At this latitude, the sun had disappeared behind the clouds by 9 p.m., but the sky clung to some traces of blue, which helped light my dinner preparations. With the almost nightly camping since entering Argentina, I was making an effort to enjoy my own cooking, as I had in Chicago. My kitchen supplies had increased and I was now carrying small bottles of olive oil, soy sauce and even garlic sauce, which I was thrilled to have discovered in Brazil. I also had a special ingredient in my rations now – dried yoghurt chillies. My aunt made these in my mother's home village outside Chennai, India. The red chillies are first soaked in salty curd (plain yoghurt) and then sun-dried. Deep-frying them to a crisp makes for a tasty condiment that's not too spicy and adds a tremendous amount of flavour. There was an intricate global supply chain in place to get these home-made goodies all the way from a village in India to my panniers in South America. For this, I was grateful to my sister, and Allen in Chicago, who were acting as my logistical coordinators.

Unrushed, I sat on my sleeping mat and ate a one-bowl dish of rice and tuna in a savoury soup as the fire roared. No one was around and once again, I spoke up to the lure of the roaring fire. We spoke about how gorgeous the riding had been that day and how comforting it was to make home with a fire next to the sea. We wondered whether future generations would continue engaging in such practices, or instead, submit completely to the technological world. Alone and without others to pass judgement, we conversed like old friends reunited. Amidst the solitude, it was another voice and also a source of company for me. I could have stayed in a hotel, but I really wasn't longing to be around strangers. I needed to find myself, and somewhere over the course of our conversation, I realized that I was on a special journey. More than a motorcycle epic, it was one of self-discovery. These revelations are not unique because many travellers have them. It is a rite of passage, an epiphany to many. Some get this through meditation, running or even counselling. But for adventurers out on the road, solitude is where we can finally find ourselves. With these fires every night, my decision to leave the corporate world had been vindicated. I was not earning a salary, but for me, getting on sanDRina every morning to take in nature's beauty before tracking down a comfortable, safe place to sleep, was an endeavour in itself.

With the wood I had chopped expended, I extinguished the fire with seawater to avoid any stray embers igniting my nearby tent, and packed up for the night right after. I awoke to a dull and grey morning that hosted a constant, slow rain. This rain is a common feature in the Chilean Patagonia, hence all the lush vegetation. The moist winds blowing in from the Pacific offload against the Andes, before the tattered remnants blow dry across the Argentine Patagonia in the rain shadow. I had to wait the rain out in my tent, which was far from spacious.

My post-camping routine every morning had been well established by then. It would take me a solid three hours to go from waking to rolling out on sanDRina. In that much time, I would've cleaned up, prepared breakfast, washed up the pots, packed up my tent and sleeping gear, changed into my riding clothes and put every little thing back in its designated place. Toiletries and clothes were in the right pannier, camping and electronics were in the top box and snacks and tools were in the left pannier. Three hours might seem like an awfully long time for a morning routine, but I was never in a rush. It was my routine. I enjoyed the slow pace of getting started for the day.

Back on the Carretera Austral, the road was paved through to the major city of Coyhaique. It even had a fancy supermarket, so after stocking up on supplies, I left the congestion behind and returned to the view of the Chilean Patagonia that I was so accustomed to by then, sharp snow peaks with lush green valleys. Passing by a few windmills, I wondered why I hadn't seen any before in Patagonia. If there's one place in the world where the winds are constant and strong, that was it. Instead, there was a billboard that seemed out of place surrounded by all the nature, from the 'Patagonia Sin Represas' action group. The name translated to 'Patagonia Without Dams'. The billboard depicted a river flowing into an electrical plug, with words reading, 'Our rivers are much more than just electrical energy'. The government was targeting the deep valleys of Patagonia with full rivers to build large dams to generate hydroelectricity. Ignoring the potential for wind-generated energy in Patagonia, they wanted to submerge acres of pristine land under water for the sake of development. And besides, large dams are not as environment-friendly as they're made out to be because of the disproportionately large footprint they leave behind, especially during construction. Submerging forests leads to the release of methane, which is a deadlier greenhouse gas than carbon dioxide as it traps more heat. The government's reasons were not valid and I was glad to see the people fighting back. This political action was an indication of Chile's high human development rate. The public had such a strong voice that the government had to spend vast amounts of money courting the local people's approval, instead of simply suppressing them and pushing ahead, which is what happened under the country's past military dictatorship.

I met a few Aussies travelling up the dirt road on rented Suzuki DR650s and we exchanged information on camping spots along the route as well as must-see sights. Such interactions are essential and coveted occurrences when touring. There is also a certain element of chance. Depending on whom you come across, you may end up in new locations that you may have never even heard about. Passing a turquoise river, I turned the corner to the jewel of Chile's Patagonia, Lago Carrera General. The massive lake spread out over the horizon, bordered with rugged and barren mountains. It was South America's second largest lake after Lake Titicaca and I was mesmerized by the unreal turquoise of its water.

sanDRina brought me to the campsite the Aussies had mentioned, high along a ridge sheltered by tall, thin birch trees. There was a picnic bench made of a few planks and a metal fire ring. As I was taking off my hefty riding boots, I saw the colour of the lake change in front of my eyes as the sunlight danced over its surface. It went from turquoise to an iridescent blue to steel grey. As though to top it off, a full rainbow appeared above, arching across the sky.

I awoke to rain again, but the sun soon came out in full force and presented me with a crystal-clear view of the lake. Continuing south along the lake, I stopped frequently to take in the shimmering waters; it was surreal. I continued to follow the edge of the lake after ignoring a left fork that would have taken me back towards Argentina, turning right instead, towards the end of the Carretera Austral at Villa O'Higgins. Rio Baker, which drains Lago Carrera General to the Pacific Ocean, showed me the way. The Carretera felt even more remote now as it climbed higher onto the mountains, compared to the relatively flat and more populated regions in the northern areas. The higher view point allowed me to appreciate the splendour of the river valley below. Rio Baker snaked through the valley, dotted with purple and white flowers in bloom.

This was the site of a proposed dam to produce hydroelectric power. It stumped me how such a gorgeous valley could be flooded over, especially given the ever-present wind. HidroAysén assumed that working on such a remote place probably wouldn't affect too many people, not taking into account that it was a treasure for all humanity. Even though the project had the rights to the land, having purchased it during the Pinochet dictatorship, they haven't been able to capitalize on it, yet.

From the only large town in the area of Cochrane, I had to make quick work of the next 125 km (78 miles) to catch the last ferry of the day. I reached Puerto Yungay with ten minutes to spare and boarded the free ferry that runs three times a day across a large fjord. There was a monument at the small port, which was once the southern terminus of the Carretera Austral, at kilometre marker 1,150. The Cuerpo Militar del Trabajo had recently extended the route another 100 km (62 miles) to Villa O'Higgins, which was only opened to traffic in the year 2000. The terrain was extremely rough in these parts as the fjord's steep cliffs prevented the southern continuation of the route, so the ferry was put in as the solution. The forty-five minute ride went by quickly and I thought back to the scene from *The Motorcycle Diaries* when Che and Granado crossed a lake on their trip from Argentina to Chile. It was majestic and humbling to have to take a ferry, accepting that we couldn't bulldoze a road through the rough terrain.

The ferry docked at Rio Bravo, after which I rode off into the thick forest. It was time to start looking for a place to camp for the night. I found a clearing among the trees, a few kilometres from the ferry landing, and set up my tent as it started to rain. The forest was wet, but I managed to get a fire going after dousing some wet limbs with petrol. Even if it wasn't enough to warm me up, a fire amidst rain is always of comfort.

I had a gloomy start the next morning, since the air was still moist from the overnight rains and the clouds overcast. There was one big mountain ridge to cross and the road signs warned me of steep and tight curves. From the summit, the view ahead was foggy and the wintry weather was bone chilling. Cold and wet, my desire to reach the end was enough to keep me going. After a few more curves and climbs, the weather turned for the better, revealing snow-capped peaks that had been hidden just ahead of me in the clouds. When the sun finally broke through the clouds, I stopped to warm up my wrinkled fingers. The route was cut right into the cliffs, as we now followed Lago Cisnes towards the end. A few more turns through the forest after leaving behind the lake and I started to see wooden fences. Within a few kilometres, I had reached Villa O'Higgins, the end of the Carretera Austral.

A small outpost with about 500 inhabitants, Villa O'Higgins had only recently been connected to the rest of Chile via the

Carretera Austral. Settled in the 1920s by European immigrants, it was renamed in 1966 to honour Chile's independence hero, Bernard O'Higgins, who was born of Irish and Basque descent in the eighteenth century. The town consisted of wooden buildings with steeply slanted roofs to survive the heavy snows during the prolonged winters.

Now, during its brief summer, the valley was rich in vegetation and the setting sun cast a warm glow over it. I found a campsite and after offloading my gear, headed down the road to the actual end of the Carretera. There was a concrete bridge with a spray-painted protest sign reading, 'No Inunden La Patagonia', translating to 'Don't Flood Patagonia'. HidroAysén had provided the entire town with free Wi-Fi in hopes of winning them over, but that wasn't enough to make the people budge; certainly not yet.

On the other side of the bridge, the road ended unceremoniously at a dock on the shores of the expansive Lago O'Higgins that spread out in front of me to the slopes of the jagged mountains ahead. This large lake straddled the border with Argentina and it was the most irregular of the large Patagonian lakes, with eight well-defined fingers, four on each side of the border. To my right was the huge Southern Patagonian Ice Field, which fed the lake. The lake is, in fact, the deepest in South America with a maximum depth of 836 m (2,743 ft), even though it only sits at an elevation of 250 m (820 ft). Besides damming Rio Baker, HidroAysén wanted to build a few dams across Rio Pascua, which drained this lake into the Pacific. Seeing all these lakes bordered with steep mountains certainly looked tempting from a hydroelectric point of view, but it would be devastating to our environment and I was glad to have reached there before another damning mistake was made.

From my campground that evening, I looked around and marvelled at the huge extent of ice in the surrounding mountains. The Southern Patagonian Ice Field lay just behind these mountains. It dictated the current terminus of the Carretera Austral. To continue south, the route had to go around the ice field, either via ferries along the coast or via land in Argentina. For me, this was the end of the road. With no ferries in place to take me further south, I leisurely backtracked over the next few days to Lago Carrera General and crossed into Argentina.

9

FREIGHTER TRAVEL

ISIGNED ON the dotted line and with that, I was ready to board the *Grande Francia*. I was in the swanky offices of Turner Lines, a shipping agent in Buenos Aires, and had just transferred about $3,000 in exchange for passage across the Atlantic Ocean on a cargo ship. I was also required to sign a liability waiver giving up all claims against the company if anything were to happen to me out at sea over the next four weeks.

Motorcycle travellers had shared stories with me of how they had managed to cross the Atlantic using Grimaldi's ships, but the only caveat was that, unlike a cruise ship, there would be no full-time medical doctor on board. International maritime law dictates that if a ship carries more than twelve passengers, they are mandated to have a doctor on board with medical facilities. To avoid paying for a doctor, most cargo ships around the world welcome no more than twelve passengers on their voyages across the sea. It's a niche travel sector known as freighter cruises. I was delighted to find out that this was still a means for travel across oceans. For me, it harked back to the days before air travel made the world an infinitely smaller place.

When I had first mentioned my overland journey from the US to India to my father, the first question he asked me was how I planned to cross the oceans. The fastest option would have been to airfreight sanDRina, but that would've been no fun and too fast. The next option would have been to send sanDRina in a crate as sea freight, but that would involve the hassle and expense of dealing with cargo agents at either end of the voyage. The third and best option for me was to use Grimaldi Lines and their roll-on/roll-off (RO/RO) ships to make the journey. When I was initially planning my trip, I had figured out a route back to India that would only require transporting my bike across water bodies on ships. I wanted to stay on our planet's surface and not take any shortcuts, namely airplanes, to remain consistent in my preference for slow travel.

My days in the Americas came to a close in the cosmopolitan city of Buenos Aires, replete with its wide colonnades and chic neighbourhoods. On the day of my departure in late February of 2011, I rolled into the Buenos Aires Cargo Terminal, close to downtown, and handed the temporary import papers for sanDRina to a moustached officer at the booth. Before entering the port, I had filled up sanDRina with bargain-priced Argentine petrol, knowing that it would cost more than double in Europe. I was officially in a customs bonded area; there was no turning back. Up ahead, in the sunny parking lot, were my fellow passengers who were heading back to Europe after their own overland journeys in South America. Clearing customs, we milled around and got to know each other while waiting for the next instruction from the Grimaldi agent who was shepherding us through the port and onto the ship.

Franz and Sandra had just finished touring southern South America for four months in their forest-green Land Rover Defender, emblazoned with snow-peak mountains on its sides. They ran an outdoor shop in southern Germany, planning and

leading canoe trips and treks, and were travelling in style with a
Suzuki DR350 strapped on the back of the jeep and two canoes
on top. Michael and Käthi from Switzerland were returning home
after a two-year trip down the Americas, also in a forest-green
Defender. They didn't sport the same accessories as Franz's, but
a honking huge spare tyre on the hood gave their 'landy' an extra
rugged look. Together, we whiled away the time, waiting to board
in the shadows of towering containers, while Käthi served up yerba
maté, the national drink of Argentina. The bitter tea had taken
some getting used to, but by then, I had developed an appreciation
for it.

It finally became apparent why we had been waiting for so long.
All the passengers were directed to a large, mobile X-ray scanner
attached to a van, since all vehicles and containers had to be
scanned before they could be loaded onto the ship. The port agents
were searching for hidden compartments, weapons and any other
items they deemed to be of interest. We all passed the inspection
and were finally taken to the berth where the Grande Francia was
docked. The ship towered above us, a clean sheet of white rising
more than 61 m (200 ft) from the dock, with the words 'Grande
Francia, Palermo' painted in large block capitals. Two enormous
blue cranes stood astride our ship, loading containers onto her top
deck. To the back of the ship was a large metal ramp angled from
the rear to the dock, inviting us to finally leave the shores of South
America.

Klaus, a German biologist who had toured South America in
his Mercedes camper van, was first up the ramp and was directed
to the sixth-floor deck. I followed him inside, circling up the
steel ramp from the first-floor deck through the ships interior.
Being the only one with a motorcycle on the ship, I was directed
to a spot near the elevators, and Nolan, a Filipino crew mate in
blue overalls, brought out some vehicle straps to tie her down.
I removed sanDRina's side panniers, spare tyres and other bags
strapped on her, and we proceeded to secure her to the eye loops

in the deck floor. There was a bit of separation anxiety as I had become accustomed to having sanDRina near me at all times during the past year. Giving sanDRina a push and seeing that she was secure and wouldn't get rocked about during the journey, I felt safe in leaving her there. Nolan helped me carry my entire luggage into the small elevator and up to the twelfth-floor deck where our cabins were.

I was stowed in cabin number 1237, identifiable by my name printed on the door. I was beaming as I opened the door to my home for the next four weeks. I had chosen to do without a cabin with windows since it would cost much more, but it was a comfortable room nonetheless. I had a large bed, desk, cupboard, attached bathroom and even a small fridge. It was a luxury compared to the average lodging I had opted for over the past year on the road.

After settling into our rooms, we all slowly gravitated to the top deck to witness our departure. The ship set sail on time at 5 p.m. and quickly picked up speed as the sun cast a warm glow over downtown Buenos Aires. We stood against the rails, each of us lost in our own respective thoughts, reflecting on our recently concluded journeys. I was bidding adieu not just to Argentina but the continent of South America. I had entered the continent almost ten months ago aboard the *Stahlratte*, and I saw it fitting that I was leaving just as I had arrived. In that time, my Spanish and Portuguese had evolved to a level that allowed me to have conversations even on politics in Argentina and Brazil. My newly acquired capability had given me deep insight into the various cultures of the continent. Feeling very much at home across South America, I wondered if my skin colour had played a part in that. I had been surprised, time and time again, at how curious people were about India. Given the shortage of Indian representation in the region, I had been thrust into an ambassadorial role for my home country. I had managed to lose my identity at certain times when I would blend in with the local people, contrarily standing proud and regaled about Indian culture in other places. Taking a large step eastward towards India, I was extremely excited to be undertaking my first transatlantic journey by sea. With black smoke billowing from the smoke stack of the ship's large engine, we powered out to the open sea.

Over dinner, my fellow passengers and I made a toast to celebrate the end of what turned out to be a successful endeavour for each one of us. Besides the overlanding passengers, there were Anthony and Marie, a young French couple returning home after a year of studying in Buenos Aires, and Jean, an African-American lawyer who was crazy enough to be making the ship journey both ways. Whereas the first night on board was celebratory, it was also characterized by a bittersweet feeling that marked the final chapter for many people's travels.

The next day, Second Mate Officer Mantilla, gave us a safety briefing. He was a short and balding Filipino man in charge of all the security issues on the ship. We were given a tour of the bridge, which is the ship's command centre, with a commanding view from the highest floor. I was intrigued to see a traditional ship's wheel right in the middle of the bridge, surrounded by rows of computers used to navigate the ship. We were told it was there mostly for traditional reasons, as well as for the fine control it offered in maneuvering the ship while in port. I guess ships in the future might have joysticks, like in modern airplanes, but tradition seemed to be holding out a little longer at sea.

Off Uruguay, the winds were picking up as we were assembled on deck to run through the fire drill. Officer Mantilla pointed out all the lifeboats on board and indicated the procedure we were to follow when the fire drill alarm sounded. Our principal source of salvation in the event of sinking was two large enclosed boats on both sides of the top deck, each capable of carrying the thirty-seven crew members and nine passengers. These were enclosed for protection against the rough winds and the bitter cold in case we had to take refuge within it. The deck was also equipped with an innocuous white barrel with an explosive lock. This, we were told, would release an inflatable raft if it detected the ship had capsized and was under water.

I saw the rest of the crew, who were all Filipino, and officers, who were all Italian besides Officer Mantilla, the next day at the end of our first fire drill, when everyone had to report for roll call. The piercing fire drill alarm was sounded on the public address system an hour before dinner. I donned my hard hat and life jacket, grabbed the cold-water suit bag stashed in my cabin cupboard and rushed to the muster station on the top deck. I wasn't surprised to see that safety was taken so seriously on board, and the efficiency with which the exercise was carried out by the crew members was reassuring. The young Filipino crew seemed to be a friendly bunch, smiling and nodding in our direction. They were assigned the operational tasks on board, such as working in the engine room, handling the cargo and basically most other responsibilities that keep a cargo ship ticking, all under the direction of the officers. This was a holiday for us passengers but work for the rest.

After the fire drill, dinner was served in the small mess hall with large windows that permitted the late light of the day to flood in. Franchesco, the steward, instructed us that we were to follow a tight schedule for mealtimes. Breakfast was served from 7:30 to 8:30 a.m., lunch from 11 to noon and dinner from 6 to 7 p.m. No food would be served otherwise, but that wasn't really a problem since we were served a three-course meal at every sitting. First, there was the tasty entrée of antipasto (cold cuts and olive oil pickled vegetables), then came a pasta course followed by two courses of meat, closing with fruits and Italian espresso coffee. This was a much larger caloric intake than my body had grown accustomed to. Eating on a frugal budget and consuming only what was necessary, I had lost a few kilos since the beginning of my journey and my only cargo pants had become loose-fitting. I could see that I would be regaining that lost weight over the next few weeks.

The meals on board, typically Italian, ended with a salad, which initially comprised of lush green lettuce, but over time, transitioned primarily to white lettuce that probably came out of the freezer. After dinner, we had to clear out of the dining room before 7 p.m. so that the officers could then have their dinner. For some reason, we were not supposed to interact with the officers. I guess some naval traditions are harder to alter.

En route north, we were scheduled to make stops in various ports, and after a few days of getting into the rhythm of life aboard the *Grande Francia*, we arrived in southern Brazil. I woke up to see that we had docked at Paranaguá, and from the top deck could see that the ramp was already down. However, it was to be a brief stop. Lines of new Volkswagen cars were ready to board, and in just a few hours, we set back out with our new cargo safely stashed in the belly of the ship. When the ship was at sea, we were not allowed near the car decks, but we were free to walk about the ship while at port. It was interesting to note all the specific safety signs around the ship. A sign next to the elevator, for instance, stipulated that the Captain and Chief Mate were prohibited from using the elevator at the same time. This was to ensure that the number one and number two officers on board would not be stuck at the same time in case of an emergency. This was similar to a policy in the corporate world I had come from, where the CEO and the next highest ranking employee were barred from taking the same flight in case there was an accident, to mitigate the risk of losing core leadership.

The next morning, we reached the port of Santos that links the big port city to inland São Paulo. We sailed up the harbour, which was on both sides of the large channel leading to the Estuario de Santos, a large natural estuary at the mouth of Rio Santos. I peered over the edge from the top deck as the ship was delicately maneuvered to its berth at the dock. Looking ahead, a vast lot was filled with a perfectly arranged mix of new passenger cars and construction equipment, ready to board. Brazil's economic might at the time was quite evident in our tours of its ports, and I was already appreciating the value of freighter travel. It gave me insight into the business of cargo that moves via sea, which is usually not visible to the public. Most of the products of our global economy travel this way, as it is the most economical means to get things manufactured or sourced in one country and delivered to almost any other part of the world. Travelling by plane, most of us lose sight of the global maritime infrastructure that keeps our economy in motion.

Tracking our journey on my GPS the next morning, I saw that we were passing by the small fishing hamlet of Picinguaba, just south of Rio de Janeiro. I had spent some extended time in Picinguaba during my travel down Brazil's Atlantic coast and thought back to the fond memories of dancing on the beach, being introduced to snorkelling and eating fresh sushi. I wanted to come back and live in Picinguaba at some point in my life. The allure of being by the sea, surrounded by tall, lush mountains and distancing myself from the civilized world was intoxicating. A few hours passed before the grand view of the most marvellous city in the world was upon us. Rio de Janeiro, with its pristine beaches and jagged mountains, was impressive to me from land and now even more so from sea. As we sailed around Pão de Açúcar (Sugarloaf Mountain), one of the prominent geologic features of this city, I remembered the time I spent there soaking in the rays at Ipanema Beach while I waited for my Argentine and Chilean visas to be processed.

Guanabara Bay, the large natural harbour that Rio sits on, was busy with activity. This bay gave Rio its importance during the early days of Portuguese colonization in the sixteenth century, as gold and minerals from the hinterland were brought there for shipping to Europe. The port is still important to Rio, but nowadays, manufactured goods are being sent to Europe instead of just raw materials.

From the ship, we had an uninterrupted view of a large favela that covered an entire hillside. Favelas are part of most big Brazilian cities, but the ones in Rio are unique because of their proximity to the rich areas of town; a side effect of Rio's rocky geography. A lack of space in the flatlands, where the rich people lived, had driven the 'faveladors' to make home on the steep hills. Besides being trapped in poverty, living there also left them at the risk of frequent mudslides during the rainy season. Instead of referring to them as slums, the word 'comunidade' (community) is more appropriate these days. Sadly, they were still easy targets for the crime gangs that Rio was trying so hard to get a handle on, before the global spotlight shone on Brazil over the upcoming football World Cup and Olympic Games.

Once docked at port, the huge ramp was lowered down. I could see dirt from the bottom of the bay stirred up by the ship's propeller, marking the trail the ship made getting broadside to the dock. Guanabara Bay, which was once a pristine and rich ecosystem with thriving mangroves along its shores, was now heavily polluted. The constant urbanization and inevitable pollution that comes with it, along with an oil spill in 2000, had dealt a massive and perhaps irreparable blow to biodiversity in the bay.

There were another thousand odd cars neatly lined up at port, waiting to board the *Grande Francia* and other ships. There was certainly no feeling of recession in Brazil as compared to the reeling markets being reported on in the rest of the developed economies.

We were allowed to deboard and enter the city for a few hours. At each port, based on the captain's discretion regarding safety, the passengers and off-duty crew were allowed a shore pass for a few hours. We had to be back on board about three hours before the ship set sail to ensure that we would not delay its departure. The other passengers had not been to Brazil yet and rushed onshore for a quick view of the marvellous city. Having already spent ten days in Rio, I went straight to town and found an internet café. I was keeping tabs on the developing situation of the Arab Spring in northern Africa, my next destination. There was no internet access aboard the ship besides a daily two-kilobyte (thirty-word) e-mail that the passengers were allowed to send via the satellite communications system on board.

I strolled through town, keeping pace with the busy crowds of Cariocas, the term used to describe residents of Rio de Janeiro. I walked past a McDonald's and noted a homeless man sleeping right in front of the busy fast-food restaurant. The McDonald's and the homeless man were both products of our globalized world. The former winning out and expanding in its global reach and the latter losing out and looking for a handout. Globalization has done wonders by spreading the benefits of economic prosperity to many millions across the world. But I believe that its inherent structure, where there are winners and losers, leaves behind a trail of inequality that seems to widen as the world's economy continues down a path of ever more growth. Like most places in the world, I noted how no one around seemed to be bothered by this man and kept walking in a hurry to wherever they had to go. I approached him and offered a granola bar that I had on me, which he gladly accepted with an 'obrigado', thanks in Portuguese.

I was walking around with Marie and Anthony and we came across some of the Filipino crew members who were having a day off onshore, relaxing with some beers at an outdoor café. They invited us for a drink, but the French couple wanted to get back to the ship in time for dinner. As we walked past people on the street, it was fascinating to note that unlike most others in the city who were on their way back home, we were getting on a ship to sail across the Atlantic that evening. We waved our shore passes to the security guard and entered the ship via the ramp in time for our multi-course dinner.

After dinner, we got on the top deck to see the push-off from Rio. After waiting a while, the harbour pilot boarded from a much smaller boat to guide us out. Ships cannot move in harbours and ports without a pilot. It's one of the oldest, least-known professions to exist, certainly to our knowledge, since ancient Greek and Roman times. It's akin to having a dedicated air traffic controller on board an airplane. Even if a ship's captain (known as the master) has been to a known port a number of times, pilots are still required as they have knowledge of the local currents, tides and any other changes in the port, which are not always evident in the nautical charts. The master is still in control of the ship but the pilot guides him around any obstacles.

We moved away from our berth and went backwards into the main waterway. We passed a sister Grimaldi ship, the *Grande Brasile*, that looked similar to ours, painted yellow and white, and adorned with two large, white cranes on her front deck. After making a ninety degree on-the-spot turn, we cruised out of Guanabara Bay under the cover of darkness and bid farewell to Rio, and finally to the South American continent. From here, it would be nine days across the Atlantic to Dakar in Africa.

With a glass of red wine, I settled into my now regular routine of sitting on a lone deck chair on the top deck, looking out the back of the ship. We were slowly moving across time zones and as we reached the end of the one at hand, the sun was setting after dinner. After crossing into the next time zone and advancing our clocks another hour, sunset would be taking place before dinner for the next few days. There would be no jet lag on our journey between continents.

With nothing else in my view besides the ship and its railing, the expanse of the ocean spread out in front of me beneath a vast sky; the horizon between the two was seemingly lost. My eyes sought out reference points to judge the distance, seeking out the border between water and sky. Yet, the only firm footing and reference point was this big hunk of metal that was motoring across the ocean. The sun set and with the clouds in the west, the evening light show commenced. First, there were the bright orange streaks of clouds in the west. They reached out over me to the navy blue background in the east, where darkness was setting in, and then those streaks morphed into hues of pink and purple that slowly grew and took over the entire sky until nightfall finally set in. Mariners often speak of the sunrises and sunsets as defining experiences of their time at sea. It is with good cause. The blackness that consumed the ship with the disappearance of the sun was comforting and unsettling at the same time. The only connection to the developed world around us was the ship, but we were self-sufficient and as long as the engine kept chugging, we would be back on land and firm footing. I was relishing the experience.

This extended time away from land gave me a new perspective on the water that covers our planet. My inner voice started to speak up, and together we mulled over the most dominant force on our planet. Where did it all come from? How could we suffer through a water crisis in spite of there being so much of it? I was uncertain as to why this was the case. Sat on that deck chair, my mind wandered, harking to my time spent next to campfires in Patagonia.

The earth was a ball of rock after its formation 4.6 billion years ago, and slowly over the aeons, water accumulated on its surface. Seeing the twinkling lights in the night sky, I wondered when the next asteroid or comet, the most likely source of all our water, would visit us. Represented by the calm ocean, the current nature of our planet is quite benign as compared to its early tumultuous history. I felt blessed for being alive during a period of stability in the life of our planet. Like most things, this period will pass and there will be events in the future that make life on Earth unsuitable for humans and other creatures. My inner voice pondered over why we, as a civilization, could not put aside our differences and work together to solve some of our most pressing failures, such as the unequal distribution of wealth. I didn't have the answers, but thinking about these matters must surely be a step in the right direction.

With no one else in sight, I smirked at how this other voice could run free on the top deck. The water all around was now home. I went back to my cabin and turned in for the night.

Freighter travel is not designed to entertain passengers. The slow progression of time leads passengers to revert to more

inventive ways to keep themselves busy. Most read books or
watched movies, but I had my work cut out. I was a few months
behind on my website and put in long hours at my 'office',
processing photos, videos and writing. I took breaks by reading
about and preparing for Africa. To keep me going, I had a warm
thermos that a stranger at a petrol station in southern Argentina
had just given me, and used that to make cups of yerba maté. The
bitter tea was soothing and had just enough pep to keep me going
through the day. I had learned from a host in Buenos Aires that
the perfect yerba maté was made with water at 78°C (172°F) –
any hotter and it would scald the tea leaves, whereas the flavour
wouldn't be strong enough at a lower temperature. After days
alone in my office-at-sea, I was finally able to gauge the exact
temperature for a perfect yerba maté and make my Argentine
friends proud.

I came out on deck frequently during the day to take breaks
from my windowless cabin and to make sure we were still moving;
a sensation denied to me except for when the ship would rock in
rough conditions. I took pleasure in gazing over the railing of
the ship. The cresting water mesmerized me. Churned up by the
ship pushing its way through the surface waters, the colours of
the crest spanned from the white on the top of the crest to a soft
blue in the turbulent wake and finally to a deep blue of the depth
that was visible in the troughs of the waves. I couldn't get over the
blueness of the ocean. The colour was remarkable. While some
of the blueness came from the reflection of the sky, most of it was
due to the way the shorter wavelength of blue light is absorbed
and scattered to our eyes. Water also inherently has a tinge of
blueness to it, which is more evident the deeper the water is.
Who needed television when nature itself was able to keep one's
mind engaged? Compared to land speeds, the ship's cruising
speed on this segment of 13.5 knots (25 kph, 15.5 mph) appeared
to be very slow, but looking down at the hull cutting across the
waters gave me a true sense of speed and appreciation for this

massive vessel to be moving at such a velocity. I would turn on my GPS every day to note down how far we had travelled. On average, we were covering about 600 km (373 miles) a day, which is how far one would get covering 25 km (15.5 miles) every hour for twenty-four hours.

There was another fire drill during which we were permitted to board the lifeboats, much to the thrill of the passengers, although the crew members were obviously not as excited, having done these drills countless times. Besides mealtimes, our only other source of entertainment was a room with table tennis and a foosball table. Klaus, Franz and I had a table tennis league going on through the journey, during which Franz and I lost most games to the agile and strong 'old man'.

Klaus had a GPS programme on his laptop with an antenna out of his window, so we could see the ship's daily progress. We were both quite excited about the upcoming crossing of the equator. Looking at the map on his computer screen, Klaus remarked how obvious it was that South America and Africa were once joined, back in the days of the supercontinent of Gondwana. Land masses are ever so slowly but imperceptibly moving and it becomes inevitable for them to join up into a supercontinent from time to time, and then, once again, break up and drift away. A rift opened up about 130 million years ago on Gondwana and after twenty million years, the split was complete and the separation of the continents began. The Americas headed westward, away from Europe and Africa. We were crossing in nine days what the continents took over 100 million years to create – the present-day South Atlantic Ocean. Geologists predict that the next supercontinent will form in 250 million years from now.

A few days later, we crossed the equator, which marked our departure from the Southern Hemisphere into the North. I kept track of the GPS coordinates and was excited to see the latitude slowly counting down to zero. The zero moment happened early one morning, which I got up to witness. Seeing 00.000 on the GPS was a thrill for this map enthusiast. I had been down to South 55 degrees in Ushuaia and now was heading back into the Northern Hemisphere. So far, it had been balmy outside on deck as we were experiencing the tail end of the southern summer. Soon after crossing the equator, it started to turn chilly as we headed into the end of the northern winter.

Around the same time, I celebrated my 30th birthday somewhere near Senegal. It was not something that I had advertised, but I was still jumped that day at lunch with a surprise tiramisu cake. I surmised that the crew must have been informed by head office and taken the initiative to do something special. The cake, the celebration and the change of dessert were the perfect distractions from life on board and everyone joined in. There is only so much celebrating you can do on board a ship, but it was made even more special by the fact that I was going to be able to prepare my chicken curry.

When we had first boarded the ship almost two weeks prior, the ship's burly cook, Nicolai, was excited to hear that there was an Indian on board. He had sought me out in the dining room, brandishing a fat bag of 'Madras Curry Powder' with a large beaming smile. I promised I would make him my famous (I assured him) chicken curry. While we were both thrilled at the prospect, I soon realized that it was just a kind gesture as Officer Mantila later informed me with regret that passengers were not allowed inside the galley, the ship's kitchen. I sulked a bit then, explaining that I was a chef and that my curry was world famous, hoping to get him to change his mind. He smiled and he said he would have a word with the captain and let me know. A few days before my birthday, I probed Mantila again. He said the head office was not allowing it on safety grounds but the captain said I could do it while out at sea, as long as we didn't tell anyone about it. At once, I agreed to making a clandestine curry on the high seas.

That night on the top deck, I reflected on how I was concluding my twenties, most of which were spent in the United States, and was starting my fourth decade on a ship in the middle of the Atlantic. This would certainly be a memorable birthday. The next day, all the passengers met in the galley in the afternoon amid the buzz of a special treat. Nicolai was a funny character that fit the stereotype of a cook on a ship; big hearted but rough on the edges, with a large pot belly. He seemed a bit flustered with our intrusion into his space but went along with it. Four whole chickens were prepared and I soon took command of the kitchen, asking for sixteen onions, twenty tomatoes, a few bulbs of garlic and lots of ginger. Jean was amused that everyone was enlisted to help as part of my offer to cook. There's no such thing as a free lunch. Sandra was chopping tomatoes, Anthony was peeling garlic and Klaus was taking photos.

Due to safety reasons, the stove did not have an open flame. Hence, I was forced to work with a sealed counter under which the burners pumped out a weak heat, in contrast to my preference. To my credit, I had managed to cook my curry on all sorts of stoves across South America, so I surged ahead and began frying onions, garlic and ginger in a large pot. Nicolai, reminding me who the actual chef was in a jovial tone, looked over my shoulder and commented that this was not how he made his curry. He continued to hover and soon interjected again when I was cutting onions. I like to deliberately cut slowly, making equal cuts across the halved onion, but Nicolai got frustrated with this slow pace. Grabbing an onion, he chopped it at a rapid pace without even looking down at it; the remaining onions didn't stand a chance. He was certainly efficient.

When the curry powder went in, the aroma filled the kitchen and smiles broke out all around, even on Nicolai. Frying the ground spices in the oil infused with onions, ginger, garlic and now chicken, created an intoxicating smell that reminded me of the best curries I had prepared over the past year. The most memorable of these was the one I had made in Cordoba, in central Argentina, in a giant steel dish over an outdoor wood fire. The strength of the heat and the flavour of the steel dish gave it a unique taste. This time, aboard the ship's safety stove, the curry was lacking that open fire taste, but different circumstances meant different tasting curries. Perhaps this one had a bit too much salt – a homage to the sea all around. With the curry done, Nicolai said he was very impressed and promoted me to sous chef.

Everyone was beaming with smiles when Franchesco served up the chicken curry at dinner. Some of the officers had joined us to take part in the curry before it disappeared, and Jean remarked how my curry had the power to bring even the officers an hour early for dinner. Officer Mantila later told me that this was the first time in his career that passengers had been allowed to cook in the ship's galley. In fact, almost everyone looked pleased with the change in cuisine after eating pasta for every meal for the past two weeks.

It wasn't my best tasting curry as the tomatoes were lacking in flavour and I had been too conservative in the spiciness. Regardless, I mused over the fact that even in the middle of the ocean, my identity as an Indian remained strong. I was travelling on this journey to discover other cultures, but in the process, I also discovered how Indian I actually am. Cooking a chicken curry from scratch for people who had never tasted Indian food or met an Indian before, is something I am very proud of. My enthusiasm for food made it easy for me to connect with people and create some genuine happiness. When I saw the smiles break out around the table that evening, I knew that being involved in preparing the curry was partly why everyone was so happy. I had made my chicken curry cooking a participatory event, and by then, I could predict the recipients' reactions. The skeptics (there was always at least one) would question how I could possibly prepare an exotic dish such as an Indian chicken curry, having just come off a bike, and that too, for so many people. It was my greatest pleasure to see them smile upon taking their first bite. I enjoyed having the ability to reach out to the good side of the skeptics through their taste buds. It was the perfect way to begin my thirties.

After nine days at sea crossing the Atlantic, we made landfall at Dakar, Senegal, on the west coast of Africa. The ship's mast flew the country's flag that we were heading for, along with the country the ship was registered at. Additionally, there was a yellow flag on the mast to indicate that our last country (Brazil) was one where yellow fever was a risk. It was novel to think that in this day and age of satellite communication, ships were still using flags. Only by being on a ship could one really experience the traditions of the shipping industry.

We were informed that we had to anchor offshore for two days since there was another ship in front of us at the Dakar port and there weren't enough free berths at the dock. Over the next two days, there was a hive of activity by the ship's crew. Officer Mantila tried a test launch of the lifeboat, which did not initially work as intended, but deployed properly later. There was a notice from the head office pinned in the communications room, where we would send our short e-mails to the outside world, stating that the ship had to be in tip-top shape before entering European waters. Apparently, the ship was not getting the highest marks on its cleanliness audits from the strict EU shipping authorities. The crew was busy banging away and chipping off old paint for a new coat.

The evening before we were allowed into port, I had gone out for some fresh air and saw a fish lying on deck. Crewman Raymond was busy fishing in the rich, cold waters off Senegal. I had seen the crew fishing when we stopped at previous ports and figured it must be their one form of release from being on the ship for extended periods of time. However, Raymond informed me that this time, the crew had orders from the captain to collect as much fish as possible for a barbeque later. All around the ship, crewmen with free time on their hands were fishing. In the end, they had collected over fifteen buckets of fish. Cadet Choru soon joined in for some fishing. He was in line to become a chief mate after many more years of experience on the high seas. They were fishing, not with rods but simply with a long line hung down from the deck, and about every minute or two, a haul of fish would come up. These waters were known for their abundant fish stocks. Raymond gave me a line that had three plastic baits strung on it, and as I had observed him doing, I lowered the line off the side of the ship. Within a minute, I felt a series of tugs and rapidly brought up the line. I was thrilled to have managed the full load of three fish per line on my very first try. I had never fished before and was delighted with my easy success. After dropping the line the next time, I was instructed to sway the line until I felt a tug, then it was time to haul the catch up. It made for a fun evening.

The next morning, I saw that we had docked at Port Autonome de Dakar, which has been operational since 1857. From the ship's top deck, downtown Dakar spread out ahead of us. Old colonial buildings contrasted with modern concrete apartment blocks and mosque minarets, adding to the cultural mix of this cosmopolitan city. Dakar's prominent location on the western tip of the African continent had ensured its importance to the colonial powers of Europe through the centuries. Before independence, it was the capital of French west Africa. A few hours after docking, the captain informed the passengers that we were allowed onshore for two hours. This was the first time to be on African soil for many of us. For me, it was more of a homecoming. I had left the African continent two decades ago after spending my childhood in Zambia, and now, I was finally setting foot back in Africa. It didn't feel like a foreign land, even though I had not been to west Africa before. It felt as though I was coming home, even if it was just for two hours.

Jean and I strolled away from the port and came across the zero mile marker of Senegal's National Highway 1. This was the start of a route from the central square heading east across the country into Mali. How I wished I could have ridden sanDRina off the ship and set out on this road. But alas, it was no longer possible to disembark from Grimaldi ships in Dakar. It had been allowed up till a few months ago and this had been my original plan. However, a couple of Belgian motorcyclists had ruined it for the rest of us. Senegal is notorious for its red tape and corruption, and these motorcyclists did not have the patience to wait a few hours for their customs papers to process and simply rode out of the port on their bikes and across the country. This situation left Grimaldi with the headache of dealing with the illegal importation of motorcycles, forcing them to pay a hefty fine.

Jean wanted to get her sandals fixed, so we found the main market and I asked around for a cobbler using my poor French. As soon as we had stepped on land, the touts were out and began tagging along, expecting a payment for giving us directions. They kept offering to sell us perfumes and other random items that they were hawking, but lots of 'non, merci' finally did it. Jean was a bit overwhelmed by their persistence and was glad that I had managed to fend them off. It was about being firm, but respectful.

We made it back into the port, and being my curious self, I began photographing the things I found interesting, from the truck drivers to the towering *Grande Francia*. Just as I clicked a shot of the ship, a uniformed port officer jumped out of his car by the ramp and informed us that it was illegal to take pictures at port and he 'could' write us a ticket for the offence. His phrasing and attitude made his intentions clear. By indicating that there was something else we could do to clear our name, he was suggesting that we bribe him.

The port officer said that we would have to see the captain to sort out the issue, scaring us into believing that we had done something terribly wrong. We were not sure what was happening but were glad to be walking back onto the ship, which was our territory, not his. He told us it was forbidden by international maritime law to take pictures in ports due to security issues, which probably had some truth to it, even though we hadn't had problems at the previous ports. We were later informed that this same sleazy officer had caught Franz and Sandra for the same offence and the captain had to save them. This time, the officer made it up to the passenger deck and demanded to see the captain. Officer Mantila saw us and winked, indicating that we were not at fault, and I understood that this was probably a common occurrence in Dakar. Apparently, the officer was seen leaving the ship later with a few cartons of cigarettes and some whisky bottles tucked under his arms.

After another delicious Italian lunch, we watched the busy port activity from the top deck, continuing to take pictures with Officer Mantila's approval. This port did not have its own cranes, like the ones we saw in Argentina and Brazil, and that was the beauty of these kinds of ships. They could visit ports lacking in infrastructure as they carried their own cranes for loading and unloading containers. It was impressive to see large 40 ft containers dangling from over 60 m (197 ft) with just four cables holding them. I wondered how often a cable broke and led to cargo being damaged. We also saw garbage from the ship's galley being winched down. There was another communique from the head office informing the ship to clear out the garbage area before landing in Europe as the German port officials were very strict about letting in dirty ships that might be bringing in diseases. I also saw other international maritime law notices in the kitchen area about pollution control. One of them said it was now banned to dump plastic waste at sea (finally!) and food waste could only be dumped a certain number of miles from shore. However, they still allowed cardboard packaging and wooden crates to be dumped far from shore. I wondered how much cargo ships contributed to the pollution debris floating around in the oceans.

After an interesting day in Dakar, it was time to set sail for Europe. Once again, the feeling that we were on board a ship sailing the high seas between continents made my skin tingle. We pulled away, taking in the fading view of Dakar from the top deck. The next evening, we had the fish barbeque. The officers were out behind the galley manning the grill. I was glad that we were allowed to have a barbeque considering how safety conscious the entire crew was. There were, of course, a few fire extinguishers nearby. The crew and officers were a fun bunch and I felt as though they wanted to interact with the passengers more, since they encouraged me to hang around with them by the grill.

I got talking with Chief Engineer Hufalar, who was from the Philippines. He had been in my home port of Madras when the December 2004 Sumatra Earthquake and Tsunami struck. His ship had been lifted over 10 m (33 ft) and dropped back down by the large waves. I probed him about some of the technical aspects of our ship. He said the ship carried 3,000 metric tonnes (mt) (3,000,000 L or 792,000 gal) of heavy fuel oil for the round-trip two-month journey from Europe and back of 24,000 km (14,916 miles), which translates to roughly 12,500 L/100 km (0.008 kpL/ 0.019 mpg). Heavy fuel oil is a very crude fuel and is highly polluting, but since it's been difficult to pass pollution laws for ships due to their trans-boundary nature, they go on burning this dirty, cheap fuel. However, Europe has enacted very strict laws regarding pollution, so the ship also carries 400 mt of light fuel oil for burning when they enter European ports. There were also 100 mt of gas oil on board, which was slightly heavier than diesel, for all the heavy machinery that was used in moving the containers around. The Chief Engineer was also late in giving us a tour of the engine room, so I pushed him on that request.

Heavy fuel oil, also called bunker oil, is not controlled by any global regulatory body for its particulate emissions, and as passengers, we felt a bit guilty for using this hazardous service seeing the thick, black smoke billowing out of the ship's chimney stack. One solution would be to throw a filter on the smoke stack to reduce the amount of particulates being sent out, but this would reduce performance and no one had been able to pass such global regulation. However, each region can set its own rules, as Europe had done. With climate change mitigation becoming a reality across many industries, it is only a matter of time before cargo ships have to do their part in reducing their carbon footprint and cutting down on their air pollution.

The fish barbeque was delicious and once again, we enjoyed the change in cuisine. After pigging out for the first two weeks on board, most passengers slowly started to refuse the second course of meat at each meal. We had to get accustomed to normal eating quantities again as we would be back to feeding ourselves soon. An interesting point about mealtimes was that we had to sit in the same seat for every meal. In the first few meals, we all shuffled around to get to know everyone, but Franchesco didn't like this since he wanted to pre-place our drink orders and forbade us from moving around. The ship certainly liked its order.

There were TVs in our cabins that were meant for capturing over-the-air channels when we got into European waters and after we got near France, we could get BBC World News. I was content without internet access on board but was starving for news about current affairs. The morning of 11 March brought the shocking news of the Tohoku Earthquake and Tsunami in Japan. I was glued to the TV from then on. This incident was slowing playing out in real time. When people in Tokyo complained about experiencing motion sickness due to the six-minute long quake, I could relate as our ship swayed in the stormy waters off of France. It was also a strange feeling to be out on the high seas, albeit on the other side of the planet and in a different ocean, as the tsunami was rapidly spreading across the Pacific Ocean. It took about twenty-two hours for the tsunami to reach Chile. I wondered what ships that were in the Pacific must be experiencing. And then, the Fukushima 1 reactor exploded due to a build-up of hydrogen inside the damaged nuclear reactor. This disaster just grew exponentially. I wondered how it would affect the global markets in the coming weeks.

As 'Fukushima' was becoming a common household name, the *Grande Francia* passed through the English Channel. We had also crossed the Prime Meridian the day before and were officially in the Eastern Hemisphere of the planet. Standing near the bridge, the White Cliffs of Dover, across the channel on England's southeastern coast, stood to my left. The South Foreland lighthouse could be seen on top of the 100 m (330 ft) high cliffs of chalk. The symbolic cliffs have served as protection for England through the ages of attack from continental Europe. Looking the other way was Cap Gris Nez, near Calais in France. The English Channel is at its narrowest between Dover and Calais, with only 34 km (21 miles) of water separating the British Isles from Continental Europe. This busy channel connects the North Sea to the Atlantic and there were numerous ships on the horizon, including an MSC container ship a few hundred metres from our starboard side (the left side of the ship).

Eventually, star gazing at night became a routine exercise for me. At around 9 p.m. every night, I found myself outside on the top deck, looking at the constellation of Orion. It is one of the most recognizable star patterns in the sky. In the Northern Hemisphere, Orion is associated with the image of a hunter. Four prominent stars draw out his four limbs, three stars in a row across the middle make his belt, and the two stars coming off the belt resemble his sword. The brightness of these stars makes them easily recognizable, even in the light-polluted city skies around the world. What was really intriguing for me was to see Orion upside down in the southern skies. At the start of the sea journey, near South America, Orion appeared with his sword looking like a tie, just as I had seen him for the past few months across Chile and Argentina. But every night at 9 p.m., as we moved north across the planet, Orion was slowly rotating. Right on the equator, he was flat across the sky with his two stars neither resembling a sword nor a tie, and when we moved into the Northern Hemisphere, he was back to his usual self with a sword. The realization was quite profound. We had just moved across a large portion of a giant rock floating through space, and rotated our position with respect to the patterns in the sky. Experiencing this gradual change made me realize the value of slow travel. If I had taken a ten-hour flight to cover this same distance, I would not have had the same perspective. Covering such a large distance at a stately pace allowed me to take note of our position in the universe. It is not the stars that are moving across the sky; it is us moving across the planet. I felt humbled and insignificant to know that the universe all around us was vast beyond our perception. This only came to me when I looked up instead of down at my computer screen or mobile phone. Not having the distractions of time, I wondered how much ancient humans or even pre-technology humans appreciated the universe. The relevance of stars in human lives increases the further back we go in history. In the days before GPS, sailors had to navigate with the stars and their sextants, and I was starting to understand how they could actually use a small twinkle in the sky to get an idea of their position in the open sea. I wondered if the cadets in training on board were taught how to use a sextant. It would certainly come in handy in case of an emergency.

Finally, after lunch one day, near the end of the journey, we had our tour of the engine room. The heavy metal door opened and we had to crouch to enter. Once inside, we were blinded by bright, green paint. It was more of a cathedral of engineering than simply an engine room as it was three storeys high. Once accustomed to the strange light, we saw the heart of the ship. Before us lay a giant, eight cylinder, in-line diesel engine made by Sulzer, a Swiss company (as stated on the accompanying plaque). They have been in the business of engines since 1834 and after employing a certain Rudolf Diesel, the world got its first diesel engine in 1898.

The sounds emanating from this mechanical symphony were astounding. Its rapid clack-a-ticking was almost deafening but a distinctly satisfying sound at the same time. I was expecting the cylinders to be much larger. Each cylinder of the engine was large enough for a man to fit inside, but I had this image, perhaps from the Titanic movie, of room-sized pistons moving up and down, which was ill-placed.

The space was tight around the engine room. I saw a few spare parts in one corner for this behemoth of an engine. I could see from the long cylinder liner that the stroke (the distance the piston moves up and down) was much larger than the bore (the diameter of the piston), and this ratio would produce much higher torque than horsepower, which was what a diesel engine on a ship would need to do. To put things into perspective, it can be said that torque is more relevant at low speeds to get things moving, whereas horsepower is more relevant at high speeds to keep the momentum.

A large mechanical lever indicated that the engine was on 'comando a distanza', meaning that the engine was being controlled from the officers on the bridge. Chief Engineer Hufalar gave us the tour of his engine control room. It looked quite different from the gleaming controls of the bridge, with its boxy control panel adorned with a large array of big, square push-buttons, some lit up and others not. Below the main engine switch was a picture of Jesus guiding a ship's crew through stormy waters, revealing the religious nature of the Filipinos.

The main engine readout was bemusing. The ship's propeller shaft was spinning at only around 100 revolutions per minute (RPM). In comparison, a typical diesel car's engine spins at around 2,000 RPM. But this vessel was all about torque and for that, low revolutions were needed, backed by immense power. Chief Engineer Hufalar told us that during the Brazil–Dakar leg, we were on schedule and were able to cruise at the slower speed of 13.5 knots (25.0 kph, 15.5 mph) to save fuel, and the output shaft was spinning at 89 RPM then. After the two-day delay in Dakar, the ship had to step it up to make it on time to Europe and the propeller shaft was increased ever so slightly to spin at 93.4 RPM, which was visible in red characters on an electronic display. That translated to 17.0 knots (31.5 kph, 19.5 mph), and ever since Dakar, we were able to feel the engine vibrations throughout the ship. On the Atlantic crossing, it was smooth as glass. It was incredible how such small differences in speed were highly relevant when the size of the object and the distances covered were scaled up enormously. While cruising at 25.0 kph, we were covering 600 km (373 miles) per day and now, at 31.5 kph, we were covering 750 km (466 miles) per day. The engine was running twenty-four hours a day.

Next to the RPM was a second readout on the display, which indicated the amount of torque being applied through the shaft. It read 293.8 kilonewton metres or 2,16,296 foot pounds. That was an absurd amount of torque. For comparison, an average car puts out around 150 foot pounds of torque. This made logical sense, however, because to move such a gargantuan object, it was all about the torque. The third readout was the amount of power being produced by the engine of 2,873 kilowatts (3,851 hp), and the last readout was of energy, which is power produced over time (or work done), of 8,337 megawatt-hours (MWh). To put that in perspective, an average house in the United States uses about 11 MWh of energy per day so the output of the *Grande Francia*'s engine in ten seconds could power roughly twenty-five homes in the US for a month.

At one end of the large control desk sat Andres, a Filipino cadet who was training to become chief engineer. He was diligently punching away at his keyboard and we saw then that this was just another office, but one that controls a massive engine ploughing through the oceans. Outside the control room, we saw the giant propeller shaft, which was probably too large for me to even wrap my arms around. It was spinning at a stately speed with copious amounts of torque. The shaft headed out the back of the ship, working round-the-clock to propel us forward.

We found out that the Chief Engineer was delaying our engine room tour because he was still cleaning up an oil spill. A few days earlier, the ship had come to a stop out in the open water for a few hours and we found out that the increased vibrations from the higher speed after Dakar had cracked a bolt that held an oil filter in place, causing the oil to spew out. They fixed the issue, but had a big clean-up task on their hands. After that, there were two more engine stops. I was impressed that we were still on time for our landing date in Hamburg.

One fact to appreciate while being on board was that the engine never stopped running (except for those three unexpected incidents), and even when it was not providing forward momentum, it had to run the generators to provide electricity and desalinate seawater. Once a ship is put into service, it is constantly running back and forth along its route with periodical crew changes. If the ship is ever docked for maintenance, it loses money, and I wondered how its oil was changed if it never stopped. With that thought, the door to the engine room was closed and we were back in the low-roofed, white corridors of the ship. It was another world beyond that door.

The skies changed as we cruised around the northwest of Europe. It was much more overcast and gloomy now and I couldn't spend as much time outside compared to the earlier part of the journey. When we were going past France, the choppy waters rocked the ship quite dramatically. I was feeling seasick, just like when the waters got dicey on the *Stahlratte*, but this time, I had an excellent remedy. Jean let me borrow her acupressure bracelet. It was an elastic bracelet with a small white ball that was to be placed between the tendons on the inside of the wrist. This placed a certain amount of pressure on my nerves and blood vessels at the spot that connected to the balance system in my head, equalizing the swaying motions. After using the bracelet for two days, my seasickness went away. Even though the ship was still swaying, my body had been trained to not feel the motions even though I wasn't using the bracelet. I was standing on the top deck, holding on to the railing and seeing the front of the ship moving up and down by the whole height of the ship and enjoying the roller coaster ride.

When I woke up the next morning, I was greeted by the eerie sight of large wind turbines poking through the dense morning fog. In front of us, in the dull, white fog, were rows upon rows of newly-manufactured cars awaiting their ships. We had docked at our first port in Europe, Emden, the westernmost city of Germany. This small town owed its fortunes to the large Volkswagen factory there and Germany's dominance in exports was clearly visible. Even during these times of a global financial crisis, the German economy was going strong with its export-oriented strategy. We picked up a few Porsches and Audis and set sail for one last night aboard the *Grande Francia*. While in Emden, the 'Zoll', German customs, boarded the ship looking for any contraband, as this was our first stop in Europe since Africa. They were not very polite and banged on my cabin door and asked, 'Anything to declare? Cigarettes, alcohol, marijuana?' They said they would search our vehicles and would call us if the sniffer dogs smelled anything funny. I was worried about the spices, but all was good. The other European passengers commented on how rude a welcome that was to Europe, contrary to South America.

At dinner that night, the Europeans joked about how I would have to start following the traffic rules again, unlike riding in South America. We exchanged contact information and thanked Franchesco for the wonderful service over the past four weeks. It had been a tremendously satisfying journey and a real eye-opener as I had seen parts of our world that were not easily visible to the general public. Being surrounded by all that water was a comforting feeling, but now, it was time to get back on land.

10

SAHARAN ENCOUNTERS

SANDRINA'S ENGINE FIRED UP and we rolled out of the Visemar One cargo hold and onto a new continent. Arriving in Alexandria on Egypt's northern coast signalled the start of my journey across the African continent. The three-day vehicle ferry had brought me from Venice after a few weeks spent preparing for Africa and travelling across Europe.

My original plan of entering western Africa via Morocco had to change after I was refused a tourist visa. Despite the issues normally associated with an Indian passport, this was surprisingly the first time in my journey that a visa application had been rejected. After multiple attempts, I gave up and changed the trip routing to head down eastern Africa. But ahead of me, the political situation in north Africa was extremely fluid.

At the beginning of the year, as I was getting ready to leave South America, I was eagerly following the people's power movement of the Arab Spring. After Tunisia's success in overthrowing their long-time autocratic regime, Egypt picked up the torch and surprised

everyone by also overthrowing their autocratic leader, Hosni
Mubarak; beginning on 25 January 2011, this took just eighteen
days of protest. He had led Egypt for the past thirty years, and like
every other 'charismatic' leader of the people, had become more
self-obsessed after the first few years in office until he assumed the
powers of a dictator. But the new age of information technology
had arrived, bringing both transparency and oversight. On
11 February 2011, Mubarak stepped down and no one (inside and
outside the country) knew what would happen next. Egyptians never
thought the day would come where they could vote freely, and now
the country was slowly stepping towards elections under a military
council tasked with leading the country through this transition.

My impression of Egyptians was that they were friendly, so the
security situation did not present an immediate concern for me.
However, the revolution had scared off most of the tourists, as was
evident by the largely empty ferry. I received confirmation from
other overland travellers who were in Egypt and the CouchSurfing
community in Cairo that things were back to normal and that it
was completely safe to travel through Egypt once again. I also had
no choice now that the route through Morocco had been closed
to me.

Parking on the docks of the Port of Alexandria, I was ready for
Egypt's notorious bureaucracy. This was the first country on my
route where I would be needing a Carnet de Passage – a bygone
document used in countries with antiquated customs procedures.
It was a customs passport of such for sanDRina, allowing me to
temporarily enter foreign countries and guaranteeing them that I
would henceforth exit with the said vehicle and not sell it without
paying the appropriate duty. The carnet was supposed to make
border crossings easier, but it still took a few hours to completely
process sanDRina into Egypt. With a temporary licence plate zip-
tied to my regular plate (Egypt is one of the few countries in the
world to still follow this procedure), I rolled out of the port into
dusty, old Alexandria.

I love the feeling of the first few kilometres in a new country, especially on a new continent. There were so many new things to process: how do people drive here, what allowances do they make for motorcycles, what are the rules for cutting through traffic, how do pedestrians act? I quickly saw that traffic rules were merely a suggestion, as two young Egyptians zipped past me on a small motorcycle and cut through the small gap between two yellow, boxy Lada taxis. The streets and all the cars parked on them were covered in dust, the first signs of the immense Saharan desert that lay ahead.

My time in Alexandria was short. I had only been granted a seventy-two hour tourist visa upon arrival, despite the reassurances of the Egyptian embassy in Paris that I would most certainly get a thirty day visa on arrival with my Indian passport. I rushed on the wide tarmac highway into Cairo, the largest metropolitan area on the African continent, and managed to find the immigration office in the busy, narrow streets of the city. Much to my dismay, the officer informed me that it was not possible to extend my visa and that I had better leave the country immediately and re-enter with a proper thirty day visa. I weighed up my options. Libya was descending into civil war. Israel wouldn't have been an easy border to cross and come back from. Jordan was also not looking particularly inviting with Syria nearby, well into its own civil war. While I nervously fidgeted in the busy immigration hall, a young man with a wry smile on his face asked me where I was heading. He was behind me in the line and had overheard my exchange with the immigration officer. Sudan, I expounded. 'Don't worry about the short stay visa,' he said, smiling. Most of the immigration officers at the airport and land ports rarely checked the valid number of days stamped on the visa, he explained, and if they did, it would only be a matter of paying a small bribe to leave the country. With no other option, I accepted that I would be overstaying my visa in Egypt and would deal with it when I got to the border. With that settled, I began exploring Cairo.

Nearly two weeks had passed in this giant of a city. I emerged out of the Anwar Sadat subway station and strolled to Tahrir Square. Having sweet tea and smoking a hookah at an outdoor café with Candela and Tiph, travellers I met through my CouchSurfing host, we enjoyed the relaxed evening. Looking across the vast square, the focal point of the Egyptian Revolution, it was eerily calm. Just three months before, Egyptians of all strata in society had gathered there and demanded that Mubarak step down. With the army on the people's side, Mubarak had no choice but to realize his time was up. I felt nervous and excited to be so close to that hotbed of political activism. Seeing the pictures on TV and then being there and understanding the significance of the location reminded me of the opportunity that overland travel presents, namely, a more intimate exposure to history. As the café shut down, we saw people gathering on the central median and chanting slogans. The revolution was not yet over.

Initially, I had been nervous to enter Egypt, but in my two weeks in Cairo, having visited old souks to modern night clubs, I saw that life was actually quite normal away from the political focus of Tahrir Square. But since the global news media primarily reported about the ongoings at the square, the image of Egypt outside of the country was one that was unstable and possibly dangerous to foreigners. This had, of course, scared away the tourists. But as I found out the next day, it also gave me a remarkable opportunity.

After seeing those sharp peaks poking out of the city skyline as I buzzed about Cairo, it was time to finally visit the grandest monument of Cairo and Egypt, the Pyramids of Giza. The sun was blazing hot as usual, and after paying my entry ticket, I rode sanDRina into the parking lot. The Pyramid of Khufu rose in front of me with its exposed jagged rocks racing from the four corners to the apex. Pictures of the pyramids come nowhere near encapsulating the scale of them in real life. The base was 230 m (755 ft) and it rose 146.5 m (481 ft) towards the hot desert sun. Standing at one corner and facing the pyramid, it was not easy to discern where the edges of this grand structure lay. What impressed me the most was the fact that the pyramid had been standing there for the past 4,571 years and was likely to still be standing for aeons to come. The exposed rocks belied the grandeur of the pyramid when it was completed, as posited by Egyptologists. From the other pyramids in the necropolis, it was known that this great pyramid was covered in limestone. It would have been an immense edifice that gleamed white under the bright sun, dominating the vista for anyone venturing close to the Pharaohs' seat of power. Over the years, either due to seismic activity or plundering for construction in Cairo, all but a few pieces of the limestone now remained.

Examining the face of the pyramid, one section had been removed, exposing the top of the King's burial chamber. Huge granite slabs placed at angles were clearly visible. Engineered by a process of trial and error, they were set to deflect the weight of the stones on top from collapsing into the void of the chamber below. Paying a small fee, I entered the pyramid at this point, an entrance known appropriately enough as the Robber's Tunnel, dug in AD 820 by Caliph al-Ma'mun, who wanted to plunder the treasures inside. The narrow tunnel that slanted acutely upward in a determined, unwavering ascent was not for claustrophobics. Who knows how long the labourers had toiled for while working on the tunnel, not knowing whether they were headed in the right direction or how far they had to chisel and hammer at the rocks within the pyramid. My own steep ascent was nothing compared to the blistered mining that its creators must have endured, illuminated only by small oil lamps and shrouded in rock dust, with no whisper of air to relieve the heat. Yet, their effort evidently rewarded Caliph al-Ma'mun. The tunnel emerges into the Grand Gallery in which sharply-cut granite slabs towered over me to the roof of the narrow gallery 8 m (26 ft) above. A group of Polish tourists was waiting to climb back down the tunnel, and once they left, I realized that I was all alone inside the Great Pyramid.

After crawling through another short tunnel, I emerged in the King's Chamber, the focus of the pyramid. It is now an empty room, 10 m (33 ft) by 5 m (16 ft) with a roof 6 m (20 ft) high, in which the only object remaining is the King's sarcophagus. Its rough finish suggested that the original intricate granite sarcophagus was probably lost in the Nile while being transported to the pyramid, and so, a replacement had been hastily put together. Egyptologists have suggested this because they've found very ornately decorated sarcophagi in other less grand pyramids. The whole room was made of granite blocks that were quarried in Aswan and floated down the Nile. Besides the feat of transporting and placing such huge and heavy blocks of granite some 4,500 years ago, what was even more impressive to me was the precision with which they were able to make cuts in the granite, one of the toughest stones on Earth.

Standing all alone in the King's Chamber, what it was to be in this ancient, grand structure, and that too, without the disturbance of other tourists, flooded over me. I tried to imagine what would drive a man (Pharaoh Khufu) to dedicate his whole life to building such a grand structure and having the power and will to employ tens of thousands of workers to erect this nearly eternal monument to himself. As I sat along one of the walls, I reflected on the various types of people that must have visited this exact chamber over the past few centuries. The pyramids have stood the test of time and have witnessed the changing faces of Cairo and Egypt over the past few millennia.

I emerged back into the blinding daylight and continued my visit of the necropolis. I wasn't hassled as much by the various camel touts and trinket sellers there as my brown skin allowed me to blend in with the locals. I had read that this grand site was a draw for visitors since its construction was completed. There was no one else in sight as I sat under a limestone outcrop in front of the second grand pyramid there, made by Khafre, Khufu's son, and had my packed lunch. I wondered how often in the aeons past had the pyramids been this devoid of visitors. Post-revolutionary phases are evidently a boon for some, and it dawned on me that the best time to visit a heavily touristic country should be post revolution. Syria nearby was well into its own turmoil, and at that time, I wondered if I should visit the grand structures that lay there just as soon as peace returns to the country.

After enjoying the bliss of post-revolution Egypt, it was time to leave the busy Nile river basin. There were multiple routes heading south from Cairo towards the border with Sudan. One went down the Red Sea coast, another followed the Nile, and then there was the path I took, through the Western Desert, the Oasis Route, looping into the Sahara to follow a string of scattered, ancient oases.

I left the cacophony of Cairo's traffic behind and soon found myself out on the open road headed southwest to the oasis of Bahariya. The landscape was devoid of form besides the gently rolling sand and rocks of the desert. The only objects punctuating the landscape were mobile phone towers, powered by solar panels, providing low cost internet access far into the Sahara desert. It was a comforting feeling to some and annoying for others who were trying to get away from it all. I teetered between both sides at various times. After I had my fill of the internet in Cairo, I was back in my get-away-from-it-all state of mind.

The dry heat of the desert was intense. Even though it was hot under my Kevlar mesh riding suit, I preferred the slight warmth of it in comparison to the burning of my exposed skin to the sun. The 400 km (248 miles) ride from Cairo to Bahariya was easy riding on the flat highway, but I stopped frequently to hydrate, downing my home-made rehydration solution (1 tablespoon of sugar, half a teaspoon of salt and some concentrated lime juice in 1 L of water). Water on its own just wouldn't have cut it in the heat, evident in the salt and sweat-stained clothing I would peel off at night.

Near the oasis of Bahariya, greenery returned to the landscape. I called up my next CouchSurfing contact, Hamada, and he directed

me to his house. Arriving at a simple mud-brick structure next
to a newly-constructed concrete house, the first thing we did was
have some sweet mint tea. For those who have not experienced tea
brewed over an open flame in a pot crammed with mint and sugar,
few things are more refreshing on a hot, sun-blasted, desert day. It
was revitalizing and delicious. Hamada, short-haired and spectacled
in trousers and a polo shirt, exuded a sense of professionalism about
him. He came from a Bedouin family and was a professional tour
guide, leading tourists on desert safaris. He had recently settled
in the town of Bahariya for economic reasons, a common trend
among many nomadic peoples in the Middle East.

Sitting there with our tea, we were soon joined by Hamada's
friend, Taheer, just as Hamada's mother brought out lunch for us.
There are no individual plates in the Bedouin habit of communal
eating. It breeds a sense of trust and creates strong bonds. And so
we sat there, eating with our hands from the plate of fried fish,
beans, aubergine, fresh tomato and pepper salad, with lots of
rice and lafa (Egyptian flat bread). It was a civilized and delicious
opening to the Saharan desert.

After a short nap through the hottest part of the day, we headed
out in Taheer's old Toyota Land Cruiser for a tour around the oasis.
Deep under the parched surface of the Sahara lay a vast quantity
of groundwater aquifers. Most of it was fossil water, meaning that
it had reached the aquifers millions of years ago and was not being
recharged by rainwater, so it remains a non-renewable resource,
much like oil. With the rate of extraction far exceeding renewal
rates, the sustainability of such water sources is not guaranteed. We
stopped at a spring where surprisingly tall pine trees grew strong
in this desert soil, beside a tank built around the spring feeding
water to the nearby area. As with most springs in the desert, the
cool waters are almost impossible to resist, so we jumped in to cool
off with the fresh water flowing from aquifers deep underground.

This was probably a common pastime for those in the area.
After an enjoyable swim, we settled down again around an open

fire to brew more mint tea. Known as the 'juice of the desert', it helps the body absorb more water than just drinking it plain, Hamada explained, as I sucked down three cups. Fortunately, my Indian heritage had blessed me with a sweet tooth to enjoy the two, heaped spoons of sugar that went in with every small cup of tea there.

Around me, water from the spring was being channelled to feed the giant pine trees and surrounding alfalfa fields, but the desert reappeared quite suddenly as soon as the channels stopped. Away from water, life quickly reverted to the desert environment, albeit specked with occasional date and olive plantations that tracked the aquifers.

Just beyond the greenery of the oasis, we turned off to the loose sand of the desert and pulled into a small property that was fenced off with thatched date palm leaves. Hamada and Taheer had recently acquired that piece of land and were in the process of building an ecolodge. There was a rudimentary structure made with date palm trunks and thatched leaves, but I was more excited to climb the nearby mound and take in the grand view of the desert all around us. It wasn't all sand in the Sahara. There were rocky mountains and plateaus as well. Up on the mound was a small plateau where Taheer laid a thin carpet and we sat in the cool of dusk, taking in the expansive view. I asked Hamada if we could sleep there and a smiled appeared on his face as he understood my love for the desert too. Taheer headed back into town for supplies and retuned with sleeping bags, food and water. We ate and talked freely as darkness settled in. It wasn't all that dark as my eyes were able to adjust, with the starlight allowing me to make out all the landforms that I had seen earlier in the daylight. It was still and calm. While it reminded me of nights spent camping under the stars in the salt flats of South America, it is important to note that every land has its own signature and the Saharan desert's was spellbinding.

I woke up at dawn to witness the desert transitioning from night to day. It had been slightly chilly at night and my sleeping bag was covered in a light sheen of sand, but I had a wonderful night's sleep out in the open desert. I sat in my sleeping bag with my shoulders covered to ward of the air's chill. The sun was just beginning to appear from behind the horizon and the dark of night gave ground, retreating through the spectrum as the rosy-fingered dawn spread across the sky. For breakfast, I saw Hamada pouring water on rock-hard bread. He said it was Bedouin bread and was prepared by initially baking it under the sand with hot coals and then left to dry under the sun until it became rock-hard. The lack of moisture in the bread allowed it to be taken on long journeys across the desert and simply needed to be rehydrated to become edible again. It sounded strange to pour water on bread but it was surprisingly tasty and not soggy as expected. We had the bread with chunks of locally-made goat cheese, freshly-cut tomatoes, yoghurt and boiled eggs. It was a fitting, delicious and wholesome desert breakfast.

  That afternoon, back in town, it was time for Hamada to head to the local mosque for Friday prayers. Out of curiosity, I asked if I could join him and he was excited to get me a jellabiya, the free-flowing dress of Arab men. With both of us sporting grey jellabiyas, having almost no hair and being brown-skinned, his mother remarked that I could pass as his brother. Since non-Muslims aren't allowed into mosques, especially during prayer, Hamada told me not to speak to anyone (since I didn't know more than a few words of Arabic) and to just follow him through the motions of prayer. We went into a small mosque that was carpeted wall to wall, and it felt strange to enter this holy place as an imposter, even if I was entering with a sense of reverence. I kept quiet as instructed and followed Hamada's motions through the prayer, after which he said he was very impressed at how well I took on the temporary role of a practising Muslim. Admittedly, you don't get to travel the world without learning how to blend in, and I was pleased to see how well my own attempt was received.

Over our last meal together, Hamada asked me to stay for longer, maybe a week or so. He tempted me with visits deep into the desert, places where there were old whale fossils and natural sculptures in the sand. I felt quite at home there. I had managed to pose as an Egyptian, so perhaps I could've even passed off as a Bedouin man and journeyed across the sands with Hamada and Taheer. But alas, I had to continue on south to the border and exit Egypt before I overstayed my visa even longer than necessary. It was a tough decision, but Africa to the south still beckoned.

A few days later when I was back on the road, the heat was starting to intensify as I neared Aswan, the southernmost city in Egypt. The sky was clear of any clouds and the sun's rays had no hindrance in their travel to scorching the earth's surface. I had drunk about seven litres of water that day to stay properly hydrated. Impressed with how well my Kevlar mesh riding suit was working out in the Sahara, my decision to get an all-mesh suit was proving to be the correct one. It was indeed hot to wear when I was stationary, but upon moving and having the air flow against my body, it was surprisingly cool even in the blistering sun. Mesh motorcycle gear is generally not looked upon favourably by riders as most of it is made with polyurethane, similar to nylon. Such jackets don't generally withstand road accidents, often disintegrating in the process. Kevlar, on the other hand, is one of the strongest synthetic materials ever made and is fittingly used in bulletproof vests. Woven with more space between the fibres than a bulletproof vest, it was proving to be an excellent material for motorcycle jackets and pants. It was not cheap, but its resistance to the multiple crashes that I'd had so far on the journey had demonstrated its worth.

All along the border between Egypt and Sudan lay a sandy desert, and so it was ironic that the only way to cross between the two countries was a ferry ride on the long, thin Lake Nasser. The 550 km (340 miles) long lake was formed by the damming of the Nile at Aswan. Heading down the eastern side of Africa, this was the only hurdle that I had to plan for, primarily because the ferry only ran once a week, and also because there was limited space for vehicles on board a barge that travels with the ferry.

I reached Aswan and immediately began the bureaucratic dance that Egypt dictates one has to follow to leave the country with a personal vehicle. With instructions from other overland travellers, I arrived at a nondescript white apartment block that housed the Aswan Traffic Court. In order to leave Egypt, I had to get a small piece of paper from the traffic court saying that I had no outstanding traffic violations. The traffic court was closing at 2 p.m. and I had arrived at 1.55. A broker (hustler) in the crowded stairwell said he could help me if we hurried. We ran up the flight of stairs, with me still wearing my heavy motorcycle gear and boots, with all the necessary paperwork in hand. The traffic court was nothing more than an old apartment packed with desks and files, stuffed with papers haphazardly stacked on shelves and on the floor. The official, who was standing up from his desk and on his way out, said, 'Oh, I'm sorry, you're too late, come again on Monday.' 'But sir, the boat is leaving on Monday!' I pleaded as I thrust my clutch of documents toward him. He saw the Ashoka emblem on the cover of my passport and exclaimed, 'Oh, you're from India? Amitabh Bachchan is great! I'll help you out, one second.' The reference to one of India's Bollywood greats momentarily stumped me, and I stared at the officer for a second with the papers held out in my hand before he took them and swept into action. My Indian passport had worked in my favour and after waiting around for thirty minutes, I received my little piece of paper. No cost for the official and just 15 Egyptian Pounds (LE) ($3) for the broker. I rushed to the Traffic Police Office and upon submitting my all-clear notice from the Traffic Court, I received another piece of paper that I was to submit to customs at the port the next day.

As I was riding around the busy streets of Aswan, I saw a baby-blue Land Rover Defender ahead of me with British licence plates. I knew there would be other overland travellers taking the same ferry as me as it only travelled once a week. I pulled up to a dashing blonde man in the driver's seat, and seeing me in my motorcycle gear, he could tell that I was also an overland traveller. He invited me to his camping spot out in the desert. Guy was travelling down from the UK with his partner Louise and they had met up with another overlanding pair, Ben from Switzerland and Ed from the Netherlands, travelling down in a Toyota Hilux motorhome. It was comforting to be around other overland travellers once again. We exchanged stories of our travels through Egypt and it became apparent that we were cut from the same cloth. All of us had left behind or put a pause on our careers to get in a vehicle and head far, far away. There were discomforts in overland travel, but Ben philosophized about the ultimate freedom that it engenders. We discussed all this at the back of their Hilux motorhome, in which they had stashed an LPG cylinder and a proper two-burner stove on which they were preparing a mutton curry and breaded aubergine. Overlanding by four wheels certainly allows more luxuries than a motorcycle. It's a reality all bikers learn to embrace. But thanks to the kindness of strangers, it means you can also occasionally enjoy the same pleasures and delicious meals; in my case, sitting under a brilliant night sky aside the shimmering Nile was part of the package.

The next morning, we headed past town in an overland convoy and reached the port where we met our customs agent, Kamal, dressed in a sweaty shirt with a warm smile. His contact details had been passed along in the overlanding community for his efficiency in getting travellers processed out of Aswan. We milled about in the hot sun, but soon had our tickets for the ferry and paid for the passage of our vehicles on the barge. At the customs house, we had tea with the official, who was quite pleased to meet all us foreigners, and after a bit of chit-chat, he stamped the exit ticket on our respective carnets. With that, we were allowed to enter the fenced-off pier and head down a rocky path, where the barge was waiting with its clunky ramp. The long and narrow barge didn't look all that seaworthy but with no other option, I rode sanDRina up and parked her between the Land Rover and Toyota motorhome. We all felt a bit of separation anxiety as we wouldn't get to see our vehicles, which were our homes, for the next few days. At this point, all we could do was just hope that they would arrive safely at the other end of the lake in Sudan.

Kamal drove us back into Aswan for one last night in Egypt. Come morning, we were back at the port, but this time as passengers for the ferry. The security screening was a mad jumble of people pushing and shoving their suitcases and sacks through an X-ray scanner. Being the only public transport between Sudan and Egypt, there was high demand for space aboard the ferry, as we saw with the rush of dark Sudanese men and women through the port terminal. I was calm and confident as I presented my passport to the immigration official, and luckily for me, he did not notice the overstay on my visa and stamped me out of Egypt. I had successfully stayed about five weeks in Egypt on a seventy-two hour visa. Take that, bureaucracy!

Exiting the port terminal, we saw our vessel for the journey, the *Sagalnaam*. The large white ferry had dings and scratches all along its sides and it probably would not pass a safety inspection in the West, but it had been happily plying these waters for years. The round windows along the centre-line indicated the second-class floor, with the first-class cabins above them and third-class travel on the roof. The cheapest fare cost LE 322 ($59) and first-class went for LE 520 ($95). We got word from other overland travellers that the top deck was the best experience, but we had to rush and beat all the other passengers to claim a good spot on the deck under one of the lifeboats to secure some shade. Ben and Ed opted for a first-class cabin and graciously offered to keep my backpack there for safety.

Our tickets came with a meal voucher, and being fair-skinned, Guy and Lu, who were travelling with me on the third-class deck, could easily enter the first-class dining room with air conditioning running, unlike the mess hall for the second- and third-class passengers below. On the contrary, I had to make an effort to look like I belonged in first-class, so I had my large SLR camera slung around my neck and wore shorts like the other foreigners. Travel on board was quite classist and for my own comfort, I had to stick out like a well-heeled foreigner, rather than my usual preference of blending in as a local.

After a hearty lunch of chicken and rice, we watched the action from the top deck. Besides passengers and their vehicles, this ferry and its barges provided a crucial trade link between Egypt and northern Sudan. Due to the strict economic sanctions imposed on Sudan by Western countries opposed to Sudanese president Omar al-Bashir's dictatorial rule (yet another in the region), most domestic and industrial goods were expensive or not available in Sudan. It was cheaper to import from Egypt than to buy locally. As such, large buckets of olive oil, augers for farming and boxes of appliances were being piled on board. Hundreds of primarily Sudanese people had boarded and by dusk, lying low in the water, our ship was ready to set sail.

There were smiles on the top deck as we shared the moment of departure with our fellow passengers. Next to us, on the fully crowded top deck, were three cheery Sudanese men who posed for a photo. I managed to gather from my rudimentary Arabic that they were heading home after a long stint in Libya working as casual labourers in the oil industry, but with the security situation deteriorating there, they had taken some time off to visit home. What they would be returning to, or even when they might next be able to find work in Libya, was all unknown. To be caught up as a foreigner in another's civil war could be problematic, and so they had turned away from it. I would have most certainly done the same thing.

As the sun started to set on Lake Nasser, we entered the golden hour of light. The long rays from the setting sun glimmered on the rippling surface of the lake. With my feet hanging off over the edge of the top deck, I felt as though I was travelling in a bygone era. I had never really travelled by boat before starting this journey from Chicago. It used to be the de facto mode of transport for long journeys before airplanes. The desert mountains that bordered the narrow lake were cast in a warm glow that reflected my own state of being. Being back on a ship once again, I felt comfortable surrounded by water, especially after the extended time spent in the sands of the Egyptian Sahara.

Once the sun dipped below the horizon, the twilight became utterly magical. The orange glow along the horizon was reflecting on the still lake, only disturbed by the harmonious wake of the *Sagalnaam* chugging its way south. As I looked around, all the passengers had stopped whatever they were doing to pass the time, from chatting to playing cards, to take in the magnificence playing out in front of us. Yet, darkness soon fell upon us, and without lights on deck, everyone soon fell asleep to the rhythmic pulse of the ship's engine.

The sun was back out in full force by morning and the calmness of the journey came to an end with the hustle of Wadi Halfa once we landed there. The remote outpost on the southern shores of Lake Nasser marked the entrance to Sudan. There was a sense of urgency among the hundreds of passengers who were stuffed on board as they exploded onto the pier. Our small group of overland travellers rushed out with the sea of humans and stuck together as we entered the concrete terminal building. Looking back at the *Sagalnaam*, it was a strange sight to see such a large boat moored at a pier in the desert. Stamping our passports into Sudan, we were all excited to be entering this country that seemed so far removed from the rest of the world.

The present-day country of Sudan, while still massive, was only a fraction of the area that was referred to as 'The Soudan' in past centuries. The name was a catch-all phrase for lands south of the Sahara that harboured black Africans. It also denoted a change in landscape, with the sands of the desert giving way to the savannahs in the south.

The region of Sudan has had a tumultuous history since recorded inhabitation began in 8,000 BC. The harsh climate and resource-rich land has been subjected to influence and intervention by external forces throughout its history. It was a part of Egypt at various times, and being close to Arabia, its Islamization happened early – albeit in part due to invasions and that Muslims were not enslaved by the Arab slavers who frequently raided the African coastline. Indeed, the root of 'Kafir', so often derogatively applied to black Africa, is actually Arabic for non-believer. In more recent times, controlling access to the Nile drove European colonial powers into Sudan, which bears a certain responsibility for the current state of the region. I had entered Sudan just two weeks before another milestone in the region's history, that of the secession of its southern region into the new country of South Sudan.

Even while Sudan happened to be in the world's consciousness for all the wrong reasons, such as the conflicts in Darfur and Abyei and for its authoritarian president, other travellers had informed me that the people of Sudan were one of the most genuine they had encountered in all of Africa. By then, I knew better to believe other travellers' perspective on the safety of a country rather than what the global news media portrayed.

We had to wait another day for the vehicle barge to arrive, and in that time, we got acquainted with the dilapidated town of Wadi, or New Halfa, that had a towering rock outcrop as its distinctive feature. This was the new location of the town because the original Halfa had been submerged when the Aswan Dam was built. Under pressure from Egypt, the Sudanese government in the 1960s forcibly moved the residents of the old town to this new location and built them a small dam, encouraging them to resettle and get into agriculture. All of it eventually dried up and the current town is a mere ghost of its former self.

During our first meal of the day after getting into town, we encountered the friendly Sudanese people, as described by other travellers. The restaurant owner went out of his way to procure different foods for everyone in our group, as we slowly got used to the intensity of the heat. He had fried chicken but he also went around and sourced falafel and fresh fruits that had arrived on the ferry.

The streets were quiet as nothing much happened during the heat of the day. Most of the buildings were made of mud bricks that would have to get redone after the rains and the streets were sandy, choking the area every time a strong breeze came through. I found affordable accommodation at the Defintood Hotel, for 7 Sudanese Pounds (SP) ($3.20) for the night. My room had a ceiling fan that blew hot air down on me, but with the cool drinking water from the clay pots in the hallway, it was tolerable.

The town came to life after the sun went down, and we gathered in the central square where the locals were focused on a football match being broadcast. All the businesses in the square were decentralized, meaning that one had to get tea from one stall, then falafel from another, and shisha from yet another. Ed pointed this out and said if it was some square in Europe, there would be one boss who would be controlling all the services in this area, ensuring efficient delivery and making big profits. But thankfully, it was not Europe and things happened at a much slower, relaxed rhythm, where everyone could run their own business at their own pace.

A striking Nubian lady served tea to us through the evening. Being a Muslim country and one where Sharia Law is enforced, alcohol sale was banned, so everyone drank tea. And they make some fantastic tea in Sudan. Our Nubian tea lady had a variety of herbs and I enjoyed her spiced tea with cumin. Northern Sudan is the land of the Nubia, where the inhabitants can be set apart by their round faces.

The next morning, we were alerted that the barge carrying our vehicles had arrived at the port. It usually took two to three days, so we were all pleasantly surprised that things were moving quickly.

Similar to how Bahariya in Egypt was the land of old Toyota Land Cruisers, Wadi Halfa was where old Defenders went to have a second or third lease on life. So we hailed an old Land Rover Defender taxi to get us to port. The road was paved and straight, yet our driver was wildly swinging the steering wheel to keep the old Defender tracking straight ahead. The poor thing could probably have used some new steering bushings.

Back at the pier, we were all happy to see the vehicle barge docked across the *Sagalnaam*. sanDRina had kept her station during the voyage. We handed our carnets over to Magdi, the local fixer in Wadi Halfa, who had a good reputation among the overlanding community. With a customs fee of SP100 ($45), he got all the required stamps, and after having our chassis VIN numbers verified, we were free to ride into Sudan. But there was one last piece of paperwork to take care of before we could leave Wadi Halfa. Upon entering Sudan, all foreigners were required to register their passports within 72 hours of entering the country, and that cost another $40. We paid Magdi $15 for helping us out and after tipping the barge captain $5, the total cost for entering Sudan, including the $100 visa, came up to a whopping $190. Just like Egypt, it was expensive to enter, but once inside, travel was cheap.

The four-wheel travellers were eager to hit the road and I bid them goodbye as I spent another night in Wadi Halfa, taking it easy. I left the next afternoon and headed south to meet the Nile. All 900 km (559 miles) to Khartoum, the capital, had been paved by the Chinese in the past few years, taking some of the riding excitement away and making the journey easy riding. Past overlanders had regaled about the gruelling ride through the deserts of Sudan, which nowadays is a thing of the past, with the Chinese trading infrastructure for oil and mineral resource rights. This was one of the motivations for me to get out and do this trip sooner than later, before it was all paved.

Sudan was one of those countries, where the external, political image was in stark contrast to the everyday reality. The news would have me believe that it was a dangerous country, and whilst recognizing that there were dangerous parts of the country, such as the conflicts in the west and south, I heeded more to the words of other travellers who told me of the safety and friendliness in the north. With this information in hand, I felt excited that I could wild camp again, having done it only once in Egypt since crossing over from South America.

At about 190 km (118 miles) south of Wadi Halfa, I crossed the small town of Abri. My GPS, loaded with the Tracks4Africa mapset, indicated a suitable campsite by the Nile just past town. When I got to the waypoint, there was nothing but a desolate outcrop, albeit with a fantastic view overlooking the Nile. I stopped for the night and began setting up my tent on the smooth rock surface as dusk descended. Just then, a young, swarthy fisherman climbed up from the riverbank and motioned for me to come and join him for food. My Arabic was still non-conversational, but the hand signs for food were universal – bundled fingers pointing at one's mouth. Trusting my instincts and overlanders' reports, I followed him down to the bank, past a grove of palms, and found a wonderful little beach that the fishermen were using as a rudimentary working camp. As his companion laboured over their open pit stove, I jumped in for a bath in the Nile with all the privacy that dusk offered. Surrounded by beached dhows and strewn nets, we ate a freshly-prepared flat bread with a fish stew that was flavoured simply with onions and salt. In my basic Arabic, I found out that their names were Bedwa and Fara; their white smiles beamed past their darkened skin. With dinner finished, as expected, tea was prepared. I sipped in silence as they exchanged a bit of banter. The Nile was flowing steadily and the moonlight reflected off its choppy surface. This was Africa. Wild. And I was content in having arrived. With my tea consumed, I got up and put my hands together with a bow to say thanks. I wasn't sure as to how well it worked, but my very Indian gesture felt appropriate at the time. They understood and nodded with a smile in acknowledgement.

I slept without the tarp on my tent to get as much air blowing through the mesh, but it was hot through most of the night, only getting slightly cool around 3 a.m. I was up at sunrise with the intention of getting on the road before it got too hot. However, after making some morning oatmeal, Bedwa came over and invited me down for tea. With morning light, I could now see the camp in all its detail. It was a small beach that was sheltered by trees and felt cosy. Bedwa and Fara were doing their rounds of rowing up the river, crossing it and laying down their net, then following it downstream for a bit before gathering up the net and its catch and rowing back up near the shore. A river flows faster in the middle compared to its edges due to friction with the banks, and thus, when rowing upstream, it's easiest to do so along the shore. After an hour's worth of work, they had caught five large fish using their home-made felucca, the name for boats on the Nile in Sudan and Egypt. It was made of beaten-down oil drums with crude wooden posts used for oars and the mast. The fishing seemed to be hard work, but their work was made harder by their crude tools. But needs must be met and on they laboured.

After spending the morning hours with Bedwa and Fara and observing their work, I wondered how the day would progress. I was trying to decide whether I should get moving or hang out some more with them. Shortly thereafter, a large fibreglass boat with an outboard motor pulled up and I met Saleh, the boss of the operation. He had a beaming smile and his lithe figure was covered in a loosely-flowing, white jellabiya, quite different from the tattered shorts and t-shirts of Bedwa and Fara. Saleh motioned for me to stay, and recognizing the wonderful opportunity, I made myself comfortable and let the day flow. Saleh showed me a gunny sack full of fish that I presumed was the combined catch of many other fishermen in the area.

Everyone got down to their tasks and Saleh gestured for me to take a look at his outboard motor. It was firing poorly and he set about cleaning the spark plug while I sat and observed, feeling no need to intervene based on my own maintenance experience. He soon had the motor running and we took a test ride on the river that had me grinning childishly at my first boating experience on the Nile (not counting the ferry).

By mid-morning, the middle of the river was flowing rapidly, making the fishermen's task of crossing it that much tougher. The opposite bank was actually the huge island of Saï that the Nile flowed around. I was told later that there were ruins among the palms with treasure hunters flying in to search for the gold bounty. The banks of the river were very steep and clearly indicative of the erosive power of the mighty river when it was in flood mode. After the annual rains in Ethiopia and Uganda, the Nile rises by a few metres before being stopped by the various dams along its length.

After doing a few rounds of fishing in the coolness of the morning, Bedwa started preparing the first meal of the day. What else would fishermen eat besides fresh fish? Gutting them, he threw the offcuts and innards back into the water, where they were quickly seized upon below the surface by their riverine companions, as the churn below the water's surface indicated. Nothing went to waste in nature's cycles. Waste and garbage are purely human concepts. Bedwa, at twenty-five, was the youngest among the fishermen there and he was tasked with food preparation. All the others were probably tasked with the same duties when they were young too.

The encounter shifted a dimension with the arrival of Mohammed Bashir, dressed in a sharp shirt and denim jeans. He had a friendly attitude and spoke English. Surprised to see an outsider with the fishermen, he asked me what I was doing there. After explaining my story, he said he was from Khartoum and was involved with buying the fish from the fishermen and selling it in the big city. He apparently spent a few days up there every few weeks, loading up his refrigerated truck with the fresh catch and heading back to Khartoum when it would be full. Mohammed proceeded to ask where I was from in India. When I said the southern city of Chennai, his eyebrows rose and he broke into a large smile. He revealed that he had actually spent a few years in Chennai studying for a pharmacy degree. How incredible! I probed further and asked at which college. When he said Sri Ramachandra Medical College, I couldn't contain my glee. That was right next to my parent's home, and moreover, my sister had studied for her medical degree at the same college. I couldn't believe that I was meeting a stranger in the middle of the Sudanese Sahara who had been but a few kilometres from my home in India. What a small world, indeed. Mohammed was gushing at the connection that had just been formed between us. I asked him about his time in India and he said that he loved it, besides the occasional racial slur that is strangely common against black people in India. He asked me what I thought of Sudan so far, and I recalled the pleasant experience of Wadi Halfa and explained that I was eager to experience more. He told me to stay a few days and that he would show me around. Having an English translator, I accepted the invitation. Saleh nodded in approval of the new bond between us all and I relished in the eudaimonia that was washing over us; a true, good and beautiful moment.

Back to the business of fish, Bedwa hauled up a full gunny sack to Mohammed's weighing scale that hung from a branch. In the few morning hours, Fara and he had caught 30 kg (66 lbs) of fish. We went over to Mohammed's truck, and inside, half the space was full of fish with giant ice blocks that kept the fish frozen until their arrival in the city. I was surprised that the ice didn't melt nor the fish spoil in the searing heat, but Mohammed explained that all the fish freeze into one solid block and thus don't spoil. Upon probing how he got into the fish business having a pharmacy degree, he said the only pharmacy jobs were with the government and they came with a paltry pay. Having an entrepreneurial streak and wanting to do something for the rural people of Sudan, he decided to give the fish business a shot.

Being a Friday, it was time to head into town for Friday Prayers at the local mosque. Everyone washed up and donned fresh, white jelabiyyas. We all went over to Saleh's house in the nearby village of Quikkah for a snack of sweet tea and sugary, fried bread snacks that were similar to doughnuts. The tea was as expected, extremely sweet with two teaspoons of sugar in each little cup, but it felt refreshing for the intense heat of the afternoon. One could only drink so much water to hydrate in the dry heat, and I was pleased to know now that tea actually helped the body get hydrated despite being mildly caffeinated and diuretic. Coffee wouldn't work, as it was too strong a diuretic; if the desert inhabitants had been drinking tea to hydrate, I wanted to learn from them.

The little town of Abri had dirt roads and colourful shopfronts selling everything from plasticware to clothes to mobile recharge minutes. Businesses were now just reopening after shutting down during the hottest part of the day, staying open late into the relatively cool night. The one modern structure in Abri was the prominent mobile phone tower near the one-storey government building. Sudan's mobile network, contrary to my original expectations, was very well established and their data rates were incredibly cheap. I had been given a local SIM card by a traveller heading north, and having plugged that in to my phone after topping up with some credit, I was soon online in this seemingly remote part of the world.

Wandering over to the town hang-out, we sat over tea and shisha to watch the town come to life as the temperatures dropped. Men at a nearby table played a highly energetic game of dominoes, replete with animated slappings of the tables and some bravado. I watched the passion that this game invoked with great interest. However, I soon took note of the garb that most people were wearing, realizing that I was showing off my legs by wearing shorts. Regardless of male or female company, this wasn't appropriate, no matter the heat. Mohammed politely explained that because I was a visitor, I was excused, but it was a lesson I took on board. While Sudan is a land of Sharia Law, I was more cognizant of the fact that it never hurts to be polite and follow the cues of local customs when in a foreign land. The last thing anyone wants to do is cause for offence while travelling.

By evening, we had returned to Saleh's house. The mud-walled, flat-roofed structure was rectangular and devoid of much architectural flair, besides the arches on the veranda and a coat of whitewash paint to reflect the sun's rays. The compound wall was higher than eye level and we sat outside the house on string cots in the cool of the evening, eating pigeon in gravy with flat bread. Dinner had been served by Saleh's wife, with whom I could not interact much because I was an outsider and also since I was showing more than a little leg. As is customary in more conservative Muslim culture, his wife and other women of the household lived in another part of the compound, away from the eyes of this stranger.

The thick walls of the mud house gave shelter from the blistering sun during the day, but as it warmed the interior, it became too hot by nightfall for anyone to sleep inside. Mohammed, Saleh and I got ready to sleep outside on the cots. As we sat there enjoying the calm breeze, I looked up at the brilliant night sky. The stars shone strong. Mohammed craned his neck to look too, quizzically examining the sky for some other object I must have been gazing at before asking me what was so interesting about the stars. It was an odd conversation that followed; one that started innocently, as I explained to him that we were looking back in time when we looked up at the night sky. All the points of light were reaching our eyes after travelling distances so far that it took years or longer for them to arrive on earth. He found the concept mind-boggling and asked me a flurry of questions: how old were the stars, how far away was the sun and what was the connection between the sun and the stars? I explained the basics of astronomy – that our sun was a star, our home star, and it shone so strong because we were very close to it compared to all the other stars. He loved the idea of us looking back in time, a phenomenon displayed every night whether or not we looked up. Here was a man who had brought his 'big city' business acumen to this rural setting, a man well versed in finance and marketing, but who in that instant seemed as enraptured as a child as I explained my own limited understanding of the universe.

Mohammed explained to Saleh what I had just told him and Saleh just nodded with a smile. I felt that he knew all this, but perhaps it was never explained to him in those words. People who live such minimalist lives understand the stars because they look at them for so long. Quikkah was off the electricity grid, and besides the few hours of generator power in the evenings, the village was devoid of any modern luxuries, which left most like me to stargaze for hours on end.

Once again, the night started out warm, finally cooling just before dawn. As soon as the sun rose up, the temperature started rising. Mohammed and Saleh went about their fishing duties, and over the next few days, I alternated between relaxing at Saleh's house, reading my books or hanging out at the fishing beach. Saleh and I grew closer over these days and I felt an honest connection with him. He showed me every aspect of the life that he had created for himself. We went through his vegetable fields that were growing strong in the fertile grounds near the Nile and he proudly showed me his pigeon coop that provided a meat source for his family. We did not speak much to each other, which is why having Mohammed around helped our communication a lot. His large smile was indicative of a warm heart and his greying hair exuded wisdom of the desert that I wanted to learn from.

After five days at Quikkah, I announced that I had to leave the next day, as my visa for Sudan would be expiring soon and there was still a large extent of the country for me to ride through till the border with Ethiopia. The sun had just dipped below the horizon, casting a brilliant orange glow across the grove of date palms that bordered the Nile. By then, I was wearing a jellabiya after feeling out of place on the first day. Mohammed said I could pass for Saleh's brother. If only I could speak a bit more Arabic!

I was in a land where I could easily shed my identity and blend in. I wished I had no constraints of a visa, as I wanted to spend more time in this unpretentious place living harmoniously with nature. Of course, Mohammed's new infusion of cash into this society was rapidly changing its dynamics, as Saleh and his people were living quite well without any dependence on the outside world. They were self-sufficient and really had no need for cash. I found out over the past few days that most people in the village spent their cash on mobile recharges, as was evident in those that had their respective phones constantly pressed up against their ears. Mohammed said these people would talk to their families and friends in other villages, whom they could only visit about once a year before the arrival of mobile phones. Now, they were able to get daily updates on their lives.

I fired up sanDRina after her slumber of a few days under the lone tree in front of Saleh's house and I bid my hosts goodbye. My stopover in Quikkah had given me a glimpse of the capabilities of human life when provided with very few resources. Lack of technology was not holding the people back. They had discovered ways to live with nature rather than see it as a force to battle. There was much to relearn from people living far away from our global urban support systems. No place made this clearer to me than amongst those who lived sandwiched between the desert and the Sudanese Nile.

11

A WILD CURRY

IN KONSO, I PULLED IN to the last petrol station for the next 900 km (560 miles). I was heading towards Lake Turkana in the remote Chalbi desert of northern Kenya. After spending several weeks amongst the people of northern Ethiopia, I had finally descended from its highland mountain culture, having my fill of the delicious staple of injera and the rich history of this ancient land. A few months earlier, as I plotted my route down the east side of Africa, I focused my attention on the one stretch that was not yet paved; from southern Ethiopia to central Kenya. From South Sudan in the west to Somalia in the east lay the harsh Chalbi desert, harbouring the massive inland desert sea of Lake Turkana, also known as the Jade Sea because of its emerald waters. The principal route south passes through the border town of Moyale before funnelling into a heavily corrugated road, infamous for ruining suspensions. Riding 250 km (155 miles) of that punishing road with a heavily-laden sanDRina was not an alluring prospect. All my worldly possessions were already straining her suspension.

Thanks to a pair of Dutch motorcyclists who had gone down the eastern side of Africa ahead of me and sent word, I had come to know of an alternate, remote route that instead went along Lake Turkana.

Receiving this information was akin to an explorer receiving word of a new, unchartered route or discovering a treasure map; the King Solomon's Mines of adventure motorcycling. My skin tingled when I first heard of it, and I let out a sigh of relief – it was the route that I had been searching for. Just ahead, beyond Konso, the barren landscape awaited on the Lake Turkana route.

It was to be an arduous off-road journey that went from the Omo Valley of southwestern Ethiopia down along the eastern coast of Lake Turkana before emptying out at the town of Maralal in the mountains of central Kenya. A remote and rough terrain with no petrol stations; just Africa and sanDRina. This was also one of the longest stretches between petrol stations in the world for an adventure motorcyclist. For those exact circumstances, I had installed the largest fuel tank available for the DR650 on sanDRina, the 40 L (10.6 gal) Aqualine Safari tank made in Australia, designed to tackle vast deserts. But even that was not going to be enough. In off-road conditions, I had seen that sanDRina consumed more petrol, reducing my range to around 480 km (298 miles) as opposed to approximately 700 km (435 miles) on tarmac. I would have to carry extra fuel, and that meant finding other travellers, the four-wheeled kind, to convoy with.

Usually, it's hard to coordinate among overland travellers because everyone has their own travel plan. But instead of finding just one other party, I ended up with four others. I was initially going to convoy with only Ferdi and Katie, a young German couple with an ever-present glint in their eyes, and their large, brown and black-shaded dog, Kayous. They were travelling in a Volkswagen Synchro 4x4 van from Germany for a loop around Africa. However, at Awasa, south of Addis Ababa, we were joined by Guy and Lu, the young British couple in their baby-blue Land Rover Defender with whom I did the Lake Nasser crossing, and Peter and Jill, an older British couple in their home-made Land Rover overlanding truck. And to keep it fun for me, there was Carlos, a similarly-aged motorcyclist from Spain, on his KTM 640 Adventure. It was rather unnerving for all of us to suddenly converge in this large group, but we knew that relying on each other would be the best way to get through the challenging route ahead. The motorcyclists needed the four-wheel travellers, and in return, they wanted our company for safety. We were heading into a land where help of any kind would be hard to come by, so everyone opted for safety in numbers. I had also bartered an agreement with Ferdi and Katie that I would cook them my chicken curry in exchange for carrying 40 extra liters of petrol for me.

Filling up all our fuel reserves in Konso, the next day, we descended down from the lush highlands that characterized most of western Ethiopia. Ahead of us lay the expanse of the Great Rift Valley. It was parched and dusty with the horizon muddling into the haze of the sky. As we drove further down into the valley, the temperatures climbed. The highlands shrank and greenery gave way to the harsh desert tans.

Just as we reached the small village of Weyto, a few hours down the escarpment from Konso, I had to slow down for a large object sprawled across the road. Ferdi and Katie slowed down behind me as well, as I waved a signal from my left hand. I realized upon getting closer that it was a large python, quite evidently and regrettably dead. Around 5 m (16 ft) in length, a large truck had run over it. Two flattened portions indicated the size of the truck and its four-wheeled rear axle. I got down from sanDRina and approached the python. Even though I knew it was dead, I dared not get too close to it. I cursed the demonizing of snakes and how it has precipitated a near-irrational fear of these magnificent animals in so many of us. Its teeth, used to grip its prey, were exposed as its head lay cocked to one side. It sure did look scary, but the poor animal was just trying to cross the road when it met its fate against the wheels of a truck. Its flesh was exposed where it was flattened and it looked similar to fish, layered and light brown in colour. The snake would undoubtedly be someone's next meal by morning. Given its size and evident proximity to human populations, I wondered whether I should be camping out that night, but there was no point in worrying. All regions of Africa are host to a generous portfolio of wildlife; it was a shame that the first large animal I came across on my journey was one so needlessly killed by the carelessness of another driver.

Just as I mounted sanDRina, a young tribal boy ran out of the bushes and stopped a metre away from me. Katie captured a photo of the stark contrast between our two worlds. One was wearing a small loincloth over his privates, most likely the extent of his clothing, while the other was decked out in high-tech Kevlar mesh gear. She said we looked like we were from different planets. My gear and helmet definitely did make me look like an astronaut, while sanDRina sported a *Mad Max* look with multiple lights, toolboxes and the jagged lines of her panniers. We stared at each other for a few moments, marvelling at our differences, before I fired sanDRina back into action and started off down the road again. I was unable to say much to him but we still waved goodbye to one another.

The tarmac soon ended, after which it would be dirt roads till Maralal. There were mountains in the distance, but the land around us was arid, punctuated only by scrawny acacia trees and thorny shrub. This was a land forgotten by modern civilization but not devoid of human history. Omo Valley, at the northern end of the Great Rift Valley, is renowned for its rich cultural diversity. Numerous tribes have existed there for aeons, all in close proximity to each other. Other travellers had told us that if we happened to be there the one day of the week when the neighbouring tribes gather to trade, we could experience their rich cultural diversity without partaking in a staged cultural visit. As we reached the few huts that comprised the village of Weyto, a cackle of human activity up ahead indicated that we were in luck. There were about 200 people spread out across the road and the market was bustling, from ladies selling grains to men selling goats. It gave me insight into the needs and produce of those tribes.

Weyto sits at the junction between the Arbore and Tsemay people, but there are eight major tribes in the Omo Valley, and each one has distinct cultural practices. I was able to identify a lady from the Arbore Tribe, as was evident from her headwear; an upturned calabash shell. She was selling a live chicken to a man from the Tsemay Tribe, who was holding their characteristic small wooden stool that is carried around to always have a seat handy. He was also wearing another major trait of the Tsemay men – a short skirt. It makes sense given the heat they have to endure. It was interesting to see that the men were wearing short skirts while the women were wearing longer ones. Everyone was so busy in their own market transactions that they hardly took notice of a bunch of foreigners walking around and taking photos.

The tribes of the Omo Valley are known to be quite violent amongst each other. Cattle raids are a common practice and are even considered an initiation rite for young males. In my travels so far, I had noticed that neighbouring cultures had a higher tendency to fight amongst themselves than with people from distant lands. But in the neutral territory of the market, most of the people presented themselves as pastoralists tending to livestock and farmers growing crops on the banks of the Omo River; the lifeblood for all the people and wildlife in the area.

Sadly, the future of all these people was in jeopardy as the Ethiopian government was building a huge dam, the Gibe III, upstream on the Omo River. It would adversely affect the lives of the tribes in the area in that the dam would obstruct the natural flooding cycle of the river that deposited its rich sediments on the banks. It allowed the people to practise flood retreat cultivation, a farming technique they'd mastered over the millennia that they'd lived in this region. It was a harsh landscape and it seemed cruel to threaten the livelihood of people in the name of development. The dam was predicted by many international research groups to be an ecological disaster. Sadly, the hydroelectricity that would be generated from it was geared for export to neighbouring countries and would hardly benefit rural Ethiopians, many of whom still live without access to electricity.

As we left Weyto, the future of the ancient cultures that had thrived in the Omo Valley worried me. This whole area was a designated UNESCO World Heritage Site for the importance it played in revealing human history through the many hominid fossils found there. Those very findings have shown us that the area has been crossed by humans and hominids for millions of years. And now, I, a hominid from a global civilization, was passing through the same region with a group of others from various cultures on a similar mission – traversing this harsh land to emerge out the other end – the only difference being that we would be rejoining a civilization that was poised to destroy the cradle of our species.

With this bitter sense of irony kicking about in my head, our convoy regrouped and headed west. We regrouped occasionally, but otherwise drove at our own separate pace. After a day of long, empty dirt roads bordered with acacia trees and the drylands beyond them, we reached the village of Turmi, where there was a rudimentary campground for travellers. One of the oddities of this landscape was that despite its expanse and barren ground, most of which was perfect for camping, we would still find designated spots. It provides some framework for travellers to navigate by, but more importantly, it also makes sure that the land does not end up dotted with the waste and scars of random campfires and open-air toilets. The setting sun cast a wonderful glow through the thin crowns of the acacia trees across the campground, under which I was content in the wilderness of Africa. Our convoy had decided that every night, one of us would prepare the meal for the group, and so I ended my last night in Ethiopia with a hot meal of pasta prepared by Jill and Peter.

The next day, before we could turn south for Kenya, we had to take a 50 km (31 miles) detour on a heavily-corrugated road to the administrative town of Omorate to have our passports stamped out of the country. This remote town was on the northern shores of Lake Turkana and it was surprising to see proper buildings and cement structures after the many miles of empty land. We hoped to make it a quick stop, but alas, the office boy told us that the only immigration officer there had just left for his breakfast. As we milled about, Ferdi reminded me that it was my turn to cook that night, and with a gleam in his eye, asked how I was going to prepare my chicken curry. When I made the deal with him, it had been only for him and Katie, but now with five other mouths to feed (and eight in total), it was going to be a major task. Peter and Jill had volunteered their kitchen, but first and foremost, I required two chickens. Ferdi and I set afoot the ramshackle town with a few shops strewn about and asked everyone we came across for 'wot', the word for chicken in Amharic, Ethiopia's official language. We were able to find and purchase two live birds from a woman in a little shack. The next step was to find a way to slaughter them, which proved substantially harder. We couldn't find a butcher, but a young boy seeing our plight led us to a small hotel that had an outdoor kitchen, where the staff was boiling up vats of cut beef for the lunch rush. I explained in sign language and some basic Amharic, which is similar in ways to Arabic, what I needed and the two lady cooks there nodded and accepted with wide smiles.

The group had gathered by the outdoor kitchen by then, but when I explained what was going to happen, most of them excused themselves with squeamish expressions, except Ferdi, Carlos and I. One of the cooks, with a green wrap around her head resembling a cooking hair net, proceeded to slice off the heads of the chickens and quickly put them under an upturned plastic tub to wait for the headless bodies to die down. Personally, I was on a self-determined mission to experience what it felt like to kill an animal for food. If I was going to be comfortable eating it, I needed to know what it was like to take its life, prepare the meat and, quite honestly, appreciate what it means to eat meat. So I stuck around, watching over the shoulders of the two ladies as they set about a task which was a daily, mundane practice for them. Once properly dead, precision cuts were made along the limbs and across the chest that enabled them to peel the skin off in one piece. It was an undeniably fascinating moment for all of us. Shortly afterwards, with the meat stashed in coolers and our passports stamped, we headed towards the shores of Lake Turkana in Kenya for a dinner of two Ethiopian chickens curried by an Indian.

Rejoining our original route, the track degraded from a hard-packed gravel road into a two-track, sandy path that drove straight into thick acacia bush land. Thorns scratched my panniers and low-hanging branches forced me to duck. This was the wild riding I had dreamed of. Following a track in my GPS and matching it to the tyre tracks in front of me, biking through the bush was interrupted only by a series of riverbeds. The Lake Turkana route is littered with about thirty crossings and we had timed our trip such that we would be there at the tail end of the rainy season, ensuring that we could cross without getting mired in mud. The steep descent into the riverbeds along with massive ruts in the loose sand was tricky motorcycling. Before accelerating into the riverbed, I would scan ahead to the other side and choose my exit path and then take the plunge and swim through the sand with sanDRina. Momentum is your friend in the loose stuff, and I kept the throttle pinned open all the way until I had climbed out the other side, where once again, the bush swallowed us up.

After a few hours of traversing riverbeds, I left the thick acacia bush of southern Ethiopia and my GPS showed me that I was crossing the border into Kenya. But all I could see was a flat, bleak desert covered in a haze as dust storms blew all around me. For all the tight security that is generally associated with crossing international borders, I smirked as I rode into Kenya with no formalities. I thought about how artificial land borders are in reality, yet, how savagely they are defended by nation-states the world over. This was no man's land in the truest sense. Bureaucracy aside, even the remote tribes that live around Lake Turkana were nowhere in sight.

But paperwork awaited us in the first settlement that we came across. In Illoret, a large village surrounded by fishermen making their living from the riches of Lake Turkana, I received a letter from the stationed policeman. It stated that I had entered Kenya on the given date with my specified vehicle. I was to produce that letter along with my passport at the immigration headquarters in Nairobi to receive an entry stamp into Kenya. That meant I would be hundreds of kilometres into a new country with no stamp on my passport. I hoped that the letter would satisfy any prying officials.

Our convoy left Illoret in a hurry to find a suitable camping spot before dark in Sibiloi National Park, a nature reserve on the northern shores of Lake Turkana. The sun quickly sank and I was challenged by the blinding light reflecting off the emerald waters of the inland sea straight into my eyes. I turned inland and the track climbed up a craggy path covered in softball-sized volcanic rocks. I was standing on the pegs and charging up the path with good momentum when I had to slow down for a huge, basketball-sized rock that sat in my path and threatened to buck me off sanDRina. Starting up an incline once again, and that too over an extremely jagged surface, required me to slip the clutch heavily before I achieved enough momentum. The riding was wearing me out and my shoulders were sore, but there was to be no rest that evening since I was cooking my curry.

We set up camp in a clearing with the lake off in the distance. The sun had set and the respite in temperature was a relief. Katie and Ferdi had a portable shower system that ran off their van's battery, and they gave me two precious liters. Ahh, the perks of travelling with motorhomes. I showered just behind the van, enjoying the freedom of having no walls.

Even though I was doing the cooking, everyone was drafted in to help prepare the curry by cutting the tomatoes, onions, garlic and ginger that are so crucial to the curry's scrumptious taste. I sweated it out in the back of Peter and Jill's motorhome, hunched over their built-in stove and cherishing that very special moment of cooking my curry in the deep wilderness of Africa. In a now familiar routine, the curry was wolfed down by all with large smiles emerging. Ferdi remarked, 'it was a good deal we had,' but I wondered who got the better end of the deal? All I had to do was cook a meal, and in exchange, they lugged through the desert a jerrycan full of my petrol. I drifted off to sleep, smelling of garlic, covered in sand and with a wide grin on my face.

While packing up the next morning, I reflected on how the parched lands around Lake Turkana have preserved numerous hominid fossils over the aeons, earning it the title of the Cradle of Humankind. The area was much more fertile back when early humans were roaming them around two million years ago. Tribes still roam those parts and their respective cultures wouldn't be too out of place if they were transported a few thousand years back in time. Alas, the land won't be left untouched by modern civilization for too long. The fierce winds around Lake Turkana are tempting for wind turbines, and recently-discovered oil under the desert was already attracting investment.

The journey continued through more sand and the further south we went, the firmer the ground became. By the next day, we had reached Loyangalani, the largest village we had encountered this side of the border. After taking a day off to rest our bones and our vehicles, our convoy continued south along our majestic Lake Turkana. Surrounded by an oven of a desert, the shimmering sunlight across this vast body of water cast a surreal setting on the route. We soon left the desert behind, climbing back up the escarpment of the Great Rift Valley. The steep ascent had us ride deeply-rutted cliff roads all the way into Maralal. This signified the end of the Lake Turkana route as we came across one of the most recognizable markers of civilization, a petrol station.

The area around Lake Turkana has not changed for a very long time and that's a rare find in today's world. It felt as though I had gone back in time, but I was also very much in the present as I bounced on the ruts and felt the sand sucking down my tyres. What an adventure! Challenging rides, exotic locales and chicken curry. Riding the Lake Turkana route was the most epic journey that I had undertaken. I had dreamed of riding in true African wilderness and it had finally happened.

12

BREAKING DOWN

IT WAS A bump like all the others that I had ridden over that morning, but this time, sanDRina's handlebar started wobbling and a screeching noise began to emanate from somewhere. You didn't need an engineering degree to figure out that something wasn't right. I coaxed sanDRina to the side of the red dirt road and stopped on the edge of a verdant green wall of elephant grass. I was in western Uganda – elephant country. Other travellers had warned me that elephants were known to charge motorcyclists, and so I kept my eyes peeled, hoping that I wouldn't have the misfortune of having an elephant step out of the grass anywhere close to me. Dismounting and removing my helmet under the intense equatorial sun, I quickly donned my sun-hat and began to inspect sanDRina. The front wheel looked just fine, as did the steering dampener I had installed to reduce handlebar vibrations. But as I moved to the rear, I was shocked by what I saw. Multiple spokes from the rear wheel were broken. Ragged and torn, they projected at random angles outward from the wheel and were undoubtedly the source of sanDRina's screeching. This, I quietly surmised, was not good. About a quarter of the spokes all around the wheel were snapped either at the rim or the hub. I had just installed this new rear wheel hub and spokes kit during a long break in Nairobi, concluded just a few days prior.

After the epic ride through Lake Turkana, I spent almost a year in Nairobi working on a research project for the distance master's degree that I had been studying for during the journey. I researched the impacts of climate change on agricultural water management practices between male and female farmers in rural parts of eastern Kenya. This research experience taught me new skills in how to systematically tackle a problem and apply those skills to human developmental issues. Now, I had a different problem on my hands altogether.

The first order of business in any such scenario is getting to a safe place for the night. The tall elephant grasses were a part of the savannah that ran along the Queen Elizabeth National Park and I was far off from any of the major cities in Uganda. Pulling out my Michelin map of southern Africa, I saw that the town of Kihihi was ahead and so I continued riding sanDRina, albeit at a much slower pace, hoping that it wouldn't exasperate the broken spokes issue. Contrary to the earlier part of the day, when I was standing on the footpegs and charging across the dirt road yelling, 'Africa!' I was now forced to maintain my sense of composure with measured riding. Africa, indeed!

After an hour, I was able to foresee my arrival into Kihihi when I saw an oncoming boda-boda rider, the name for motorcycle taxis in those parts of eastern Africa. It sped past me, hauling two large water containers – a sure sign of civilization. Soon enough, the dirt road met the tarmac of the town. I stopped at the first lodge I came to. This single-storey, concrete building was not much to look at, but it had a gate, which meant that sanDRina would be secure overnight. The young boy at the front table, Gordon, who introduced himself as the owner's son, said he knew a good mechanic in town who might be able to help after I had explained my problem. Swapping sanDRina for a new, shiny Chinese scooter, now ubiquitous in east Africa, we rushed over. Surrounded by greasy parts in a cluttered shop, the mechanic said he could replace the hub with another one, though I would have to provide the replacement. The old hub and spokes were still in Nairobi, but that was now over a thousand kilometres from where I was. Sensing what I was thinking, Gordon threw me a bone, explaining that replacement parts could be sent via a courier service on the local bus network. While there was no direct bus from Nairobi to Kihihi, he assured me that many things in town were sent from the big cities of Nairobi and Kampala via private bus networks. I was taken to a begrimed office where I was told that a small package would cost 15,000 Ugandan Shillings ($6) to be sent from Nairobi to Kihihi. It was a good deal and the bus agent gave me the details of their office in Nairobi where the package was to be dropped off.

Back at the lodge, I turned on my mobile phone to call my partner, Aki. She had stayed back in Nairobi as I continued my journey. We met a few months into my stay in Nairobi and had fallen madly in love with each other. On our second encounter, we decided to start living together. The relationship was intense and exhilarating. Aki was an anthropology researcher from Japan and we met at one of Nairobi's many expat parties. She was distraught that after four months of living together, I was going to leave her and my life in Nairobi that I had built over the past year. I had secured a research position at a large agricultural institution and had formed an interesting friends circle, but Nairobi was always going to be just a stop for me, not the end. In spite of all this, she was very understanding of the commitment I had made to completing my journey in India. As I got ready to uproot my life once again, I was torn between hitting the road with sanDRina and staying with Aki and starting a new life in Nairobi. So it was with no surprise that she was the first person I called up. The days when Gus in Chicago was the first person I would call with a mechanical issue seemed so far gone. But that's how adventures play out. She was happy that I had called and understood the problem I was experiencing. Jokingly, she asked if this meant that I would give up and return to her. But I had to say no. I had already committed to getting back on the road. I had to see it through to its finish in India. It was a tough choice, but to turn back on it so soon after leaving would have been a disservice to both of us. I had a dream to realize, and if I didn't leave then, it would forever haunt me till I eventually did. Aki was sensitive to this, perhaps better than I, and so we parted ways. Now she was the key to my staying on the road. She understood the severity of my situation and volunteered to help get the package delivered quickly.

Next up, I called Milan, who was an ace mechanic in Nairobi. He happened to be of Indian origin and I befriended him soon after arriving there. We had worked on sanDRina together and replaced many of her worn parts over the past twelve months. One of the large parts we had replaced was the rear wheel hub as the bearings had become too loose. Milan understood the urgency as well and started reworking my old hub the same day – it was still lying next to him on his shop floor. In the time that Aki took to reach Milan's shop, the hub had been reworked and packed with the old spokes. She took the package and rushed to the bus service's office on a boda-boda, handing it in just in time for the night's journey to Kampala. In their own way, developing markets can be extremely efficient.

By the end of the next day, Gordon had received the package, after which I spent another day having the local mechanic mount the old hub and spokes into sanDRina's rear wheel. After a few test rides, I was beaming with a wide smile as this major problem was now sorted. Aki was delighted that she had helped me in my journey and I officially gazetted her as a member of my international support team. She had put on a brave front and was very positive every time I called, but I knew our separation was as hard on her as it was on me.

I got back on the trail heading south out of Uganda, pleased that a major crisis with sanDRina had been averted so quickly. After paying homage at the genocide memorial in my few days across Rwanda, I crossed the border into western Tanzania. Straight ahead, on the main highway that was heading eastwards, lay the famous wildlife national parks of Tanzania, such as the Serengeti and Ngorongoro, but I had already experienced a lot of game parks as a child so I gave them a miss. I was seeking the remote roads along its western border down towards Mozambique. At Nyakanazi, south of Lake Victoria, I turned south from the highway. I smiled as the tarmac ended past the junction; it was good to be back on dirt.

The road from there for the next 1,200 km (746 miles) was simply called Regional Road B8 and moved along western Tanzania. It was slated to be all off-road, with the exception of a few patches of tarmac through some of the towns along the way. This remote road had a gnarly reputation amongst the adventure motorcycling community. Travel blogs and forums were full of photos of trucks and bikes mired in thick mud along this track. However, I picked my season just right, once again, and arrived there towards the end of the dry season. In a few weeks, the rains would start and its hard-packed mud surface would turn into a sucking clay soup, making it dreadful for most vehicles to traverse it. In such times, bicycles becomes the best mode of transport for they are light enough to float on top of the mud. I shifted up the gears into fourth and fifth and stood on the pegs just cruising, gratified about riding a motorcycle off-road in Africa. The red road was lined with green brush. I thought back to my time on the TransAmazonica in Brazil, a similar road that wasn't a challenge when dry but could become a nightmare amid moisture.

I was cruising at 85 to 90 kph (56 mph) on the empty sections of the road, slowing down to maybe 40 kph (25 mph) as I passed through villages. The speeds were a tad high, but I was in a buoyant mood and there was something just so intoxicating about riding at a high speed off-road. 90 kph is not a high speed compared to the

200 kph (124 mph) I used to cruise at on my rides in the US astride a sport bike, but for a dirt bike loaded down with metal panniers and adventure gear, it was exhilarating. Speed is a relative term. It is not the same as velocity, which is the absolute number that you are riding at, say 90 kph. Speed is a sensation that one feels, and on a dirt bike, where the vibrations are pronounced by the big single cylinder thumping in the engine, 90 kph feels fast. And that was key for me – feeling fast.

The later part of the afternoon was approaching and since I was making good time, I pulled off on the side of the road for a break. sanDRina and I needed to rest our muscles. Despite my improved skills, her rear suspension was taking a beating on the bouncy road. Back in Bolivia, I would gingerly go over every bump on the road due to my lack of experience in off-road riding. Now, many months and thousands of kilometres ahead, I finally had the hang of it. To master off-road riding, one needs to ride fast. The aim is to skim the top of the bumps. While this reduces the sensation of the bumps for the rider, the bike's suspension works overtime and the oil inside the shock absorber heats up as it compresses and releases with each bump. I remembered the advice from Carlos, with whom I rode along the Lake Turkana route in northern Kenya. He said that taking a break to cool the suspension would ensure that it wouldn't fail during a bout of fast off-road riding.

Like most places in east Africa, a crowd of onlookers soon formed to inspect this strange man and his machine. When I'm in the mood, I play it up and put on a show and entertain them with photos and maybe share a bit of what I'm snacking on. But that's only occasionally. Most other times, I seek a remote place to stop and take a break so as to have some peace and quiet. When someone does stop and stare, I recognize that I am passing through their land and that they have every right to do so. It doesn't bother me any more, but there is something unsettling about having strangers observe my every action, whether it is sipping water from my hydration pack or adjusting the wires running from my iPod. Such people are usually very congenial and give me space, but the kids in Ethiopia were my least favourite onlookers. They were oddly aggressive and would instantly ask for money or a pen or sweets. And if I didn't give them something, I was bound to get stoned. Most overland travellers through Ethiopia had stones thrown at their vehicles. So when a few young kids started gathering around me in western Tanzania, I was quite impressed when they kept their distance and just sat on the mud ridge on the side of the road. First, there was one, then two, and within a few minutes, about ten. They just sat there politely and simply observed me. At the time, I had been munching on dry dates, and so I shook a few into my hand and offered it to them. Very orderly, their tiny hands reached forward and took one or two. I took their photos and showed it back to them, which brought big smiles to their cute faces. Many of them had enlarged stomachs on their small frames; an indication of malnutrition, which is, unfortunately, common among children in rural parts of Tanzania and the rest of the developing world. Their staple food consisted of ugali, a maize-meal porridge, and beans. It obviously wasn't enough.

From there, it was still 30 km (19 miles) to the first town of Kibondo. The sun was beginning to settle over the mountains to my right which also serve as the border with Burundi. I bid goodbye to the kids and plugged in my earphones pumping out a classic rock off-road playlist. After struggling a bit with the well-worn zipper on my bulky Kevlar mesh riding jacket, I was all suited up. My Arai XD helmet went on next, followed by my Teknic gloves. I looked ready for battle – a battle with the elements. I slid my right leg over the high seat, and once balanced with both feet, I fired up sanDRina. A smile spread on my face, as it usually does when I'm about to go riding. I worked my way up the gears and was back again in fifth, cruising at 90 kph (56 mph) over the hard mud road.

I passed a few villages, waving at the police check points stationed at the edge of each village. There were no hotels or places to stay for the night in these villages and that's why I was aiming for Kibondo, the only sizeable town before Kigoma, further ahead on the shores of Lake Tanganyika.

All of a sudden, sanDRina died. Died is the appropriate word because death signifies the end of something that was alive or in motion. Her engine did not even splutter; it just lost power. She cut out and sidled to a slow, inevitable stop. Her sudden death seemed like she had run out of fuel, only that there had been no gasp beforehand. Moreover, it didn't make sense since I had just topped up her massive fuel tank at the junction with the main highway. Not having much time to think, I turned the fuel taps to reserve. She fired up right away. I was glad she was running again but I still felt unsettled. Why had she stopped running in the first place? Within a few minutes, her engine stopped again. This was a problem that I had to tend to right away.

I checked the battery voltage meter fitted to her handlebar, jerry-rigged from a semi-truck catalogue in the US for such situations. Most motorcycle batteries need to be at 13.2 volts or higher, and if the voltage monitor was reading anything less than that, then it was probably an electrical issue. The monitor was reading 13.4 volts, so it wasn't an electrical issue, or at least, it wasn't a battery issue. It sounded like an issue with the fuel system. I reasoned that sanDRina was not getting fuel to flow into her engine. The issue could've been anywhere from the fuel tank to the carburettor to the spark plugs.

I had to inspect the carburettor. But I couldn't just open it up by the roadside. Flanked by massive rain ditches, maize fields on my left and dense forest to my right, the road had also become a funnel for dust kicked up by passing vehicles. I had just passed two massive Coca-Cola trucks, slowly lumbering their way down the route, making deliveries in the villages and towns. Unlike a motorcycle, they couldn't move at high speeds off-road and simply resolved to going up and over every bump with all six of their axles and thirty tyres. All that commotion creates enormous dust clouds and I had just ridden through two of them. I knew these were lumbering up behind me. To expose the carburettor to more dust and grit would undoubtedly lead to further complications. Yet, the day was ending, which meant there would be more traffic on the road. I flagged down a big, old Bedford truck that had a crew standing in the open bed at the back, returning from a mining or construction site. I explained my situation to the driver in broken English to match his understanding, and asked how much it would cost to put my bike on the truck and head to Kibondo. He asked for 80,000 Tanzanian Shillings (Tsh) ($40). That was too much. He was clearly eager to overcharge this 'mzungu' (foreigner in Kiswahili). Being frugal with my money, which allowed me to live for so long without an income, I scoffed at his offer and tried to bargain down. But he was heading away from Kibondo, which meant that I would be inconveniencing him.

By now, a few other people had gathered around us as the truck was effectively blocking the road. Just behind the truck, a man got out from his run-down Toyota Corolla, one of the most common vehicles that I had come across so far in Africa and Latin America. Since he was a teacher, he spoke English and understood what I was trying to do. I asked him if he could ask two of the men to help me push sanDRina into town. It was about 5 km (3 miles) away, and there were a few hills to cover, making it a strenuous challenge. The frugal traveller in me figured paying two guys to help me push sanDRina was the best option. Two guys jumped down from the truck, lean and muscled as you would expect labourers to be. With 5,000 shillings apiece, they were ready for action. One of them got behind the bike holding my top box, and the other got a hold of my right pannier. I was on the left side with my hand on the clutch lever. I couldn't reach over and get to the front brake to slow us down, and instead, engaged first gear and simply pulled in the clutch so that we could roll the bike. This was not the best idea in terms of clutch wear, but at the time, it made the most sense. I was huffing and puffing as we pushed up the steep hill. I was still in my riding gear and consequently sweating buckets. I could feel the sweat coursing down my skin, soaking the layers between my gear and causing them to knot up under my arms and between my legs. I kept drinking from my hydration pack hoping this torment would end soon.

At the top of the hill, we all took a breather. Asking them to meet me at the bottom, I told them I would sit on the bike and coast down to the trough and wait for them right where my battle with gravity would come to a halt. It was wonderful to be moving again on the bike, with or without the engine running. They came running down and we started again up the next incline. For a moment, I wondered what I had gotten myself into by restarting the journey after Nairobi. But I just laughed. It was all part of the adventure. The good and the bad. It's what makes the experience and I knew this would make for a great story one day. Right then, I was a Kevlar-encased pool of sweat and grime that had to get to town.

The next decline was fairly long. I was coasting down and just as I reached the trough, I tried sanDRina's engine start button and she came back to life! I was so overjoyed and caught up in my emergency of getting to town that I quickly waved to the two helpers and rode off as fast as possible towards town, or at least as close to it as possible before she died again. But she didn't die and we kept going. I tried not to smile knowing that the problem wasn't fixed, but I just had to. I started seeing a few roadside shacks selling bananas and mobile recharge cards, and then a mobile phone tower around a corner which meant that Kibondo was very close.

The mud road ended at the edge of town, and sweet, sweet tarmac welcomed me back to civilization. There was a hotel on the northern edge of town that seemed to be an old colonial house. This would've been ideal, as I wanted some space to work on sanDRina that was away from all the commotion. I was out of luck, however, as the guard at the gate said they were full and directed me to another lodge out of town. I nursed sanDRina left at the main junction and proceeded down the hill and out of town. Just as I got to the end of the tarmac, sanDRina spluttered again. My heart sank as a knot grew in my stomach. The lodge was a kilometre out of town. I knew I wasn't going to make it. Not wanting to leave the tarmac, I rode back up the hill and just as I got to the junction, she died again. There were many shops around and people were walking by and I was drawing a lot of attention. I pulled the choke on the carburettor to give it more fuel, but she wouldn't start. Stumped, I didn't know what else to do.

Luckily, sanDRina had stopped right in front of a small bike mechanic shop. The proprietor was a lithe, fit man wearing a sleeveless, red Coca-Cola shirt. He came up to me with a friendly smile and, in broken English, told me it was probably a fuel issue. He introducing himself as Ramadan and I immediately felt relieved as someone cool-headed was there to finally help me. His bike shop comprised of a shed with his tools and Chinese bikes in various states of disrepair strewn about in front. He told the crowd to create some space, as by now, I was the biggest attraction in town. We pushed sanDRina across a plank over the concrete drain that separated the road from the shop. Inconsistent with my attitude thus far, I found it tough to just laugh off my misfortune this time. I felt then that my journey was pivoting and the story ahead would be quite different from what I had envisaged when I left Nairobi.

A hundred curious faces looked on as we removed the carburettor. Ramadan blew into the fuel inlet pipe and pointed out that there was too much resistance with the float needle, a small piece of metal that moves up and down in the carburettor regulating the fuel flow. Maybe that was the problem. He said we would need some sandpaper to smoothen out the valve, but with daylight fading, the hardware shops were closed for the day. With the crowd still watching curiously, Ramadan took a sample of fuel from sanDRina's fuel tank that was now lying on the ground. Bubbles appeared when he rubbed the petrol between his fingers, which was not normal. He suggested that there was perhaps water in the fuel, which was a common practice used by vendors to cheat customers. I recalled how I had fuelled up with petrol from a jerrycan. I had almost a full tank, having used only about 5 L (1.3 gal) so far of my 40 L (10.6 gal) tank. That would be a lot of money to just throw away, but Ramadan knew what I was thinking and told me not to worry. He called up the local boda-boda drivers and convinced them to buy my tainted petrol at a discounted price. Apparently, their Chinese bikes could handle a little water in their petrol, whereas my fancy Japanese motorcycle needed the purest petrol possible. I was simply going along with all this, not knowing any better. Petrol was retailing for Tsh 2,500 per litre ($6/gal) and Ramadan sold my fuel for Tsh 2,200/L. It was not a terrible loss to get rid of water-infected petrol. We bought some fresh petrol from the nearby fuel station and sanDRina fired up at first go. I was smiling, but not for long. She died again within ten minutes of running. Oh great, I thought, it wasn't the fuel. Maybe it was the sticky float needle after all, but that would have to wait till the next day.

I left sanDRina at his shop and hopped on a boda-boda to the only proper hotel in town. Not having a functioning bike, I didn't bother checking all the accommodation options and just settled for Hotel Sankere, the swankiest place in town. At Tsh 20,000 ($12.40) per night, it came with a hearty breakfast the next morning. There was a quarter piece of chicken, chapati, noodles, boiled plantains and beef and potato soup. Thinking about the day ahead, I slowly made my way through the large meal and was good to go till dinner.

I arrived at Ramadan's little shop just as Kibondo was coming to life. We bought some fine sandpaper and carefully sanded the valve jet for the float needle so that it could move effortlessly. sanDRina fired up but then died again within ten minutes. Ramadan confidently stated that it wasn't a fuel issue and that it was perhaps something to do with the electrical system. A small voice inside my head told me otherwise, but having a more experienced mechanic around pressured me to suppress the voice.

We removed one of the spark plugs, and upon starting sanDRina, we noticed that the spark looked weaker than expected. To find out which component was producing the weak spark, I told Ramadan to bring one of the Chinese bikes he was working on close to sanDRina. We proceeded to first send the spark from the DR's ignition coil to the Chinese bike. It didn't fire up. Next, we wired up the ignition coil from the Chinese bike to sanDRina's spark plugs and she fired up, running good for about ten minutes. There was no way to run her longer without overheating the engine. I was convinced that there was something wrong with sanDRina's ignition coil, so I went and bought two ignition coils from the local parts shop that were meant for the Chinese bikes. The DR is a dual spark engine, and thus, I had determined that two ignition coils designed for the smaller 125 cc bikes would do the job on sanDRina's 650 cc engine. I installed the new coils, but sadly, that didn't fix it. Again, sanDRina ran for about ten minutes and then died. I was beginning to get extremely frustrated. It seemed to be an ignition coil problem and I determined that sanDRina needed a proper DR replacement.

Retiring to my room at the Sankere, I patiently and methodically navigated the slow 2G internet on my phone to post about my woes to other motorcyclists. Hoping they could help me figure out what was going on, I sent out some e-mails to the DR motorcycle community in South Africa. I pulled out my multimeter and started probing all the electronics to see if something else was also failing. I had carried it all the way from Chicago just in case I ran into electrical problems and I was finally putting it to good use. My readings from the capacitor discharge ignition (CDI) unit, considered the electronic brains of the bike, were not in line with the specifications in the maintenance manual on my laptop. Maybe the CDI had finally come to the end of its life, but these units hardly ever fail. Two DR riders in Johannesburg, Dave and Craig, from the WildDog motorcycle online forum, replied to my post. They had a spare ignition coil and a CDI lying around from an unused bike and said that they would be glad to send them to me. Shocked but relieved, I was in luck. I resigned to patiently waiting in Kibondo for the parts to make their way to me. Craig was going to ship the parts to Nairobi, from where Aki was going to send them as a bus parcel via Dar-es-salaam, the capital of Tanzania, onward to Kibondo. On the phone, Aki laughed at how she was quickly becoming an expert in the bus parcel business of east Africa. She asked me if my previous travels were plagued with so many bike problems, to which I defensively assured her that sanDRina ran great from Chicago to east Africa. It was just in the span of the past few days that she had experienced two major problems.

Relieved at finally locating the problem with sanDRina and her replacement parts arranged for, I could zone out of bike-repair mode and take stock of my surroundings. Kibondo was a minor town on the way to Kigoma, sitting on the edge of a ridge with the expansive savannah down below. Morning sunrises were a peaceful time to walk around before the hustle and bustle of the town took over. There were people selling basic groceries and phone accessories. Others were engaged in bicycle repairs and baking bread. I went to the central market daily and bought some fresh produce for my meals. Since I was staying longer than expected, I moved into a cheaper room priced at Tsh 10,000 ($6.20), which came with an attached bathroom but didn't include breakfast. I set up my trusty MSR Dragonfly stove on the table in my room and enjoyed the time preparing meals. It also helped pass the time. I quickly ran out of my small bottle of sesame oil and picked up a bottle of local palm oil for Tsh 1,000 ($0.62) that smoked viciously and gave everything I cooked an orange tinge but hey, I had to use what I could find. My supply of oats was limited, and not knowing how long I was going to be there, I reverted to a breakfast of bread with peanut butter, which was locally available and cheap. Served up with smashed bananas, it made for a hearty breakfast. Avocados were available in the market and I frequently whipped up avocado salads. I had a decent supply of dried soya chunks for my protein intake but decided to make red beans one day, seeing them readily available in the central market. It took so long to cook on my little stove that I gave up and dreamed of a mini travel-size pressure cooker and reverted back to soya chunks. I got friendly with the hotel staff and they invited me to join them for lunch, which was usually ugali with beans. No plates were used and everyone just dug into the pot it was cooked in. Communal eating might be frowned upon in most cultures, but there was something trusting and reassuring about eating from the same pot or plate as others. I also passed the time by reading up the course work for the last set of exams for my master's degree.

After ten days of waiting patiently and coordinating with Aki in Nairobi, the parts had finally arrived in Kibondo. To my frustration, it still didn't fix the issue. Once again, sanDRina ran for ten minutes and then died. I was losing hope when my inner voice told me that it was just a motorcycle. It was designed by humans and could be fixed by humans; I was just lacking the knowledge on how to fix her. I called up Gus, my old mechanic friend and mentor in Chicago, and he suggested I run the bike without the generator (stator) plugged in. I did that and she ran for longer than ten minutes, which brought a big smile to my face and lifted my spirits. However, it wasn't possible to continuously run sanDRina without a stator as that would damage the electrical system. Perhaps the stator was faulty, so I decided that it needed replacing. I e-mailed the group in South Africa to no avail. I knew it was available in the US but it would've taken a few weeks for any parts to arrive from there. It was getting near the end of September, and I had originally planned to be in South Africa by the first week of October to take the last exams for my master's degree in Johannesburg. After much deliberation, I made the call to leave sanDRina in Kibondo and bus it back to Nairobi to take my exams, receive the spares from the US, and then get back to Kibondo, hopefully with a solution in hand.

The arduous, two-day bus journey back up the bumpy road was strenuous, and I hoped sanDRina would be safe, tucked away at Hotel Sankere in Kibondo. Aki was elated that I was coming back to her. The separation had been hard on her and she had been putting on a brave face. Being able to help out with sanDRina's problems had provided her with a sense of involvement in my trip, but she still struggled with why I had to continue my journey. She questioned the purpose behind it all and if there was something I was trying to prove. My only answer was that I had told myself that my journey would end in India and I wanted to see it through. She respected my commitment but was jealous that I was more committed to sanDRina than her. I myself struggled with why I was still on the road when an amazing partner was waiting for me. At the time, I told myself that I had to get back to sanDRina, revive her and then see where the journey took me.

Over the next few weeks in Nairobi, I took my exams, received the stator from the US and joked with friends about my recent troubles with sanDRina. Aki had also managed to find a worthy job in New Delhi, as that's where I thought the trip would end and where we could continue our lives together.

With the stator in hand, I hopped on a rickety bus out of Nairobi, wondering what lay ahead for me. Arriving in Kibondo two days later, I rushed to Hotel Sankere and was thrilled to see sanDRina still standing there, patiently awaiting my return. The hotel staff were happy to see me again and asked if I would be staying for long. I hoped not. The following day, I installed the new stator and when sanDRina did not die after running for more than ten minutes, my hopes lifted. I went out for an hour's test ride on the road leading out of Kibondo and she ran just fine. I contained my excitement, and the next day, I hit the road south out of Kibondo.

I stood on the footpegs, cruising once again at 90 kph over the hard-packed mud roads. I was euphoric to be back on the road after nearly two months of trying to sort out sanDRina's troubles. It felt liberating and I was thankful the rainy season hadn't kicked in yet. I spent a few days in Kigoma, on the coast of Lake Tanganyika, and took in its grand views with the towering mountains of DR Congo on the other side. This rift valley lake is the second deepest and second largest lake in the world, after Lake Baikal in Siberia. It's the world's longest lake at 676 km (420 miles), extending all along the southwestern edge of Tanzania. My planned route would move parallel to the lake as I headed southeast.

Leaving Kigoma, I passed the small town of Uvinza, after which I was fully in the jungle with the mud road ahead covered in large puddles; the rainy season was slowly making its way in. I was lost in my music and thoughts of how wonderful it felt to be on a motorcycle in a remote part of Africa when once again, sanDRina died. The realization that I hadn't really solved this issue hit me hard and I had a terrible sinking feeling. Just like before, she would start up if I let her rest for a while. I went along like this for a bit, with her dying every few minutes. I was looking at 200 km (124 miles) through the jungle up ahead, whereas Uvinza was a few kilometres behind. I first tried to resuscitate sanDRina by replacing the spark plug and the ignition coil with a spare set, and she ran for a bit longer before dying again. There was no traffic on the road, and dark, bulbous rain clouds were lurking ahead. Tropical rains in the afternoon are as consistent as clockwork. To avoid getting stuck in the torrential rains with a dysfunctional motorcycle, I turned around and slowly made my way to Uvinza with sanDRina dying every few minutes.

It took over an hour to cover the few kilometres into town, and just as I pulled into the aptly named Sleep Lodge, the clouds opened up and the water poured down as if to add to my misery. sanDRina was looking sad with the rain pelting down on her and I was feeling dreadfully low. I didn't know what else I could do to fix her. I felt I had tried everything I could think of. It seemed to be some sort of fatal issue with the electrical system. There may have been a short circuit somewhere in the wiring harness, but I didn't have the energy to strip the bike down and remove the entire harness to search for it. I was ready to give up. I had lost my confidence in the bike. I figured it had been a good run up until then, and I started making plans for getting back to Nairobi on a truck. It wasn't easy and I spent a few days languishing in the doldrums, wondering if I was really ready to stop my journey.

I got on the internet and shared my plight with friends who had been following my journey. All of them kept encouraging me to continue and a few, in particular, were reminding me to check and recheck everything from the basics. Maybe it wasn't an electrical problem. Maybe it was something with the fuel system, they said. But I had checked the carburettor and it all looked fine.

I called up Aki and told her that I was ready to stop and come live with her in New Delhi, ready to start our life together once again. I was feeling very weak emotionally and had lost the strength that I had earlier. Once again, I wondered why I was struggling so much in a remote part of Africa when my partner was waiting for me back in civilization. I was shocked when Aki told me that I wasn't welcome in New Delhi. She said there was no place for me in her life. I sank to rock bottom. This was it. Not only was I getting ready to give up on a journey for which I had left everything behind, but now, my partner was breaking up with me, as well. I couldn't understand it. Why was she doing this to me now? I needed support, emotional support, and I was being shut out. I tried to plead with her, but once her determination to end our relationship was clear, anger welled up in me and I hung up on our call. I was angry at myself for being vulnerable and letting someone else dictate whether I felt needed or not. I was angry at Aki for breaking up with me. And I was disappointed at what I had led myself into.

I was sitting in my boxers under a torn mosquito net at the Sleep Lodge in Uvinza. Clutching my phone, my anger told me that I had nothing going for me beyond where I currently was.

There was no partner waiting for me. There was no life in New Delhi and all I had was this journey. That voice spoke up; the voice that was always there for me. It told me that I had better figure out what was wrong with sanDRina and complete my journey. It would be my only resolution. There was no other option. Slowly, my anger ebbed and I began to breathe properly once again. With my new resolve, I soon fell asleep.

The next morning, I confronted sanDRina. The sun was out and I pulled back her rain cover. I stared at her long and hard, thinking back to my friends' words. Perhaps I was overlooking something very basic. I put my ego aside and in a very calm manner, thought about how sanDRina was dying every few minutes. It could either be an electrical problem, where I had replaced almost every major electrical component, or it could be a fuel flow problem. I opened up the petcocks in the fuel tank and they seemed quite clean. Next up in the fuel line was the fuel filter that I pulled out from under the tank. The plastic casing was covered in grime and the insides were equally dirty. Somehow, incredibly, I hadn't checked the fuel filter all this while. I had moved it to a new location on the bike during my rebuild in Nairobi and it was out of sight now, tucked away under the fuel tank – out of sight, out of mind, as the saying goes.

The clear plastic fuel filter had a paper core, which I realized could easily get blocked if there had been any water in the petrol as the paper would swell and block the pores, obstructing fuel flow. Along with water, I guess I had taken on some dirty fuel because there were grimy particles inside the filter. It hit me like a tonne of bricks. I realized why sanDRina was repeatedly dying after running for a few minutes. It dawned on me that this partially clogged filter was allowing the bike to run for a few minutes at a time until the sediments got into every pore and chocked the carburettor of fuel. After resting for a few minutes, the sediments would settle out of the pores at the bottom of the filter and sanDRina would fire back up again, until the sediments would get disturbed, rise up and choke the pores. That was it. I had cracked this enigma. With lifted spirits, I rummaged through my spares kit for a new fuel filter that I had with me the entire time and installed it with ease on sanDRina. She instantly fired up. Unlike before, she was throaty and clear. I revved the throttle and I sensed a new-found responsiveness from her engine.

A group of kids had gathered around and they sensed my joy. I was ecstatic. It had been the fuel filter all along! My first hunch of this issue being a fuel-related issue was correct, but I had stopped my diagnosis at the carb and didn't inspect the entire fuel system. Abuzz with the fact that I had finally found the culprit, I couldn't even be angry with myself at that moment. I donned my gear and went for a 60 km (37 miles), one-hour-long test ride north of Uvinza and sanDRina sounded sensational, revving effortlessly through all the gears. I rode with a new gusto and was back in my element. The successful test ride surged up a great new energy in me and I knew I could carry on and finish riding through Africa. I wasn't ready to give up. I just needed a big push to keep searching for the root cause, and, at last, I had done it. I fuelled up once again from jerrycans on the roadside, as there was no other option. I wasn't worried this time, since the new fuel filter had a copper core that would not get clogged even if there was water in the fuel.

My spirits were soaring as I shifted my focus away from bike maintenance. I could now see the beautiful little village of Uvinza. Storms were coming through every afternoon and kept the landscape lush. A little old lady sold me some rice from a shack as I restocked my supplies. I bought some mangoes from a group of kids who were all very shy at first, but after I took some photos and showed it to them, they went berserk and started making the funniest poses. Their joy reminded me of why I was in Africa. It was not to complain and whine about bike problems, but to see and experience this amazing continent, which I was once again ready to do.

A motorcycle is a machine and it only fails if its operator has neglected to maintain it or if it wasn't manufactured properly. I had been listening to the audiobook of *Zen and the Art of Motorcycle Maintenance* and it prompted me to stop paying attention to the weak emotion of hopelessness when dealing with a frustrating problem, which the author calls a 'gumption trap', and to simply tackle it rationally. With the issue resolved, I could now let the positive emotions of achievement and success flood my brain and bring me back on track.

The next day, I got back on the muddy trail south and had no problems whatsoever with sanDRina. She really was cured of her ills. I thought about the countless weeks I had spent barking up the wrong tree and how it had probably led to my break-up with Aki. I was not angry with her any more and realized that I probably seemed very weak in wanting to give up my journey and return to her with my tail tucked between my legs. But it pained me that she did not stand strong with me in my weakest moment. It also showed me that in the end, this game of life is really with yourself. Figuring out how to rely on your own emotional strength made for a better strategy, as opposed to solely relying on others and being let down when the vagaries of human emotions fall through. This is not to say that there's no use in having a partner through life, but just that it is better not to be utterly dependent on them for emotional strength.

As I cut through the hundreds of kilometres of mud roads that followed, dodging the rain clouds, splashing through puddles and embracing the charge of riding a motorcycle through remote roads, I discovered the joys of adventuring once again. Aki got in touch to apologize and said that she did not want to be the reason I ended my journey. I thought about that and it made sense. I was using her as a reason to stop. I realized that it was only once she broke up with me that I was able to get some clarity. Once my anger subsided, I had figured out the simple issue that had been plaguing sanDRina the entire time. As I rode further along Tanzania's southwestern highlands, I smiled, thankful that Aki had broken up with me and liberated me from my weakness. Not to say that being in a relationship was my weakness, but at that moment, I was better off being free rather than having someone or something else to choose instead. I got over my indignation with Aki and she asked for us to get back together, but I wasn't up for it. I wanted to be free and finish the journey.

13

HOMECOMING

A S THE METAL GATE lifted, I twisted sanDRina's throttle and we rolled ahead. The next country on my journey beckoned, but it wasn't just any country. This was home. Or at least it used to be.

I had just entered Zambia. The sign at the Chanida border with Mozambique declared that it was a friendly country, which the customs and immigration officials certainly attested to. I had to use my carnet to check sanDRina out of Mozambique, but in Zambia, it wasn't required and I was simply given a free temporary import permit. Smooth and organized, with parallels to the customs procedures at South American border crossings, this was as good a sign as any that Zambia was progressive and that it had its bureaucracy sorted. The fact that I was also made to buy road insurance at the border sealed the deal. I rolled on the throttle and smiled broadly as I headed away from the border and towards Katete on a well-maintained tar road.

A few days before, I had received word that my visa had been approved from a family friend in Lusaka, Zambia's capital. I was surprised at how difficult it was for Indians to acquire a Zambian tourist visa. I had to have a local Zambian formally invite me and get prior approval from the immigration authorities before I could enter the country. It was different thirty years ago when Zambia openly invited Indians to settle in the country, as my family did.

In 1983, when I was just two years of age, my family moved to the small town of Chipata in eastern Zambia, where we lived for the next decade. My father, an agricultural scientist with the UN's Food and Agriculture Organization, was stationed at a research centre near town. My family says those were the best years of their lives; the years as a young family. Life was good in Zambia. The economy was growing and the political situation was stable, Zambia being one of the few African countries never to have had a coup or military dictator. Holidays were spent lounging on the shores of Lake Malawi and enjoying the wildlife of South Luangwa National Park. I saw lions and elephants out on the savannah before I ever saw them in a zoo. I had my first taste for road trips in rickety, old Land Cruisers, having crossed borders before I could even write. My time in Zambia played a fundamental role in who I had grown up to become. This 'home country' visit was in every respect a pilgrimage and a deep trip down memory lane.

The clouds were gathering as I turned east on the main highway to Chipata. Memories of the lush green and graceful landscape came flooding back in. The land was ripe and verdant as I had entered right in the middle of the rainy season. Ahead of me, I kept an eye on a localized rain cell that eventually crossed my path as I neared Chipata. The short burst of heavy rain was just as I had remembered. When I was growing up, it was dry for the most part, and then for just a few months at the end of the year, it would rain intensely. With rain gear on, I just smiled and welcomed the cooling staccato drum of large raindrops against my helmet, shoulders and chest as I drove through the deluge.

Cresting one last hill, a large 'Welcome to Chipata' sign stood across the highway. It exuded a certain magnificence, if not confidence. Looking fresh from the rains, it was modern, emblazoned with a glossy graphic of elephant tusks laid over a large advertisement from Airtel – an Indian mobile phone network.

It had been over twenty years since my family and I left Chipata and moved back to India, but I remembered the layout of the town impeccably. The main highway from Lusaka heading to the border with Malawi cut through the middle of town. There was a beehive of activity along this corridor. Street vendors sold food, plastics and hardware alongside a seemingly legion supply of cobblers. A swanky new hotel in the middle of town stood just before the intersection that I knew would lead me home.

I turned right and headed towards Chipata Hospital. The public golf course was to my left, which I used to cross on the way home from primary school. I took a left right before the hospital. I knew exactly where our old house was. Another left and I turned onto the familiar road. The bamboo fencing still appeared to be the same and the two lofty trees at the gate still stood sentinel, in bloom with purple flowers. But as I neared the gate, I saw a sign that read 'Mukels Guest House'. Interestingly enough, our old house had been turned into a guest house. It was a discovery that delighted me. I had tried to find a hotel nearby with plans of visiting later, but there were no rooms available at the only hotel in the vicinity due to a major conference that was taking place. In merely swinging by, I was presented with the chance to stay in my old house.

The veranda on the old colonial bungalow had been extended and enclosed, but otherwise, our family home looked just the same. I was overcome with emotion to be there. As I rode over the large exposed roots in front of the gate that I used to pass over every day with my bicycle, my brain was engulfed with a wave of distant memories rushing back all at once. I remembered the innumerable outdoor parties, where chicken and dosas were cooked up on a half-cut oil barrel barbeque stand, with cars and jeeps filling the driveway. Our guard dogs, Fido and Defa, had to be tied up on the right side of the gate whenever we had guests, but they were the gentlest of pups in my memory. The garden out front was still there, but the neighbouring driveway, where I skinned my knees so many times while learning how to ride a bicycle, was now covered with grass; I considered that to be a positive change. Smiling in glee at the vivid images in my mind, I pulled up to the front door. The five large steps at the entrance, painted in dull red, were just the same. I wondered if guard dogs still slept on them as ours used to.

Inside, I declared triumphantly to the young manager in the living room, which was now the reception, that the building we were in used to be my house. The limber young man smiled and welcomed me warmly, before politely informing me that it would cost 125,000 Zambian Kwacha to stay for the night, which was roughly $25. It was a lot more than I would usually pay for a night, but I would have gladly paid $100 to stay in my old house. Despite being denied a cheeky request for a 'past resident discount', I gathered my things from sanDRina and headed towards my old bedroom that I used to share with my sister.

On the way back in, I began my exploration. The veranda, where aunties and uncles used to play endless rounds of Rummy on any given Sunday, had been extended and converted to a restaurant area that now blocked out the natural light that used to pool into the living room. The old fireplace that we never used was still in place, as was a hefty bookshelf built into the wall to the left. I would take bulky encyclopedias from it and read through them before giving my father a summary at the end of each day. That had been when I was older, of course, but I had still resented it at the time. I was eager instead to be playing with my toy trucks in the mud outside under the mango tree, whose exposed roots provided the perfect miniature off-road course. But I was thankful to my dad now. Those readings had stirred a curiosity in me for the things in life that could be traced back to why I was undertaking this motorcycle journey. I still wanted to experience the world I had read about in those encyclopedias, and it seemed fitting that my travels would lead me back to where the curiosity stemmed from.

From the living room, there was a corridor to the left leading to three bedrooms. The one on the left used to be my parent's room, the one on the right was a spare room and up ahead, at the end of the corridor, was our room. I remembered this corridor being much longer given the size of my little feet; always scared of something or the other, I would run to my parent's room in the middle of the night. But now in just five steps, I had reached the end. As I opened the door, the fading light lit up the room and I beamed with delight. I was back in my old room. To anyone else, it was just a random motel room in a small African town, but for me, it was home. I put my bags on the bed and looked inside the bathroom. It was still the same – a bathtub on the left, where my father would give me haircuts followed by glorious bubble baths, and a large window looking out the back.

I flopped down on the bed with my hands outstretched and eyes closed, exulting that I had finally made it back to Chipata. My childhood friends, whom I was still in touch with thanks to the ease of online communication, were utterly jealous that I had been able to go back as they too cherished growing up there. As I looked around the room, once again it appeared to be rather small, seen through the eyes of an adult. As a child, the room appeared large and cavernous. The walls were now covered in a glossy off-white paint that probably made it easier to clean compared to the simple whitewash that I remembered. On the back wall, there used to be a large map of Zambia that had triggered my fascination with maps. Besides tracing the Chipata to Lusaka highway, I had wondered then what Mozambique was like, which I knew now, and also wondered about Namibia, which I would soon find out.

That evening, there was a power outage, and the manager said they couldn't prepare dinner as the cooking range was electric.

I wandered into the kitchen to cook on my camping stove and realized that their cooking range looked like it was still the same one from my time in this house, with four electric coils and an oven underneath. Using my headlamp, I set up on the kitchen table where I used to help my mom make cakes (she would allow me to lick the batter after we were done), and made a simple meal of egg-fried rice. I cherished that moment, revelling in the thought that I was actually preparing a meal in the same kitchen that set me on a course to use my cooking to connect with people all over the world. This was an eudaimonic moment if there ever was any. It was true, good and beautiful, as the Greek philosopher Plato said of eudaimonia; broad terms that are self-evident when they are experienced all at once. I was beyond being content, in a state that surpassed happiness. I was in a state of flourishing by being back in my old house and by deriving positive energy from the vivid memories. This is what eudaimonia meant to me and I was elated to find it at home.

The next day, I strolled through the public golf course that was adjacent to our house and remembered feeling the wind in my face while cycling there; a precursor to my motorcycling life. I wondered if that little boy had ever dreamt of riding a motorcycle across continents back then. A little further up the road, I came across my first school, Hillside Basic School. The blue and white buildings appeared to be just as I remembered them, albeit with a fresh coat of paint. School was in session but I was allowed to walk around after I told the guard that I was a past student. He smiled and let me through. Sitting on a bench under a large tree, I reflected on how this insignificant small town in Africa had played such a pivotal role in my life. I had come full circle. What a privilege it was to come back and visit the very land that had given me a bounty of opportunities the world over. I had been nomadic for the past few years but my wanderings had brought me home, even if it was just for a visit. By being in that physical space, there was a certain reinforcement of positivity in me from the earlier stages of my life that I could apply to the present, in case there were mental struggles ahead. The vagaries of adult life have a way of clouding and doubting the 'good old days' as cynicism takes over with age. In realizing that my past was indeed true, good and beautiful, I was investing in my future state of well-being.

I was back in Zambia during an important moment in its history as the country was about to rebase its currency. They were lobbing off three zeros from the denomination of the Kwacha for a number of reasons, namely psychological confidence in the currency and making the imports that people depended on cheaper. During my first run in Zambia, the Kwacha was strong and pegged to the US dollar, but in the late 80s and early 90s, poor policies were catching up with the country's economic stability, which is when high inflation set in. That was also when many long-time resident expats moved out of the country, including my family. From a peg of 1.20 to the dollar, the Kwacha was now trading at 5,250 to the dollar. After the new year, it would be 5.25 to the dollar. I actually saw every item in a supermarket priced at both the old and new Kwacha. Most of the products were imported from South Africa, displaying Zambia's dependence on food imports. It was also amusing to see a variety of Indian food in cans, such as 'Delhi Beryani'. This was almost certainly due to the popularity of Indian food in south Africa, but I wondered how many people in Chipata consumed its canned version – just enough to keep it stocked on supermarket shelves, I guess. Whereas I'm curious about strange foods, when it came to canned food and its preservatives, I passed. As I entered east Africa and travelled south, it was intriguing to witness how Indian food had spread into the local cuisine. Chapati and samosas were very much a part of the staple in a lot of areas, and I wondered if my family, along with the many other Indian migrants, played a role in that by sticking strong to our food culture or perhaps there were even earlier connections between our cultures.

I took sanDRina for a ride and headed a few kilometres out of town towards the Msekera Research Institute, where my father had been stationed. A sense of pride washed over me as I rode into the tall-treed campus. My father had been working on improving the yields of various crops by controlling their impacts from pests, and his work led to better seeds being available in the local and regional markets. Further down the road, on a muddy track, was the very first house that we had stayed in upon arriving in Chipata. I opened the bamboo gate and no one seemed to be around. I yelled out to avoid coming across as a trespasser but there was no response, and so I moved inside. The squat, single-storey house was still there but less well kept than our bungalow. The large garden no longer had the grass that we used to play on, but the trees were still there. Something about the large mango tree in the garden drew me closer and I sat on a low branch and swung my legs, lost in thought for ten minutes or more, feeling like a kid once again. I wondered if other kids who came to this house after me knew that the backyard opened up to a large prairie where it was easy to get lost in the tall grasses. I wondered if the gap in the neighbour's fence had been closed up. Was the living room still grand with its French windows? It's marvellous that the brain has the capacity to keep such intricate details stored away for decades, and serve them up so easily when appropriate.

Seeing the afternoon rain clouds approaching in the distance, I headed back towards town and rode a few kilometres past it on the way to the border with Malawi. I pulled off on the side of the road under a large tree and reflected on how it was on that very stretch that music and being on the road had become fascinations of mine. My father would take us for evening drives in our boxy Nissan Bluebird sedan, during which we would listen to old Hindi songs. He would ask me to identify every instrument in the song, giving birth to my obsession with music that carries on to this day; I need to be listening to music any time I'm on the road. sanDRina's licence plate and my moniker of 'Jammin' goes back to these moments in Chipata.

Returning to town, I was exploring the condition of the nearby houses of my childhood friends when I turned a corner and saw ominous, dark rain clouds sweeping in fast. Heavy rain was just minutes away. It feels lovely to say that I ran home for safety. Just as I entered the veranda, thunderous rain began pelting down. Similar to my childhood, I enjoyed watching the heavy rain from the large windows in my bedroom. The storms were just as intense as I remembered them. They swept in fast in the afternoon and were finished within half an hour.

The best part about fast-moving rain is the clear skies left in its wake. I stepped out once the rain passed and took in the marvellous unblemished sky. The mango tree near the entrance of the house had dropped a few ripe ones. I relished the sweet meat as I sat on the front steps. My mother would feed me on those steps as I cycled round the driveway, taking a bite after every round. I picked up some of the red dirt. I used to play in it and probably ate some too. I was happy to note that some of that dirt was on sanDRina, and not being one to wash my motorcycle, I would probably carry some of its redness onward to India.

Back in my room, I pulled the curtains aside and couldn't get over the fact that my amazing motorcycle was parked outside. I used to stare out the same window and wonder what kind of life lay ahead for me. Who knew that I would end up riding a motorcycle from the US back to Chipata and onward to India. sanDRina was connecting all my homes, and, of course, she herself was my home on the road.

The next morning, it was time to leave. I put on my hefty motorcycle boots in my old bedroom and had one last look around. As I fired up sanDRina, I thanked my old house for giving me such a wonderful childhood, grateful for the chance to be able to come back. With another chapter concluded and my farewells said, I opened sanDRina's throttle and headed out of town.

From Chipata, on the eastern edge of Zambia, it was 570 km (354 miles) to Lusaka. I had been driven on that road many times as a kid in old Land Cruisers and I was going to be journeying on it for the first time myself. At the junction town of Katete, I ran into a group of motorcycle travellers from South Africa on big BMW R1200GSs, the mack daddy of adventure bikes. They were making a loop of southern Africa. They had blasted up Namibia, were in the process of cutting across Zambia, and after hitting the beaches in Malawi, they planned to blast down Mozambique before getting home. Their quick trip was indicative of the quality of roads and ease of border crossings in southern Africa, probably the most advanced in the whole continent.

As I got to the Luangwa River Valley, which neared the halfway point of the route to Lusaka, the terrain became hillier. With the first-rate roads, it made for exciting riding. Being the rainy season, wild mushrooms had sprouted everywhere, which young boys were selling by the sides of the road in large buckets. I bought a few large ones for dinner, resisting the urge to buy an entire bucket as insisted by the boys. They had a confidence in their smiles that I had not seen in the other African countries I had travelled through, so far.

Crossing the Luangwa River Bridge, I headed down a small dirt track to the aptly-named Bridge Camp that provided a wide vista of the large, winding river below. The bridge had always been a national strategic asset and was still guarded by the military; no photos were allowed. I remembered crossing this bridge many times during my childhood trips, using it as a halfway marker to home when we would come from Lusaka.

In the fading light, a lone fisherman headed down the river in a dugout canoe. The Luangwa River flowed from the northeast of Zambia through the wildlife parks of North and South Luangwa National Park. It connected to the Zambezi at the Zimbabwean border before flowing across Mozambique to the coast. When living in Chipata, our family used to visit South Luangwa National Park quite frequently. It was now being heralded as a hidden gem of Africa, receiving increasing attention from safari tourists who usually head to the well-known Serengeti, Maasai Mara and Kruger national parks. It was bound to happen at some point, but Zambia still remains a bit off-the-radar.

Back on the road in the morning and after a few sublime hours of smooth motorcycling, the increase in traffic marked my arrival at the capital city. Pretty soon, I was lane-splitting my way to a GPS waypoint to pull into the driveway of Verma uncle, the family friend who had got my Zambian visa approved. He was a long-time resident, and just like my father, had come there in the early days to help with Zambia's agricultural sector. He had become a renowned scientist for his work on improving yields of maize that is made into the staple food of Zambia; nshima, similar to ugali in east Africa. His wife prepared a delicious and simple Indian meal of rotis with dal and drumstick. Drumstick, or moringa, is one of my favourite Indian vegetables, and it is grown locally just for the large Indian population who have been in Zambia for over 100 years. Unlike Indian migrants who went to South Africa or other parts of the continent, Indians who came to Zambia (or Northern Rhodesia as it was known before independence) were not indentured labourers, but artisans and business people. Contrary to the uneasy relations between Indians and the locals in other African countries, such as Uganda in the 70s, Zambia has been good to its Indian community, which is maybe why so many stayed and prospered.

The next day, I was set to visit a special girl. Following directions, I arrived at the Children International Centre in Zambia. I had been sponsoring a child with them for the past few years. For $22 a month (of which 80 per cent goes to the child), they promised to rescue one child out of poverty and give them a solid start to life by providing education, nutrition and guidance. I had read that it was rare for sponsors to visit the recipients of their aid due to the remote locations in which Children International operates, but that wasn't an issue for me. I was curious to see how the programme worked, but most of all, I was curious to see this particular child who was getting a leg-up in life. The benefits of focusing on just one child as opposed to spreading the provisions across a community could be debated over. My rationale, much like the programme's, was that by securing the future of at least a few individuals, their contribution to their respective societies in the future would be greater than distributing the same amount of money among everyone at once. There were plenty of other aid agencies taking the route of spreading charitable resources across entire communities, but I was curious to see if the individual strategy had any merit. I had chosen to sponsor a child in Zambia deliberately, as a way of thanking the country for the wonderful childhood that it had provided me with.

Joan, one of the programme officers, took me around the centre and showed me all the facilities and services they provided to the sponsored children. There was a dedicated clinic that ensured that children and their mothers were in optimal health. There was a library filled with young children, all reading various books, and in the main hall, volunteers from the community were handing out items to families, such as mattresses, plates and cups. After a group photo with the energetic and joyful volunteer ladies, it was time to finally meet the girl I had been sponsoring, Abigail.

I saw her sitting in a lovely green check dress with a gentle smile. She was seven years old and I'm not sure she understood what was happening. Abigail's mother sat next to her but without much emotion. She might've been unsure as to how she was supposed to react to the man who was giving money to support her child. Still, we made the usual pleasantries as I tried to speak with them both. There wasn't much else to do since we couldn't really communicate, so we took some photos outside by the swings. It was then that her mother called out to Abigail as 'Abi'. I was stunned, pleasantly so. As a kid, my nickname had been Abi, too. It felt as though our unusual relationship was meant to be. I couldn't convey my exuberant emotions to her besides smiling with glee.

I was a part of the 'haves' of the world and I felt obligated by values instilled in my childhood to see that the number of 'have-nots' was reducing. My family had taken on sponsoring an orphanage in Chipata when we lived there. On Sundays, we would drive out to the countryside where the orphanage was and hand out food provisions and treats, and I would spend time playing with the kids my age. Years later, I asked my parents what had prompted them to get involved in charitable practices. Besides being generous and caring, they wanted to instil in my sister and I a sense that we were no different in essence to all other humans, even though we were lucky enough to be socio-economically privileged. As a child, it was simply a fun afternoon with other kids, but as an adult, it allowed me to travel through numerous cultures with an open mind and see the general goodness but unfair disadvantages that exist across humanity.

While taking photos with Abigail, there was a group of young boys hanging around who wanted their picture taken as well. I turned my camera to them as they struck up a bunch of fun poses. They had a lot of character and were making signs with closed fists in a cross that I later found out was the symbol of a popular rap group in Zambia. One of the kids had a glint in his eye and I had a feeling that he would get far ahead in life. He seemed to be an extrovert in comparison to Abigail, who was shy and reserved. I wondered if this was a facet of their gender. In most lesser-developed countries, the boys usually get more of a boost in life as a result of the almost-universal influence of patriarchy. This had been the driving force behind my decision to sponsor a girl child. Women have, without a doubt, contributed as much to the current progress of civilization as men, but have had to endure unfair gender biases along the way. I hoped that securing an education and good health for Abigail would allow one more woman to flourish into adulthood and contribute to Zambia's future. With that, I bid goodbye to Abigail and her mother, strengthening my stance in believing that this indeed was a fruitful programme. My visit to the Children International Centre had filled me up with great joy and hope for Zambia's future.

I spent the next few days applying for my visa to Namibia and had engaging talks with Verma uncle. I refer to him as 'uncle' because in Indian custom, any elder man, whether related or not, could be referred to as uncle. One of the interesting topics we discussed was world hunger. He revealed that to feed the entire world, it had been calculated by agricultural scientists that it would take only 850,000 sq km (328,186 sq miles) of fertile land, and Zambia, a very fertile country, was around 750,000 sq km (289,577 sq miles). That meant we definitely had more than enough fertile land in the world to feed everyone, yet a billion people still go hungry every night, whereas one and a half billion are overweight. After travelling the world and living in Zambia for so long, he was thinking in global terms. Similarly, I had taken on the viewpoint of seeing humanity as one after having traversed across large parts of the globe myself; all its warts and hopes in one potpourri. I wondered if I would have still gained the same perspective had my family stayed on in Zambia and endured the rough years of high inflation. Uncle had thrived, so perhaps I might have as well, seeing the same boyish curiosity of the world in him that I myself possessed. I had no regrets and was ever thankful for how my life had played out, bringing me back to Zambia at that moment.

Our perspectives did not always align, as uncle did not see the value in my sponsorship of Abigail, thinking it a waste of money. He felt that tackling society's systemic problems, such as hunger and inflation, would bring about sustained change more effectively. He was probably right to some degree. Living among rapid development had made me very individualistic, and so, perhaps I felt more compelled to help an individual instead of the collective. Staying back in Zambia might have indeed engendered a more collectivistic view in me.

I also wondered what life might have been like if my family never came to Zambia in the first place. Would I have taken on a stronger Indian identity if I spent my entire childhood in India? Would I have been as comfortable in wild and remote places had it not been an integral part of my formative years? But that's the thing with the past – one can only question with 'woulds' and 'shoulds' without reaching a conclusion. Instead, I prefer to see the past for what it is, unchangeable and true, and live in the present, here and now. Ignoring the unpleasant parts of my past in Zambia, such as bouts of malaria and being disciplined for breaking things, I chose to focus on all its positive aspects instead.

My visit to Zambia had been more than I had expected. I had managed to sleep in my old house, refresh old memories and get a sense of where my home country was heading. If Zambia manages to get its inflation under control, there would be a bright future ahead and perhaps I would come back some day for a longer stay.

14

NATURE AT ITS GRANDEST

THE SKY WAS BESIEGED with clouds. Spreading all the way from the horizon, they lingered over me; white and harmless, yet ominous. Perhaps it was a sense of foreboding that I saw in them? Or it could have just been another long day in the saddle. My mind would drift – pensive, stretched – before alighting on the next visual. My body, tasked only with keeping my right wrist firm on the open throttle, was steady. I was preoccupied at that moment by the grey tarmac whizzing by endlessly at high speed. My eyes and mind wandered: 'how many kilometres have I covered already today?' Ignoring the odometer, I pushed my brain to process the basic arithmetic. It had indeed been a long day.

I was riding across the entire Caprivi Strip in one day. From the eastern border town of Katima Mullilo, it was about 500 km (311 miles) to Rundu, the next major town. After entering Namibia just the previous evening, I was making quick work of the distance for a number of reasons. My visa for South Africa was issued in Nairobi about two months before, leaving me with just a month to enter and wander around Namibia. Larger than France, this nation's presence has long been defined by the Skeleton Coast on which the two expanses of the Namib Desert and the Atlantic Ocean meet. But there is far more to this corner of Africa. As rich in landscapes as its history and its people, Namibia has a reputation for enchanting its visitors. But it is also one of the least densely populated countries in the world. This was a land for those seeking solitude; something I could definitely use.

Aki and I had made up since the time I had almost thrown in the towel in western Tanzania. My mind was troubled because her messages to me were mixed. She was now in India and apparently waiting for me at the finish line, but even that seemed unclear. We would have to work out where we stood only once I crossed that line. So on I journeyed, uneasily straddling my hopes for a relationship and the desire to be free and on the road. I had finally launched into Namibia, embracing it as one last hurrah. Free of oversight, I had committed to enjoying the journey ahead just as it was, packing away my relationship concerns at the bottom of a figurative pannier, to be dealt with when it was time.

Compared to the other African countries I had ridden through up until then, Namibia was the most developed. For 500 km (311 miles), the road through the Caprivi Strip was in impeccable condition with coloured markings on the edge of the tarmac and large signs warning of possible elephant crossings – another way to warn motorcyclists such as myself to look out for large piles of fresh elephant dung. Roads aside, Namibia was still working on doing a better job at economically integrating its indigenous black African population. The nation had only gained independence from South Africa in 1990, having suffered the same injustices from apartheid that its southern neighbour bears the scars of. Most of the nations that I had visited had come a long way since their independence, but Namibia was still labouring through the early stages of what seemed to be a long journey. Progress could be seen everywhere, but straying from the road would expose one to the base realities of the challenges they face.

To my left and right, lush groves of trees spread out across the sun-beaten savannah, clumped in random dots, comprising the last vestiges of forest turned grassland. The Caprivi Strip itself was an odd geopolitical feature. Extending 500 km (311 miles) east in a finger of land just 50 km (31 miles) wide, it protrudes from Namibia, linking its territory to the Zambezi River. German colonizers had negotiated this land so as to have access to the waterway and the border with Zambia, in order to establish river connections with its territories in east Africa and the Indian Ocean beyond. However, the vagaries of the water in the Zambezi and its politics made river access to the Indian Ocean unattainable for the Germans. Today, the Caprivi Strip, resembling a panhandle on the map, is covered primarily in protected forest land and open grazing land for the local people. To the north is Angola, with Botswana to the south. And to the far west ahead lay the giant sand dunes of the Namib Desert that had captured my imagination since my childhood days in Zambia. Like the photographs in the encyclopedias my father made me read as a child, they were within reach.

These thoughts ran through my mind as the kilometres slowly rolled by. I regularly ignored the odometer on such days. The unrelenting meter of progress made the journey onerous. It was better to just sit back, open sanDRina's throttle and let my thoughts flow. Runners, trekkers and swimmers, all experience it. When you hit your rhythm, you no longer feel the effort. Your movements become mechanical and rhythmic, allowing your mind to wander free. Motorcycling was no different, and on long days such as this, I would find kilometres and hours would sometimes pass in this unburdened manner.

Yet, the world always finds a way to mark the passage of time. Towards the end of the day, the white clouds had merged, transforming into mighty thunder cells – heavy, dark and vast – over the land. I followed my GPS towards a marked camping site, and soon after, arrived at N'Kwazi Lodge right on the Okavango River near the town of Rundu. Lodging was expensive in Namibia since it was more developed than the other countries I had ridden through in Africa, and so I was keen on camping frequently over the next few weeks. I flung open my one-man tent in the lush green grounds just as the first drops started to fall. The owners of the lodge were elderly white Namibians who had been there for a few generations. A local lodge staff member came over and gave me a room key, saying that I should stay inside one of the cottages due to the heavy rain that was coming. The proprietors were showing sympathy for a frugal traveller in the low season, and I gladly accepted the charity, especially as I would still only pay the camping fee of 60 Namibian Dollars (N$) (US $7). An elegantly thatched roof and soft bedding awaited. After 500 km (311 miles) of the endless highway, it was a treat.

I had come to this lodge in hopes of taking a boat ride on the famous Okavango River, but the rains had upended those plans for the day. Enjoying the location and hospitality, I decided to stay another day, indulging in a proper bed and reading up on Namibia's history. I studied its map to get the lay of the land into my head, noting the major towns, primary roads and sites of interest. A route started to form in my mind, consisting of some epic natural and ancient human sites. I had done this frequently on my travels. While I knew the entry and exit ports of the country through which I was travelling, I would leave the route between the two unestablished. I had learned that routes would present themselves at the right time – sites on maps would beckon, friends and strangers would offer me advice and tips, and on other days, delays such as this storm would point me in another direction.

By the afternoon, my boat had arrived. It was a home-made contraption; two canoes with a platform tied between them, powered by an outboard motor. It was bedecked with a gazebo to protect its only passenger from the sun. It had a certain ridiculousness to it. As we began motoring, I sat on the front edge of the platform and skimmed the bottom of my feet on the rushing surface of the river.

I had been fascinated by the Okavango River after seeing BBC's *Planet Earth* nature documentary series a few years ago. I learned then how the Okavango, flowing from the highlands in Angola, drained inland instead of into the sea like most other rivers. It drained into the aptly-named Okavango Delta in northern Botswana, flooding a large desert area every year that sustained a vast ecosystem. The lodge owners had told me that the river had only started its annual rising a few days back, owing to the heavy rains that were now lashing the region. Within a few weeks, the water would be reaching the delta and the flooding would commence. Contrary to the expectations people have when embarking on a safari, it turns out that not every trip is a wildlife documentary. The storm cells overhead proved to be more entertaining than the marsh-lined banks that were hiding most of the wildlife within its dense expanse. As the towering clouds roiled overhead, the winds squalled and flattened the sea of reeds and elephant grass in waves. We pulled over at a large sandbar in the middle of the river as it fanned out. John, the helmsman and sole other occupant of the safari canoe, handed me a placard with a large grin that had the words 'Illegally in Angola' written on it. I posed for a silly photo with the placard as he explained that this sandbar would become exposed before the river rose higher every year and was technically a part of Angola. This was because the water coursed south of us, but the actual bank to the north, signifying Angolan territory, was a hundred metres further away. We did not wait for long since the storm began to build, and so we rushed back to the lodge as the thunder rumbled from the gorgeously sculpted clouds. Nature was resplendent even in its wrath. I managed to duck into the lodge's canteen just as the heavy rain started lashing down, leaving me to ponder the conditions of the roads for the next day over a hot mug of tea.

Departing the lodge the next morning, I was faced with large muddy pools on the dirt track back to the main road. I wondered if that was what lay ahead when the tarmac would end in a few days. My plan had been to head to a waterfall site directly west of Rundu, but that road was supposedly very rough, and with the recent rains, I didn't want to get stuck in the mud. Instead, I chose to head southwest to the large town of Grootfontein and then back northwest towards the waterfall site. Filling up at a fancy modern petrol station at Rundu, I felt like I was back in the US. I could pay with my credit card at the pump and there was an array of drinks and snacks at the convenience store. It was crowded, just like a gas station would be during a holiday weekend on an interstate highway in the US. The modernity was jarring. Seeking out the open expanses away from it all, I set out once again.

Leaving Rundu behind, the smooth tarmac highway passed through gently rolling flatland that was dotted with herds of cattle and goats, some dashing across the highway as I approached. Always accompanying the livestock were Namibian herders, who looked quite modern with their jean shorts and t-shirts. However, they still looked poor, relative to those I had just seen at the petrol station. The divide in Namibia was still stark. A few hours from Rundu, I passed through an 'Animal Disease Checkpoint' marked as the 'Red Line' on my map. It was crowded with livestock, minibuses and shops selling mobile recharge cards and fried snacks. I realized that I had crossed into a different Namibia on the southern side. There was no more loose livestock about. The people disappeared and fences ran along the highway on both sides. When I did see livestock, they were behind fences and gathered by the roadside. This was the predominantly white part of Namibia. South Africa's long rule, and prior to that, Germany's colonization of Namibia, was still evident in this distinct separation of black and white.

As I neared Grootfontein, I stopped outside a ranch gate advertising camping. The owner of Die Kraal, a lithe and white

Namibian man, came out and said that camping was officially closed since the bathrooms were run down, but gave me the green light if I wanted to pitch my tent for free and stay the night. Encouraging me with a gentle laugh, he claimed that it was the only place with free camping in all of Namibia. I took up the offer as he showed me around the back of his ranch house. He took me to a site under a large tree that had a barbeque ('braai' in Afrikaans) stand built in concrete. I was soon to learn that it was a quintessential part of camping in Namibia.

There were still a few hours of daylight left, so I unloaded my panniers and set off for the Hoba Meteorite site. Passing through Grootfontein, I was shocked to see a stop sign. It had been many thousands of kilometres since I had seen one and I came to an abrupt halt. My instincts kicked in as I remembered how in the US, there was invariably a policeman nearby ready to give me a ticket if I failed to stop completely. As suspected, there was indeed a policeman in a patrol car near this stop sign. I yelled out to him for Hoba and he pointed to the west. I was riding straight into the gorgeous late afternoon sun when the route to Hoba became a dirt track on the other side of town. The corrugations were not that pronounced and I beamed as I stood on the pegs and upped the speed on a lightened sanDRina. I was itching for more off-road riding.

I soon arrived at the meteorite site, which was empty besides two Toyota Land Cruisers with South African plates and roof tents mounted atop. The ticket office was closed because it was a Sunday, so I wandered through the gate freely and past a thick grove of trees, and there it was. A massive boulder that didn't look like any rock I had ever seen before. Squat, square, shiny and most certainly, other-worldly. It had excavated a shallow crater as it crashed into Earth 80,000 years ago. An amphitheatre had been built around it on which I sat to marvel at this meteorite. It was about 3.7 m (12 ft) across and said to weigh over 55,000 kg (1,21,254 lbs). Its surface glinted in the fading sun, hinting at its metallic iron composition, which is how it had survived the fiery journey through our atmosphere. It was probably much larger before it had entered the atmosphere, but the heat caused by the entry friction would have burnt off a large chunk. What remains is the largest known meteorite and lump of naturally-occurring iron on Earth. I touched it with a feeling of reverence and rubbed my fingers on the smooth surface. I was touching something that had come from outer space. It was really no different that touching any other metal on Earth since it all initially came from outer space, but it helps to put our lives in perspective when you consider the sheer enormity of what else lies beyond the world as we know it.

As I was walking out, the Land Cruiser troupe called out and invited me over for some snacks. Erez, his wife and daughter were Israelis from Cape Town and were touring Namibia with a friend. They were immediately impressed to learn that I had been on the road from the US. When I told them I was looking forward to going deep into the Namibian wilderness, they regaled me about their trip through the interiors of Kaokoland, a large remote area of northwest Namibia. That was scheduled to be my next challenge, and so I probed them for details on the conditions up ahead. They had ventured far off the regular route through Kaokoland, warning me that fuel was scarce and that I wouldn't be able to make it without travelling in a convoy with a jeep to carry extra petrol, just like the Lake Turkana crossing. They told me stories of how they got stuck in the loose sand and that everyone had to make an effort to free their vehicles. They evidently had a good time and I was grateful for their used map of Kaokoland, covered in valuable notes and 'intel' for the route. It looked like I was set.

Back at my campsite under the large tree, I saw that a wheelbarrow full of firewood had been brought over. As the fire got going effortlessly thanks to the dry wood, I realized that this was my first proper campfire in Africa. It seemed strange for me to venture through such a large continent and get a campfire going for the first time, just as I was nearing the end. This was because I

had been bush camping in all the other places where I did not want
to alert others of my presence. But Namibia was a well-developed
country and camping in a safe place such as at this ranch meant
that a roaring fire would be no issue. And so in its good company,
I prepped my dinner, satiated with where I was.

With a newly-purchased off-road tyre strapped to the back
of sanDRina, I left Grootfontein the next morning and headed
northwest on the smooth highway. Crossing back over the Red
Line, livestock was once again roaming freely across the road. The
towns looked worn and weary, dotted with rusting cars on the side
of the road and a high number of bars. The population was once
again predominately black and I wondered why there was such a
distinct difference in Namibia north and south of the Red Line.
More than an animal control line, it seemed like a control line for
black people.

I was on the road to Angola. I wished I could enter that country
but its visa requirements were quite strict and convoluted, making
it difficult to attain one. I heard from travellers who had passed
through that it was filled with natural wonders and an interesting
mix of Portuguese culture in its architecture and food. But alas,
I had to turn left at the border and head west. All of a sudden, I
saw a drop in the land ahead. I had been riding on a vast plateau
and ahead of me in the lowlands till the distant horizon, the
earth was a lush, green expanse of forest land that expanded into
Angola. Although the view was distracting, the road demanded
my attention, snapping back and forth in a series of hairpin turns
as we navigated the steep descent. At the base of this cliff, the
tarmac gave out; there was even a sign to inform me. I used to
love seeing that sign in the US. It suggested to me that the state
had determined it just wasn't worth it to pave the road beyond a
certain point. I had reached the start of the wilderness, and just
where the pavement ended, was a campsite called Hippo Pools,
run by the local Himba tribe.

A Himba lady, wearing nothing more than a loincloth and covered head to toe in their signature red ochre paste with her breasts exposed, greeted me at the reception building. In her basic English, she warned me of crocodiles, as they were known to come ashore at night from the Kunene River that separated Namibia and Angola. In spite of this, I figured that crocodiles were not such a big threat and took the decision to camp near the river. It was a calculated risk of the dangers of a hungry croc against superb views of the river that flowed past at a seductively calm and measured pace.

My front tyre was at the end of its life and it was time to switch it out with the new off-road tyre I had bought in Grootfontein. The current Heidenau front tyre had been mounted back in Hamburg, Germany, almost two years prior, and had lasted me a good 28,070 km (17,446 miles) all across Africa. Amazingly, I didn't get a single flat tyre in all those kilometres. Just as I took out my tools to do the tyre change after setting up my tent, I heard a loud clasp of thunder. A thunderstorm was approaching the campsite over the nearby ridge. I had to race the storm to swap my tyre out.

As I fished around my various tool bags, a vital piece of my kit was missing. A U-bolt that I had fashioned into a bike lift, allowing me to raise one end of sanDRina slightly off the ground, was nowhere to be found. With the urgency of the impending rain, I gave up on finding the U-bolt and rolled a large boulder over, positioning it under sanDRina so as to lift her front tyre off the ground. The clock was ticking, but I was rather pleased with my fieldcraft, and soon enough, I had the old tyre removed. Just as I mounted the new one onto the wheel rim but before I could set it in place, thunder struck once again. This time, the dark clouds were right above and I could see sheets of rain coming for me, obscuring the land behind in a deluge. With the front tyre still in tow, I ducked into my tent just as the rain unleashed. The tent cover lashed in the strong winds and I held the cover up with my hands outstretched. It was a wild experience to be tucked away in a small one-man tent crowded next to my exposed front tyre, subjected to the full force of a thunderstorm. I brought the tyre in with me because any water that got into the tyre before it had been set would lead to rust. Just as suddenly as the storm had descended upon the campsite, it had moved on to seek the next traveller to chase into a tent. Within ten minutes, the storm had passed and I emerged to a fresh, clear sky, under which I fitted the front tyre and proceeded to help sanDRina off of the boulder.

Just then, a convoy of three pickup trucks pulled into the campground. I waved to the group of white Namibians as they decamped from their trucks and started setting up. Maru and his family were on their way back home to Rundu after a two-week fishing trip in southern Angola. I was intrigued by their travels but they were more impressed by mine, and so they invited me to join them for dinner. Their camping was at another level. They had an electricity generator, a fridge, an ice-machine, a moderately well-stocked bar and, of course, wood for a braai. It wasn't quite camping, but who was I to complain when Maru was offering me a whisky to ward off the evening's post-rain chill. We exchanged travel stories through the evening and I felt comfortable surrounded by people who also valued the experience of spending time outdoors and roughing it; beyond the generator, fridge, ice machine, and bar, of course. The only word of caution they gave me was to remain in the campgrounds. The risk of snakes and other animals was just too high in Namibia. Given the company, I wasn't about to object. With a bellyful of steak and potatoes, I tucked in for the night.

I was awoken by raindrops steadily falling on my tent cover. I was eager to start the off-road section of Namibia, but with all the rain, I opted to stay another day, hoping this low-pressure system would pass. I spent time sorting through and organizing my belongings, during which I realized that I had been carrying a spice shaker since the US and had hardly used it. Instead of stashing it back away, I saw the mama Himba woman preparing the midday meal for her family. It was a simple meal of maize porridge with milk powder, for which I offered her the spice shaker. She obviously recognized it for what it was, as her face lit up with a large smile and she gratefully took it. Opening up the Cayenne pepper compartment, she proceeded to nearly empty the chilly spice into the food as I looked on in some trepidation. I was assured, however, by an interpreter who was at the front desk, that this was nothing unusual. The Himba, as it turns out, love spicy food, but due to their desert heritage, don't have access to it very often. With that, I left the mama Himba to serve up a rather novel, peppered maize porridge.

It evidently did nothing to upset her family's stomachs as her children sat around afterwards quietly watching me while I worked on sanDRina. I had rolled her under the awning of the reception to protect her from the rain as I fixed up a short circuit in my 12 volt charging plug. I had all my tools laid out, and in trying to involve the kids, I asked one of them to hand me the screwdriver. A young girl, maybe eight years old, dressed only in a loincloth and bands of elaborately-coloured beads around her belly and arms, handed me the tool. I tightened the bolt on the battery and handed it back to her, and she put it back in its place in the tool roll. They were well-behaved kids and appeared to be quite bright. This was despite them not attending school due to their remote location, which I learned earlier from the interpreter. The elders of their tribe gave them an education on how to survive and thrive in the harsh desert environment – knowledge that us modern people could learn from. Instead of migrating to urban centres and adopting our global culture by wearing pants, skirts and shirts, they chose to stay out there in the desert and keep to their loincloths and red ochre paste. How strange that we might call them backward or undeveloped just because they didn't follow our modern signs of development. They chose to hold on to their cultural roots even if that was seen in some perverse way as 'offensive' to modern society. How anyone could take offence to indigenous people choosing tradition over reform and conformity has never made sense in my mind.

Leaving Hippo Pools behind the next morning, I stood on the footpegs as the road climbed up and over the ridge. It was extremely rutted by the heavy rains and I almost lost balance a few times. I told myself to calm down and take it easy. There was a long way to go before the pavement started again, and up next, were large pools of water to cross. These were not mere puddles, but mini ponds. For the first few, I gingerly went around the perimeter of the pools to avoid any unseen deep parts hidden under the water, but after the first few, my patience faded and I just charged straight through the next set. It was as much fun as any child would have charging their pedal bike through puddles. My feet were soaked, but this was all offset by my childish grin. But of course, confidence can get the better of you. As I was charging through a large pool, sanDRina's front tyre slipped on a slimy and mud-coated bottom. My right leg shot out against the shallow bottom to prevent us from falling, managing to save sanDRina and my dignity from a muddy dunking. Safely across to the other side, I stopped for a breather and told myself to calm down once again.

I continued timidly with no more drama through the next set of crossings, heeding my rational side to slow down and take it easy. The track passed near the Kunene River a few times as I headed west to Epupa Falls before reaching a fork in the road at Swartbooisdrift. I followed Erez's advice and tracked on the better-maintained southern route. Wide yet unpaved, it passed through greening shrub land and over multiple shallow dips. These were seasonal water channels that were soon to fill up and start flowing across this landscape. It seemed like I was just in time. Soon, the rains would flood the region and it certainly wasn't worth it for the government to build hundreds of bridges over these channels.

As I approached an upcoming dip, I saw a detour sign. Perhaps the water was too high to cross at the dip, and so following the path through the shrubs, I came out onto the banks of a fast-flowing river. Thirty feet ahead of me on the other riverbank, I could see where the path continued. This was the first real river crossing I would have to undertake in my journey across Africa, and I hadn't the faintest idea of what to expect in doing so. Not that I expected crocodiles and hippos to be lurking in the currents, but the riverbeds, hidden beneath silt-laden water, could hold all sorts of hazards for not only me, but sanDRina as well. Knowing I would not be able to lift her out of the water on my own if we were to fall, I looked around for help. Fortunately, the crossing had attracted a few local herdsmen and their goats, who offered to walk in front to show me the way across the river, for a tip.

I gently coaxed sanDRina down the bank and into the current, feeling the rocky, loose bottom beneath her wheels. The murky, chai-coloured water, filled with sediment, was over two feet high and flowed over and into my tall boots. We successfully crossed most of the river, but just as I reached the other side, the front tyre hit a large submerged rock and I lost my balance. sanDRina and I fell right into the flowing river. Her engine cut out and my adrenalin kicked in. I was breathing heavily in my hefty gear and managed to quickly scramble up, thankful not to be hurt. The herdsmen saw what happened and rushed back to help me lift sanDRina upright. I prayed the carburettor was not flooded and was relieved to hear sanDRina fire up right away when we dragged her upright. I revved her engine, desperate to get out of the river. Searching for an exit, I realized the bank was too steep at that section. But the river was flowing quickly and I wanted to be back on land. I pointed at the steep bank and rode the front wheel out, which wasn't a smart move since the exhaust pipe went under water and started bubbling. I continued revving the engine to make sure water did not enter the exhaust pipe. Modulating the clutch in first gear, sanDRina wasn't moving forward as her rear wheel was slipping on the muddy bank under the water. The herdsmen lifted sanDRina by the panniers and we ever so slowly climbed out of the water and finally onto the bank. I was breathing very deeply and was completely wet from the chest below. I removed my helmet and jacket to calm down. The herdsmen came over and patted me on my back. We shared a laugh at the mishap. I tipped them generously for their help, after which they went on their way. Fortunately, there wasn't much damage. The right pannier had got dented against a rock underwater and I hoped my belongings inside were still dry, but that was more or less it. So, other than a bruised ego and sodden gear, I was relieved to be on the other side. But I didn't know how many of these crossings I still might have to make. There was no guarantee that I would always find herdsmen to help, but I was committed to the route at this point.

Back on the move, I wondered why my riding had been so troubled recently. It was not particularly challenging, except the river crossing, but my mind hadn't been fully focused. Was it Aki? Was keeping her in my thoughts distracting me? This was strange to me. Before Kenya, I had felt no stress when encountering difficult terrain and hadn't really had that many mishaps on the road either. But it seemed that after Kenya, my journey had been troubled more often. It was easy to think of her as the cause, but maybe it was true. Love can trouble any man. Maybe I was better off not having someone to love. I remembered the remote riding in Patagonia and how stable and at peace I was then. But now in Namibia, I no longer felt at ease.

I reached Epupa Falls and camped once again by the banks of the Kunene River. But this time, there was a constant roar. The river spilled over a large series of boulders creating a powerful waterfall; a sight to behold. The hike on the opposing ridge gave me a wide view of the expansive falls. It turned out to be a series of them falling over a distance of a few hundred metres, interspersed with giant baobab trees that clung to the exposed rock. Epupa Falls slightly resembled Victoria Falls – what it lacked in grandeur, it made up for in remoteness. Angola was on the other side of the valley, and I took one last look across the river, hoping to travel through there someday, before now putting on my blinders and heading south.

The next day, the road south brought me to the town of Opuwo. Surrounded by dry shrubs, the desert had encroached into the city, evident in that there was sand covering the sidewalks and traffic medians. I was filling up at a Shell petrol station when a white Namibian man leaned out of his green Toyota Hilux pickup truck across the fuelling island and asked which way I was coming from. He was delighted to hear that I had spent time along the Kunene River as he managed a lodge right by the river. I asked him if there was a good campground in town and he said the best one would be up the hill at the Opuwo Country Hotel. Thanking him for the tip, I headed up a craggy, dirt track up the knoll that towered over the town and pulled into the fancy-looking country lodge. Staying at the cottage rooms would have been too rich of me, so I was glad to see their campground was well appointed. Each site had a thick natural grass square for pitching tents, a paved concrete table with an electrical outlet and access to well-maintained bathrooms.

After pitching my tent, I headed back to the lodge to take in the sunset. I was getting used to a certain level of comfort in these camps, a virtue of the popularity of camping in Namibia. I settled into an infinity pool that flowed over the edge with an awe-inspiring view of the valley down below. I was waiting for the perfect light when an elderly black gentleman came over and politely enquired as to where I was from. Always happy to chat, I told him about my journey. That was all it took for us to begin conversing, and soon after, I joined him and his wife for a drink. After a bit of banter about how elegant the lodge was, we came around to the topic of what we all did for a living. He replied casually and in a very offhand manner that he ran the region we were in. After further inquisition, I discovered that I was having an evening sundowner with the local governor. I was amazed by how friendly and open he was, striking up casual conversations with strangers. Of course, those are the skills of a consummate politician, but there was no pretence behind his interest. Much like myself, he was just keen to know a few things about those he came across.

We continued to chat for an hour or so, during which I stepped away to quickly take some shots of the sunset, which had reached a magical hue. The governor was, in fact, a retired diplomat who had been summoned out of retirement by Namibia's president to help integrate the tribal people into the modern world. It was a delicate task he faced. The government wanted the tribal people to hold on to their respective cultures, but also adapt, which meant giving up some practices. In some respects, this was progressive because it would bring about fair and equal treatment for women and access to education for all children. Its reality, however, meant that there would be fundamental cultural changes in their tribal societies. Taking into account the societal gains and cultural losses, on balance, it was beneficial to the tribes as well as Namibia, but there was no indication as yet whether the tribes were altogether welcoming or understanding of all these changes. Throughout my travels, I had noticed a conflict between traditional ways of life in all its variety and the growing national pressure to integrate into the global economy. Rarely were the two mutually compatible, I had found. Ultimately, it was a personal decision for the people and the groups. Not everyone craved the attributes that today's global society deems to be beneficial, whichever way you spin it. The tribal people in Namibia have been living off this harsh land for thousands of years and will continue to do so, as long as we don't interfere in their ways. And with the impacts of climate change upon us, wasn't there something for us modern people to learn from people who live closer to nature? I tried to voice some of these concerns to the governor. He must have heard this reproach multiple times by then and simply smiled, saying that my impassioned, nuanced stance and bald head reminded him of Gandhi. Sipping my beer, I smiled and said that my father would undoubtedly be proud to hear that. After my conversation with the governor, I walked back to the campsite under a dazzling night sky.

Such occurrences were one of the unpredictable pleasures of my journey. I never quite knew who I would be speaking to at any time in the day. The governor was, to date, the highest ranking dignitary I had had the chance to entertain.

I had planned to continue my ride south the next morning. Enjoying a warm bowl of oatmeal for breakfast, I appreciated the view of sanDRina as the sun shone strongly through the thorny trees. Almost everything was back in the panniers except for my tent, which was sitting on the grass. As I picked up my tent with both hands, I immediately felt a jolting pain on the first knuckle of my left middle finger. I threw the tent down and jumped back. I figured I had probably cut it on a sharp blade of grass, but then, my finger went numb. This was no blade of grass. I flipped the tent over and there sat the culprit – a small, brown scorpion with a fat tail full of venom.

My first thought was, 'I'm a biker, I'm tough, the pain will just subside.' You live and learn. The numbness soon spread, moving swiftly through my hand and to my wrist, which is when I realized that without treatment, the venom would eventually spread up my arm. What if it reached my heart? People die that way, I remembered. I rushed over to my only neighbours, an elderly German couple who were packing up their Toyota Hilux and its roof-mounted tent. When I explained what had just happened to Wolfgang in a restrained panic, he offered to drive me to the main lodge, while Martha told me to get my papers. I grabbed my passport, phone and money pouch. The scorpion was still on my tent, so I snapped a few photos of it in order to help identify it later.

Wolfgang drove to the lodge like a paramedic on duty, but the receptionist told us to go to the clinic in town. The German rally driver in training raced down the rutted path. He continued to make small talk with me about my trip and India, which I knew he was doing to keep my mind off the unbearable pain. The sting brought back the sensation I had felt when I ripped the ligament in my knee from its stump – a deep-seated throbbing, a sensation unknown to the nerves near the skin. For a brief second, I marvelled at the complex feedback mechanisms that were built into our bodies. When we reached the clinic, I showed the young doctor the photo of the scorpion and his eyebrows rose upward in a response that no patient wants to see. He explained that the fat tail indicated the venom was very dangerous and that I'd better rush to the nearby government hospital. Pausing only to inject some local anaesthetic into my finger, he pushed me out the door as the venom began to pulse past my elbow. I jumped in the Hilux and we rushed across town to the hospital where a guard intent on doing his duty, which seemed to be not to let anyone in under any circumstance, stopped us at the gate. Only after yelling that it was an emergency and flashing our foreign passports did he stand aside. I ran past the empty lobby and burst into a busy room labelled 'Casualty Area'. I quickly explained to the nurses what had happened and gestured that the venom had reached my shoulder. Still, no one reacted to my urgency.

The head nurse, sitting at a desk by the window, slowly raised her head and asked me for my passport. I almost yelled, 'Are you serious? You want to do paperwork first before saving my life?!' My temper was boiling but I knew better than to show it because these nurses were the key to my survival. I threw my Indian passport on the table and she just laughed while rolling her eyes. 'No. Where is your Health Passport?' 'I don't have a health passport! I only have an Indian passport!' She proceeded to open a new booklet, a health passport from the Namibian health ministry, and started filling in my details. I cursed bureaucracy under my breath and mustered all my willpower to keep it together for a few more minutes. Once she was satisfied with the paperwork, she directed me to the treatment room. Another nurse brought two vials containing a potent anti-inflammatory and a steroid. She gave me the shots in my butt and the relief was immediate. I sighed deeply as the numbness in my hand started subsiding. I was going to live after all. I lay there for another hour, feeling woozy from the steroids, before I was able to walk comfortably again and maintain my balance. Thanking the nurses who were all smiles now, I paid my dues and walked back slowly up the hill and to my campsite. Wolfgang and Martha had left after dropping me.

Everything was as I had left it and I was glad to see that the scorpion wasn't around. The pain from my arm had subsided but I couldn't fully flex my fingers. The nurse had explained that it could take a few days to regain full sensation in my fingers. There was nothing to do besides wait because I wouldn't be able to pull in sanDRina's clutch without a fully functioning left hand. So I settled in to stay. It was with some trepidation that I ventured back into my tent that night, constantly scanning my environs for my Namibian nemesis. I thought I had been stung again a few short hours later when I was awoken by a searing pain, once again in my left hand. I quickly turned on my headlamp fearing my nemesis's return, but I was alone. It was, I realized, the painkiller wearing off and the underlying residual pain resurfacing. Unable to sleep due to the excruciating pain, there was nothing more that I could do but pace the campsite under a dazzling starlit night. I nursed my arm through gritted teeth and kept my eyes peeled for the resident scorpions. Fortunately, after an hour or more, the pain finally subsided enough and I managed to fall back asleep.

Three days passed at the campsite as I waited for my hand to get back to normal. I was itching to get back on the road. Finally, on the fourth morning, I went to sanDRina and pulled in the clutch all the way. It was a moment of triumph. I was filled with glee to learn that my hand was finally functioning normally. I packed up again, but this time, using two sticks to lift the tent up and check for any demons. Not seeing any, I let out a sigh of relief and laughed at my newly-developed fear of scorpions. I wasn't scared of much, having conquered most of my fears (the dark, heights and snakes), but scorpions were new on the list.

Back on the road, I was pleased that my little run-in with the scorpion did not lead to any serious troubles, although it did result in an increasing sense of self-doubt. Riding past endless kilometres of desert land, my mind was wandering to places I did not want it to go. I wondered if the recent spate of mishaps were all somehow connected. A rational mind would view them as mere coincidences. However, doubt can lead one to form a narrative between seemingly unrelated events. Perhaps brooding so much about my relationship with Aki was not allowing me to fully be in the present and tackle challenges with clarity of mind. But how could I blame her for the scorpion sting? Was it my mind that was stinging me? I was looking for meaning where there was nothing to be found. The sting was just plain bad luck. I had camped in numerous places where snakes and scorpions could've been under my tent, but they weren't. I was in the desert and scorpions were expected to be found there, but my irrational state of mind didn't want to hear that.

The dirt road was surprisingly smooth and the green terrain around Opuwo quickly faded into a light shade of brown. The whole of Namibia could be considered a desert land, but it was by no means flat. There were ridges to cross and mesas to ride by. The flat-topped hills looked artificial but they were simply products of erosion. The sun was beating down. It was hot. The water in my hydration pack had started to warm up, and so I added a powdered sweet ice tea mix to distract me from chugging down a hot drink on a hot day. Being the first day back on sanDRina since the scorpion sting, I thought I would take it easy and ride less than 200 km (124 miles), but by noon, I had already reached my intended destination for the night, the small outpost of Khowarib. I pushed on. The intense heat was still quite bearable and my mind was settled by now. In a few hours, I reached the next outpost of Palm Wag, which was where Erez had told me I would find fuel. Two vintage petrol pumps stood in the open air, dispensing the lifeblood of modern civilization. It was still too early in the day, so I decided to push further and get to my next destination of Twyfelfontein. The names of these places in Namibia were fun to say. They came from the Dutch who once inhabited these lands, but the names sounded like they were from the *Lord of the Rings'* Middle Kingdom.

Crossing the Red Line again, within a few kilometres, sitting on the road ahead of me were two springbok – a white-bellied antelope native to southern Africa. This was my first proper wildlife sighting in Namibia. Known for their elevated bounce while escaping from predators, they can survive for years without water as they get a sufficient amount from grazing on succulent desert plants, similar to the vicuñas of Bolivia. They soon scampered away as I approached, but right when I rounded the next corner, I found myself flanked by zebras to one side and giraffes on the other. At first, I wondered why a horse head was sticking out from behind a tall acacia tree, but when I realized it was a giraffe, I stopped to enjoy the presence of the large and graceful animal as it stared ponderously at me from about 30 m (98 ft) away. I slowly reached for my SLR camera and snapped a few pictures, before its offspring sauntered out from behind the brush. This sudden profusion of wildlife stumped me, and it was only when I zoomed out on my GPS map that I realized I was passing through a private nature conservancy. As the giraffes strode off, I continued down the track.

The land was dry but there was beauty in the starkness. Towards the late afternoon, the road dipped down into a canyon and the tall mesas all around mesmerized me. It seemed to be hallowed ground and felt undisturbed beside the dirt road I was on. A few kilometres further, I turned for Twyfelfontein. There wasn't much there besides a sandy campground amongst scattered acacia trees, but the main attraction was a series of rock engravings by ancient peoples that I visited the next morning.

The area was arid with sandstone cliffs rising out of the flat landscape. The name of Twyfelfontein is Afrikaans for 'unreliable spring'. As per the story, a Boer family settled in the area in the early 1950s and tried to sustain a farm from the unreliable spring among the cliffs. Unable to survive, they moved on. But before them, humans had been coming to this area for 6,000 years and maybe longer, experiencing a mystical connection with the spring. It was now festooned with thousands of exquisite rock engravings across its flat sandstone walls. There were giraffes, kudu and even an enigmatic lion with a pugmark at its tail. The engravings have been attributed to shamanistic rituals. I was intrigued by how humans had been living in this land for so long, and yet, thankfully, civilization had not made its way there. Looking away from the site of the rock engravings, I was more impressed by the vista of the colourful sandstone mountains across the small valley. In this relatively flat landscape, Tywfelfontein was the only free-standing feature in the area. Considering it had a spring, it was no wonder that ancient peoples had found a connection with the site.

Leaving Twyfelfontein, I stopped at the nearby Petrified Forest. I had read about the process of petrification in school books, where minerals replace organic materials and create fossils, but it could not have prepared me for the intricate details of the trees that were now preserved in the petrified rock. The dry conditions of the Namib Desert were perfect to preserve such natural artifacts for aeons. Next to the petrified trees were these grotesque-looking plants called welwitschia. They were large, low-lying plants that characteristically had two large leaves flopped on the ground. It was blooming season and so I was treated to its flowers, which resembled pine cones but with a shade of brilliant red. A signboard at the entrance to the petrified park said that these plants were referred to as living fossils, as they were known to be hundreds to thousands of years old. The harsh climate and scarcity of water meant natural selection, the mechanism of evolution, favoured plants that took the slow growth route. They were known to survive by tapping into groundwater and pulling moisture out of the fog that rolled in from the coast. Ah, the coast! I was yearning for it after all this time in the dry interior.

Taking a break from the sizzling afternoon sun, I stopped in the town of Khorixas and spent an hour cruising the shopping aisles of a local supermarket. I was there primarily to soak in the air conditioning, but as I have done in other countries, I tried to get a read on the local culture by seeing what was for sale. Sadly, they only had a lot of chips and other types of processed food on sale. It seemed to be a lower-income part of Namibia as was evident by the run-down cars outside.

I set back out into the heat, leaving the town behind. I found my rhythm on the wide gravel road, relishing the undulations of the desert. I was tracking west now and the low afternoon sun was directly ahead. I tipped the sun beak of my helmet forward to block the blinding light, and after a while, I had to stick my hand up to protect my eyes from the glare. Beyond the glare, I could see it. There was a lump in the land that was slowly growing bigger. The surrounding land was extremely flat except for this natural protrusion. My GPS labelled it as the Brandberg Massif, my destination for the evening. As the sun neared the horizon, the massif grew bigger until I suddenly found myself at the base of Namibia's tallest mountain. Its name in Afrikaans and German means 'fire mountain', and rightly so, as with the sun setting, the barren dome-shaped granitic intrusion was ablaze in a deep-orange glow. This was a geologic anomaly as granite usually forms in large bands under the earth, but this massif stuck out like a sore thumb. Brandberg towered in front of me – its scale relative to the surrounding desert was dramatic. I imagined how ancient people must have felt a similar deference and perhaps given it spiritual significance. It turns out that they did, and I would find out exactly how the following day.

There was a campsite at its base and the lovely girl working at the front desk decided to give me a free bundle of firewood after I told her that I had been on the road from the US. I was impressed with how many free things I was receiving from white Namibians. She also told me I could collect whatever firewood I needed for the night from the grounds, even though that was generally discouraged as it disturbs the local environs.

With my tent set up under the expansive canopy of a large tree, I went about gathering firewood. Just a few feet from my camp, there were large basketball-sized chunks of elephant dung. It was surprising that such large animals could thrive in the harsh desert. The Brandberg Massif and its protruding terrain trapped moisture from the coastal fogs that in turn helped sustain a thriving desert ecosystem.

I had a roaring fire going on the braai stand before it got dark. The desiccated wood lit up with ease and quickly turned into hot embers. Instead of using my petrol-fuelled camping stove, I made a small coal stove using three large rocks and slowly pushed hot embers into it. I cooked a meal of rice with vegetables and salami on the coal stove, which took longer than usual, but I had nowhere else to be. In fact, I relished cooking my food slowly powered by a fire that I had got going. I felt most at home in such settings – surviving with ease in harsh climates with minimal human interaction. My friendly inner voice came to the fore and as I ate the hearty meal, it started talking to me about what life was going to be like after my trip ended. It would need to end soon since my funds were running low. Moreover, it reminded me, I had promised myself I was heading to India. The voice asked me if I was still sure of that plan. I was starting to feel quite at home in Africa, so I wasn't quite sure if I wanted to stay in India anymore after the trip, but I still had to go back and see if there was anything for me there. Of course, Aki was in Delhi, but deep within, I knew that we did not have a future together ... yet, the sap in me wanted to see her again, regardless. Even though breaking up with me was exactly the push I needed while stranded in Tanzania, I had lost trust in her. We had a great connection for a few brief months but our relationship wasn't meant to go the distance.

The voice proceeded to lay out the benefits of being in India, such as a large, new land to explore in the north, opportunities in a growing economy and the chance to contribute to my citizenship. Thus far, I hadn't done much for my country of birth, besides regale positive aspects of its culture to people I came across on my journey. Given the many ills plaguing India, I felt compelled to make a difference. I wasn't sure how exactly I would do that but the prospect was alluring. With that in mind, I turned in for the night.

The clear skies of the night were replaced with a thick fog in the morning, casting an eerie cloak over the campground. The peaks of the massif were shrouded as well. I always revelled in the changes that nature threw my way while travelling. As the sun rose higher, the fog cleared and I rode sanDRina into the Tsisab Ravine, the starting point for a hike into the interior of Brandberg. Fearful of snakes and another encounter with a scorpion, I elected to make the forty-five-minute ascent in my motocross boots. If you've ever tried to walk uphill in ski boots, it's a comparable experience. Stumbling in the heat, I dragged my weighted feet and made the slow ascent free of any bites or stings. The ravine and its steep rock surfaces were uninhabited except for the small desert animals that thrived there, such as the rodents that were scampering across the large boulders. As we trekked up, my guide, John, a local Damara man, explained how his forefathers would come to Brandberg for spiritual reasons. This became apparent when we came across a small cave that housed the famous White Lady rock painting. The ethereal figures it displays were painted by San and other local tribes centuries ago, but they were only discovered by Europeans in the early twentieth century. The most prominent figure on the wall is a man covered in white with an antelope in front of him. The first European travellers to discover this figure determined that this was evidence of early European presence in the region. It was later deduced that the figure was actually a local shaman covered in white dust that usually kicks up during shamanistic dance rituals; a practice that was still alive among the San and other local tribes.

With Brandberg slowly fading in my rear-view mirror, I found myself on the road to the coast. This was no ordinary coast, however. I was on my way to the Skeleton Coast. It was named after a book title that chronicled the sinking of a ship along the treacherous coast. It was one of many that have sunk along that stretch in Africa, often battered by unrelenting Atlantic waves or lost in the dense fog. Currently, I was facing a straight road in the hot sun heading west. The searing ground created mirages in the distance. I saw shapes of boats, houses and other blobs dancing in the heatwaves. I stopped in the middle of the empty road and looked all around. There was nothing. No sign of human activity besides the electrical posts running alongside the road. The earth was getting whiter now, reflecting the sun's rays more so than before. As I continued down the road, I realized the mirages had been of the ocean. All of a sudden, the haze cleared and I saw a wide band of blue across the horizon. I had reached the coast. Crossing the breadth of southern Africa, 5,000 km (3,108 miles) on from Beira on Mozambique's coast, I stood atop sanDRina's pegs gazing out to the Atlantic Ocean.

I camped by the coast that night at the only lodge in this desolate area. I pitched my tent at Cape Cross and hurried down to the beach. Buffeted by a clear salt-laced wind, immense waves crashed onto the shore with an intense rolling thunder. This vast expanse of water in front of me was a relief to my eyes after all those months surrounded by the desert, scrub and savannah. I sat on the sand alone, for there was no one on the beach around me, and soaked in the cool wind and dramatic waves. The sky was clear, but as the sun dipped, it never reached the horizon. Instead, it bowed out behind a thick band of haze that rose up from the ocean. So it was on my first day on the Atlantic coast that I gazed back west towards South America and my journey's start in Chicago, while the sun set, still high above the horizon. The Skeleton Coast was a strange land indeed.

In the morning, the weather had turned and the beach was grim. The fog hung low to the ground, through which I could hear the incessant pounding of the waves somewhere ahead. Back at my campsite, I saw that my neighbours were getting a large fire going and they invited me over. Mike and his girlfriend, Denise, were just about to cook up a traditional Dutch dish called 'potkjie', which is a mix of eggs, bacon, meat and vegetables all put in a metal cauldron and then placed atop a fire. They said they were from the nearby city of Swakopmund and were just out for the weekend.

Thanking Mike and Denise for the hearty food, I headed to Cape Cross's major attraction, a vast seal reserve. It's one of those sites that don't translate well from nature documentaries because you always smell and hear these places before you see them. Black seals covered the beach as far as I could see and the noxious smell emanating from thousands of them was overbearing. It was thrilling to see so much wildlife in one place, but the stench cut through, and so I stuffed my neck gaitor into my nostrils in an attempt to block out at least some of the gut-wrenching fetor. The seals, of course, weren't bothered. It was calving season and baby seals were crawling about responding to the loud brays of their mothers while male seals fought for territory over prominent rocks. Amongst them was a relic of a slaughterhouse and it was an odd sight to see so many seals lying around, carefree in the sun, on the very ground that hundreds, if not thousands, of their own had been killed. Maybe it wasn't all that odd. Such animals are probably far more familiar with death than we are.

This extensive seal colony had been here long before humans ever showed up. The seals' guano, the source of the putrid funk, is rich in ammonium nitrate and drew the first Europeans to these lands a few centuries ago. They mined the guano and sent it back to Europe to be used for fertilizer and gunpowder. They also clubbed the seals for their fat and meat, ensuing in gruesome operations of seal slaughter. Horrid as that might sound, the number of seals never went down regardless of this human harvesting. In fact, seals had become a major problem for the Namibian fishing industry since their numbers were rapidly growing. Seals are known to eat up to one-third of their body weight in fish each day. The unrelenting harvest of orca whales in the area in the past few centuries had freed the seals from a natural predator. Consequently, humans had to step in and cull them. It seemed so typical of our take-it-all attitude towards nature. By over-harvesting whales, we have created an imbalance in the natural cycle, leaving us in charge of controlling the whole cycle now. Somehow, we just can't let nature be.

After bathing in the stench of the seals for an hour, I finally headed out, trying to put as much distance between me and the colony as possible. Still, the smell carried after me with the wind down the coast. A short ride south brought me to the very German-looking city of Swakopmund. The low-lying buildings had exposed timber that resembled houses in southern Germany. They would seem appropriately placed in the Alps, but they stood out on the shores of Africa. After stocking up my supplies at the well-appointed local supermarket, I left this strange mark of civilization to head back into the wilderness.

Just like the Brandberg Massif, another peak rose up from the horizon ahead of me. I was back inland in the flat Namib Desert. I turned away from the coastal tarmac and got on a gravel road heading towards this natural anomaly. Spitzkoppe, which is German for pointed dome, rose prominently from the desert floor. The giant granite dome, which is now a protected site, invited me to come closer. One of the campsites inside the park was hosting a large group and their overland truck under a stunning rock bridge. A little further, I found an uninhabited campsite at the base of an arch in the smooth granite boulders that spanned at least 10 m (33 ft) and stood 3 m (10 ft) above a surrounding rock. It seemed like a wonderful place to stay the night. Being a wild campsite, it had no facilities besides a dry-pit latrine.

I removed sanDRina's panniers to make a stool and bench for the night. I then flung open my tent, which had to be pegged down since the breeze was extremely strong. I quickly raced up the steep granite wall next to my home for the evening to get a view of Spitzkoppe and the surrounding granite peaks as the magical hour around dusk commenced. Ducking under the arch, I reached a vantage point that had me about 5 m (16 ft) above the desert floor. I had to carefully maintain my balance as I stood on a small dome, the furthest out I could stand without falling. I clicked away at the light show nature was putting on display all around me. The three-sixty-degree view of nothing but large, orange-hued, smooth granite peaks and flat desert land allowed my spirit to soar. I couldn't get enough of these wide-open spaces in Namibia.

Other humans must have certainly stood in the very same spot as me. There was evidence of the San Bushman in the nearby rocks by way of their rock paintings. Their ancestors would have probably visited this cathedral of rocks from millennia ago. There is something about a conspicuous feature sticking out from its surroundings that draws humans in. These were just large and wonderfully curved granite rocks, but what made them unique was the lack of other such structures in the vicinity. With the setting sun in front of me, I closed my eyes in contentment. When I opened them, the sun had dipped behind the horizon. The sun's orange glow still shone strongly and filled the sky with a smooth orange light that slowly faded into the black of the east. As the moon rose, I could see Jupiter in conjunction.

I headed back down to my campsite and started a roaring fire with branches I had collected from the nearby brush. I sat on my pannier with a bowl of soupy rice and soya chunks. I felt at peace and my mind was calm. My inner voice and I reflected on how magnificent it was to experience the grandeur of our planet and our place on it. It was much easier in such places, far away from civilization and modernity. With no other humans around, the voice reflected how it didn't matter which country I was a citizen of. It only becomes an issue when humans feel the need to label others and place them under specific categories. I thought about how the San Bushman are called so because of where they are from, which made me realize that nationalism is just a global extension of tribalism. The voice scoffed at this and told me about a future where we outgrow the nationalism that is currently practised. Once humanity attains that level of cultural development, we can achieve grand feats, which I imagine would include the end of poverty, unlimited energy and other boosts in humanity's development. But instead, we resist true global development by wallowing within artificial borders and sabre-rattling with our neighbours. I felt content to let these thoughts run free for they might not sit well with others. As the fire neared its end, I turned in for the night.

Just as the light started filtering into my tent at dawn, I woke up and rushed back up the granite slope. The rising sun cast a deep, intense auburn glow on Spitzkoppe and the surrounding granite peaks. The light seemed unreal. The stone arch behind me was set ablaze against a deeply saturated azure sky. As the sun rose higher, that magical light was soon replaced by the blinding harshness of daytime. Back at my camp, I relished a bowl of oatmeal sitting under the brush and wondered how many other humans over the aeons had been in my position.

Leaving Spitzkoppe, I passed through Windhoek, the capital of Namibia, to spend a few days with a family friend. With my clothes washed, supplies restocked and a new rear tyre on sanDRina, I was back to the desert. The tar road ended an hour out of the capital and I was once again in my comfort zone on the gravel roads. The dry brush of the desert spanned all around and the big sky enveloped me.

After crossing the Tropic of Capricorn towards the end of the day, I had reached Solitaire; a fitting name for a solitary hamlet in the middle of the desert with no other large settlements within a few hours. There was a modern petrol station with a rusting old car out front that had succumbed to the desert. I jumped in the attached campground's swimming pool, excited by the simple presence of water after spending the entire day in the heat and dryness. There was no one else at the campsite and that's just how I liked it. I wanted to be away from others. I walked away from the site towards a clearing in the grasses and sat on a bench there, awaiting the evening light show.

In its descent, the sun cast an incredible array of colours onto the clouds overhead. There were deep shades of pink and orange framed against the blueness of the darkening sky behind. It was the most vivid of sunsets I had seen in Namibia. My inner voice spoke up again. It was me, but it felt like another being who I could pose questions to. I thought about how such a great deal of beauty could exist in our world while, simultaneously, our collective human condition experienced a great deal of sadness. He said it was just a matter of perspective, of course a privileged perspective, not taking into account unfair situations such as being born into poverty or having disabilities. Natural beauty could be found the world over, but it was on a grand display here in Namibia. It is also an individual's responsibility to pick out the beauty from around them instead of wallowing in the sadness that is an inevitable part of human life. I felt sad at that moment. The trip was nearing its end. After south Africa, I would be reaching India. I was nervous for the end but extremely grateful to have been given the chance to experience the twilight in the Namib Desert. The strength of nature's beauty, which at the time felt like a show put on exclusively for me, reinforced in me the notion that no matter how sad I felt in the future, knowing that this beauty existed here would give me strength to carry on.

After another hot day through the desert roads, I reached the tourist destination of Sesriem. It was a remote outpost but with modern facilities. This was due to the large natural attraction nearby, namely the giant sand dunes of Sossusvlei, which are accessible only on four wheels. Once I was set up for the night, I cooled off by the pool. I was lying on a chaise when a man in Speedos approached me and asked if I was able to get on the Wi-Fi of the campground. I hadn't bothered since I had internet access through the mobile network on my phone. He asked if I could help set it up for him on his phone. Changing back into shorts and a t-shirt, I wandered over to his campsite. Yannick, from southern France, was travelling around Namibia with a friend of his, Naas, from Cape Town. They had rented a Toyota Corolla and its open boot showed that they were well-stocked with food and drinks. After setting up internet access on Yannick's phone, he invited me to stay for a beer. The cold and aerated brew was much appreciated. I told them about my annoyance over how motorcycles were not allowed in the park, and they immediately offered to take me with them in the morning. After an evening of stories and pork chops from the braai, we were up before sunrise for the hour-long drive into the park.

Sossusvlei was the leading attraction in all of Namibia. Owing to the large number of visitors, the government had paved a 60 km (37 miles) track from the park entrance to the sand dunes, making it one of the few paved roads outside of urban areas in Namibia. Slivers of dawn were sneaking up around the horizon as we cruised on the smooth road with small dunes on both sides. After about forty-five minutes, I could make out large shapes all around us. They were sand dunes, but not like any I had ever seen before. They soared above the desert floor. The first large dune we came across was blandly called Dune 45. We parked and started climbing up the ridge. The light to the east was growing stronger with every minute and our party was determined to reach the highest point for sunrise.

We quickly ascended the dune. It felt strange to take a step onto the loose sand of the ridge, only to have it spill out to its sides. It was not easy to walk on. I remembered walking up a snow ridge at Aspen Highlands in Colorado with hefty snow boots. The steps in the sand produced a similar sensation. For every foot we climbed, we lost at least half in the shifting sands.

There were others around us as well. Soon enough, we found our spot at the top of the dune. Sitting on both sides of the ridge, everyone's attention was rapt at the rising sun. Finally, the first rays broke free from the horizon and shone brilliantly across the dune landscape all around. I immediately understood why these dunes were so captivating. It was the colour; all various shades of orange. Of course, the grandness of the dunes was also captivating, but the colour was stupefying. I had seen dunes before in Egypt and Sudan, but they were the typical colour of sand; light brown, almost yellow. These dunes were orange, whereas some in the distance were dark orange. That was due to how old they were. The Namib Desert is considered the world's oldest desert. It formed around fifty-five million years ago and has been arid ever since. In comparison, the Sahara is only around seven million years old.

The problem with sunrises in the desert is that as soon as the sun fully emerges, it gets extremely hot. We descended from Dune 45 and went deeper into the park to Sossusvlei. Once parked, we boarded an open-top park jeep for a few hundred metres further across deep sand for the grand attraction of Sossusvlei. 'Vlei' is the Afrikaans word for marsh and 'sossus' is the Nama (local tribal language) word for no return. The basins amongst these dunes were endorheic regions, with whatever water that collected in them not draining to any external bodies of water. The water, from the rare rains or moisture from the coastal fog caught by the sand, pulls salt minerals from the sand that accumulate over time in the vleis. But for most of their existence, the vleis are dry and the salt left behind forms a flat, white pan, which is blinding in the stark desert environment, similar to the salars of Bolivia. We walked a few minutes across a small ridge in the scorching heat towards the grandest attraction of all, Deadvlei, and its towering sand dune called Bid Daddy. Deadvlei was iconic to me as I had been seeing photographs of it since I was a child. Compared to the other vleis in the area, Deadvlei had large, dead acacia trees trapped in its salt pan. They were devoid of leaves, of course, but still left standing, frozen in time. The heat and the radiation from the vlei seemed to char the trees solid black. The bark had cracked all over the tree trunks. It looked surreal, almost as though they were suspended in a painting and ready to rejuvenate if only some rain would fall.

Surrounding Deadvlei were the largest sand dunes I had ever seen. Bid Daddy, at the far end of the vlei, soaring almost 325 m (1067 ft) above, is one of the largest sand dunes in the world. It is an enormous wall of rust-orange sand rising from the desert floor. I had seen an iconic photograph years ago with a motorcycle parked in front of a deep orange sand dune, which had immediately sparked a desire in me to go there. This was one of the strangest places in the world. It was inhospitable and thankfully for that reason, free from any nearby development. Hence, its stark beauty would be preserved for the future.

I packed up my things back at the campsite and hit the road. I was more comfortable moving at a moderate speed on the bike rather than walking around in the desert. Standing on the footpegs, I reflected on my experience from earlier that morning. A dream several years ago that stemmed from a photograph had brought me to the very location it originated from. I felt gratified to know that a dream, if pursued, could become reality. It was only a small dream, but I knew that having some kind of end goal to drive me would result in experiences along the way that would help me grow, adding flavour to my life. As I soaked my cooling vest at a petrol station before getting back on sanDRina, I started to look forward to the end of my journey. I felt satisfied with all the places I had visited in the flesh as well as in my mind, and now, it was time to take the next big step.

15

INCREDIBLE INDIA

'BUT I DON'T need a visa!' I almost shouted to the immigration officer. I had needed a visa for every country I had been to, but this was the one exception since my passport bore the name of the country I was entering. I was at the international arrivals hall in Chennai airport, having just landed from Cape Town, via Doha. The officer had flipped through my passport, and upon seeing so many other visas, had somehow presumed that I was a foreigner and asked me for my tourist visa. How he had made this mistake was beyond me. Was there something about the way I looked that made me appear foreign? I showed him the front of the passport and tapped the Ashoka emblem on it with my finger, ensuring that he took his eyes off the visas to acknowledge that I was, in fact, in my home country. Barely even looking in my direction, he dismissed his error and stamped me in. I was, it seemed, back home.

sanDRina, on the other hand, was still at sea. She was coming from Cape Town, and while I had intended to join her on this leg at sea, I had been unable to find passage. As a result, I had reluctantly resorted to taking a flight. The distance I had covered in ten hours of flying north from Cape Town to Doha had taken me two years on land. This really helped put things into perspective. I wasn't sure how to feel upon arriving at what seemed to be the final destination of my journey. It was finally time for me to prepare for the inevitable. In no certain terms, my life had been irreversibly changed since I had left Chicago three years and 94,934 km (59,002 miles) ago. Waiting at the end of it all were the realities of life, relationships, society and my own bottoming bank balance. All the things I had escaped for so long were waiting to bite me, but I had one last journey to make.

With sanDRina cleared from the Chennai port a few weeks later, I was ready to start the final leg of my odyssey – an upward traverse from south to north India. I am originally from Chennai, and I had never visited north India before I left for the US several years ago. I had barely been halfway up the west coast, the furthest north being Bombay (renamed Mumbai just before I left).

Spending a few weeks at home had been a real treat, as I had not done so since my schooling years. My mother took great joy in cooking each of my favourite dishes ranging from crispy-fried coccinia (ivy gourd) to prawn curry to appam (rice pancake) with coconut stew. These, of course, were served with yoghurt chillies, just like the ones that had been shipped to me in South America and Africa. In the midst of it all, I did not get the chance to prepare my now famous chicken curry for my parents, because the kitchen at home was supremely my mother's domain. Besides, she had become a vegetarian in my absence.

The day before departure, I was in the same state of fervour and anticipation as when I had restarted my journey after Nairobi. I managed to make my multi-year journey feasible by thinking about it in smaller bite-sized chunks. I had a busy day of sorting through all my gear and packing it on sanDRina. Certain that I was going to stay in India after the trip ended, I was able to leave behind a lot of spares and other random gear that I had carried with me so far. When I was on the road in Africa and South America, I never knew where and for how long I would be, and thus, ended up carrying parts such as a spare rear wheel hub, multiple tyre tubes and enough fuel line to set up another bike. It sounds ridiculous, but I was prepared for contingencies. I proceeded to sort my gear into mechanical and electrical spares, medical supplies, camping gear, electronics, clothes, toiletries and snacks. Organized into packing cubes of various sizes, they were then fit into the panniers to make full use of the limited space. Everything has its place on sanDRina, but with a few things moved around, it would take me a while to get accustomed to where everything was.

The day was also busy with welcoming relatives for a Satyanarayan Puja (a religious ceremony) at home at the insistence of my parents. They were relieved that I had finally made it home after this arduous journey without anything untoward happening to me. I had only seen them once during my journey, when I had taken a break in Kenya, so the relief was palpable. They were now concerned for my safety through India, but I reassured them that I could handle whatever India threw in my way. But just to be safe, they were going to ask the gods for their blessings. Being a 'good boy', I complied.

I had never understood my parents' commitment to religion. Having noticed this in me, my father had told me to at least have faith in some supreme power. What I did respect was nature and its impersonal and unknowable features that fuel the universe, and in turn, all of us. My father understood this, adding that some people call that god, except for them, its personal. He always had a way to tighten my loose ideas in with his firm beliefs and that's precisely what I respected about him.

We had several talks on our terrace, sipping single malt whiskys in the cool evening breeze; something I had always loved about Chennai. He revealed that he was still trying to process how I had managed to convince him to let me go to the US for college at the tender age of eighteen. It had been an unprecedented move in our extended family. He was also curious as to where exactly my courage to undertake such a journey had come from. It was obvious to me – it came from him. The events of his life had provided me with a blueprint for my own. He had moved his young family to a remote corner of Africa and thrived. That, in my view, was courageous and adventurous. I had also seen a photograph once of my father on a bright yellow dirt bike that he said was used for field inspections in Chipata. I was cut from the same cloth. Of course, with age and being surrounded by the general conservatism of their social circle in India, my parents preferred less risk and hoped I would share the same view as well. Perhaps I would in my later years, but right now, sanDRina beckoned once more.

That morning, I realized that I had incorrectly set sanDRina's valve clearance check in Cape Town, so I set about adjusting it to the specifications in the maintenance manual. My 'pedanaina' (uncle in my mother tongue of Telegu) from my mother's village had come to town for the puja and I was delighted when he wanted to help me with the valve job. He used to encourage me as a child to tinker by taking things apart on the family farm and learn how to put them back together. He had only studied till the 8th grade, but had learned how to repair borewell pumps, tractors and radios. My desire to study mechanical engineering started with childhood holidays spent on the farm with him. And so, the two of us spent a few hours together working on sanDRina. He was surprised at how easy it was to understand the mechanisms inside her engine. I saw that as a validation of my taste in motorcycles. The Suzuki DR650 has a robust, well-designed engine that wasn't overly complicated, as more modern motorcycles are. Pedanaina, however, did not understand why the front wheel had to be so large. I tried to explain that it allowed me to absorb the shock of potholes and bumps with ease. Having used a Bajaj Chetak scooter (similar in style to a Vespa) his entire life, using its miniature wheels to ride off-road around the farm, he felt sanDRina was a supermodel, superfluous but alluring. We finished the job, pleased with the smooth clickety-clack of the valves. He sat astride her high seat but declined to take her out for a test ride, shy of her powerful engine.

During the Satyanarayan Puja, we sat around a makeshift shrine with a holy fire in our living room and followed the motions of the pujari (priest) through a series of incantations and songs. I had heard most of these growing up and felt pleased in being able to recall the words. Afterwards, I had the pujari also bless sanDRina and our journey through India. sanDRina had faithfully carried me across four continents, and now we were on our fifth. At this juncture, there was no way that I was going to exclude her from such an important ceremony. Blessing vehicles in India is not uncommon. Originally a tradition applied to horses and cattle, it has now been extended to new trucks, cars, motorbikes and scooties. The priest was entirely unfazed by my request and was obviously used to fulfilling similar requests. We cracked a coconut at the front gate, rolled sanDRina over some limes and draped her in long garlands of marigolds. I had no idea how long these would stay on her, but maybe it would work in my favour in case I got pulled over by the police. All set with blessings from the gods, I tucked in for the night.

I departed Chennai and headed south, accompanied for a few hours by the Madras Bulls, the local Royal Enfield motorcycle club. It was sweltering even as the Bay of Bengal was visible from the smooth and fast East Coast Road. It was early in the day and the heat grew constantly until it climaxed at about 42°C (108°F) in the late afternoon. I was travelling during the hottest time of the year on the Indian subcontinent; maybe I just wanted to suffer one last time. The actual reason was that I was trying to avoid the monsoon rains, which I knew could potentially make travel by road almost impossible.

Outside the old temple city of Trichy, I sat under a shady tree drinking refreshing coconut water. I yearned for the chill of the

upcoming Palani Hills. I turned onto the familiar route that took
me up to the cooler climes of Kodaikanal. The heat from the plains
gave way to the chilling air filled with the fresh smell of pine and
eucalyptus. This was one of my many homes. I had spent ten years
of my childhood up on those hills at school, and I was returning
after so long on a motorcycle that I had ridden all the way from the
US. I smiled at that thought, twisting and turning up the enjoyable
Kodai Ghat Road, all the way up to 2,150 m (7,055 ft). Ghat roads
are the name given to access routes in the mountains of the Western
and Eastern Ghats that cover south and west India, and I planned
to ride on as many as I could.

The verdant forest gave way to shacks and then concrete
buildings. Before I even knew it, I was in the centre of town. At
the Seven Roads Junction, I saw that familiar white gate. It was
my alma mater, Kodaikanal International School. I wasn't allowed
in at the main gate and was instead directed to the alumni office.
Yvonne, the alumni officer, recognized me since I had been writing
the yearly update on our class. She welcomed me back with a warm
hug, and upon hearing my story, immediately asked me to speak to
the current batch of students. Two nights later, I was standing in
the Covered Courts, our outdoor basketball courts, giving a small
speech to the graduating class. I told them about how one of the
senior boys during my middle school years rode into an assembly
gathering with his father on a big black motorcycle. They had
ridden from London to south India in the mid-90s and I had been
awestruck that people could still undertake such epic journeys
today and live to tell about it, what with all the negative news that
is generated about every country. I remember marvelling at the
photographs of their journey through Afghanistan and Pakistan
that were put on the walls near the cafeteria, wishing to be a part
of something as special. They had camped by the road and were
welcomed by strangers. According to them, the world was a lot
friendlier than it seemed. These ideas had planted a seed in my
mind that had now matured. For obvious reasons, the school

principal wasn't too keen on me emphasizing on the bit about quitting my job. Instead, I explained how it was possible to achieve even a herculean task if you put your mind to it. With hopes of inspiring the kids, I was pleased to see the intrigued expressions on their faces. A number of them approached me after the talk. Some were simply curious about sanDRina whereas some posed for photos with her. One girl was beaming with joy upon hearing that I had visited her home town of Mbeya in southern Tanzania, which had a climate similar to Kodai.

Over the next few days, I visited some of the old haunts of my schooling days, such as the nearby bakery and Tibetan restaurants that were run by refugees who found the chilly climate of Kodai to be a good fit. I ran into my old dorm parent, my physical education teacher, but what really surprised me was when some of the maids and cooks launched into gleeful whoops upon recognizing me. I grew up in front of them over an entire decade at Kodai, and I felt that they collectively played a part in how I had turned out. Whereas it was reassuring to see that many parts of the school campus and town were just as I remembered them, there was also a slew of development. The popularity of Kodai had risen tremendously since my time and I wasn't too pleased with all the new construction and mismanaged development of hotels and restaurants catering to the crowds coming up from the hot plains. But this was progress, inevitable and necessary.

Having my fill of nostalgia, I descended back down to the plains. The twisty hairpin turns were a joy to ride down and I realized that for the first time, I was navigating them myself. All the previous times that I had been up and down this ghat road were in the back of a bus or a taxi, and I remember feeling queasy at the time, but it was so much fun now. The temperature rose as I neared the plains, but thankfully, the cloud cover as well as a few raindrops fought off the heat as I continued south. Soon, I arrived in Kanyakumari, a geological imprint in almost every Indian's mind as it is the very southern tip of the Indian peninsula.

My arrival brought out a large crowd that put me under a barrage of questions about my travels and sanDRina. They weren't aggressive, just overly inquisitive. Some people were confused when I said I was from Chennai, as they obviously mistook me for a foreigner since hardly anybody else rode a motorcycle that big or with full riding gear. They were even more surprised to hear that I was headed for Kashmir. Suddenly, the crowd dispersed just as quickly as it had formed. Among the few tourists and street hawkers, I looked out at the protruding Thiruvalluvar Statue. It is perched on a rock outcrop a little ways from the coast. I was at the southernmost tip of India, about to embark on my last lengthy journey straight north to the Himalayas. The spontaneous gathering of the crowd and their response to my appearance made me happy. They had treated me like a celebrity of sorts. It was a grand send-off on the final leg of my journey and I couldn't help but smile even though my stomach was in knots. sanDRina roared into life and we turned north toward the finish line.

A few hours later, I crossed the state border into Kerala. The Malayalam script on the welcome board reminded me that I was a foreigner to the upcoming states since I didn't understand any of the local languages; I would have to get by in English. I headed inland and took a state highway north to avoid the busy coastal highway. The road was in excellent condition and embraced the Keralan hills beautifully. The ride proved to be exhilarating as I navigated multiple climbs and drops on the sinuous road. This sliver of a state sandwiched between the Western Ghats and the Arabian Sea accommodated a population density so high that the traffic was ever-present and it was outright crazy. There was a lack of respect for the painted lines on the road and vehicles overtook one another whenever they could with the slimmest of margins. In the past few days riding through my home state of Tamil Nadu, I had developed an understanding of the local driving habits and could somewhat anticipate whether or not an auto rickshaw (tuk-tuk) driver was about to make a random U-turn. It seemed like everyone was in a race of their own. I knew that driving on Indian roads was mostly a free-for-all, but Kerala was on another level and I loved it. sanDRina was a powerful, sharp and agile vehicle compared to most of the other small motorcycles and underpowered cars that surrounded me. She had always proven to be a pleasure to ride. The naturally undulating landscape shrouded in the lush forest cover had me grinning as I rode as quickly as I could through traffic.

When I crossed into the state of Karnataka the following day, I noticed red and blue lights flashing in my side mirrors. I figured that I had finally been caught for my spirited riding over the past few days, undoubtedly above the official speed limit. When I pulled over to the side of the road, three police officers in their characteristic brown uniform exited their jeep and slowly advanced toward me. This was a situation I had prepped for mentally and I had my game face on. I was ready to talk my way out of this run-in with the law, prepared to pay a reasonable bribe if necessary. Up until now, I had only paid a single bribe, that too for US $3 in Honduras for overtaking in a no-passing zone. I had been stopped numerous times by the local police in South America and Africa, but managed to get away without paying a fine each time. I was quite proud of myself for that. But I knew India was a different ball game altogether. Policing in most states and territories is just business. Holger and Anja, whom I had ridden with in Peru, told me that riding in India had been the most stressful country for them. Several other long-term travellers had also shared with me horrible stories of being shaken down by the police in India. And so, I left the engine running and even left my helmet and gloves on. I was not planning on stopping for too long. It was part of my strategy when stopped by uniformed officers. I had a monologue ready, explaining that I had just ridden through Kerala and was urgently trying to get to a phone to call my sick mother, but surprisingly, there was no need to do so.

The moustached chief approached me and broke out into a large smile. They were evidently a little bored on patrol and my passing had piqued their curiosity. What better way to find out who I was than to just pull me over. We started chatting away and they asked me what kind of motorcycle sanDRina was, where was I riding from and where I was going. This went on for a few minutes, with each of them asking questions and expressing some surprise at my journey before I brought our roadside chat to a close by asking them if we could all take a photograph together. They were all smiles. A few pictures and handshakes later, I was on my way again and laughing at the ridiculousness of India, which I had both forgotten and strangely missed.

Up ahead, I crossed into Goa, the quintessential holiday destination in India due to its picturesque beaches and cheap alcohol. I was there during the low season and the pre-monsoon humidity was thick in the air. I pushed on further with my sights set on the mountains up north. Before that, however, I had about 2,000 km (1,243 miles) of central India to ride through. I spent a few days in Bombay at the request of an old Kodai School friend, Arunoday Singh, who was now a Bollywood star. Along with a few other friends from my schooling days, I had a night out in the town and it was intriguing to get a taste of the Indian high life. But the concrete metropolis of Bombay is claustrophobic to nature lovers and I was glad to leave. The highways narrowed from eight lanes to six and then four as I passed through the city's suburbs and out onto the Golden Quadrilateral Highway; the new highway system connecting the four corners of India. I was truly headed into foreign territory. In contrast to riding up the busy, fast-moving, two-lane coastal NH-17 national highway, the four-lane NH-3 was full of trucks in every lane and I felt as though I was riding through an obstacle course. I was dodging almost-stationary trucks that were throwing out thick clouds of oil-coated diesel fumes from old engines as they strained against the inclines of the ghats at 40 kph (25 mph).

The Indian summer sun was beating down with full force but I was surviving the ride with my cooling vest and hydration pack. I pulled over on the side of the highway, halfway through the state of Madhya Pradesh, and noticed a few small houses surrounded by lush, green paddy fields. I had noticed that in India, just like in Ethiopia, people would approach me out of curiosity within a few minutes of my stopping anywhere on the road. A young village boy came over, respectfully nodding his head as he came closer. I nodded back and smiled. He had a large sickle in his hand and I had seen him working in the fields. His lithe figure was draped in worn shorts and a loose t-shirt. We were both Indian, but I still felt like an outsider, not only because of my hefty Kevlar mesh gear but also because I could not speak Hindi, the national language. Thus, our encounter was just a series of polite nods. He was respectful and well mannered, which I can't really say for most people who are curious about sanDRina and I in urban areas. In all my travels, I've seen a greater sense of civility in rural areas than in urban areas.

A few hundred kilometres later, I left the wide highways and got back to smaller roads heading northeast to Khajuraho. The roads were in a poor condition and I was riding in and out of gigantic potholes for most of the day, with brief respites on newly patched up tarmac. To add to it, the scorching power of the sun was almost overwhelming. If I lifted my helmet visor while riding, it felt as though I was sticking my face inside an oven. Covering my body in head-to-toe gear, I had protection from the sun and the fierce hot winds. People kept asking me why I wore such heavy gear since it looked so uncomfortable in hot climes. I did indeed feel hot in it when I would suit up, but as soon as I got moving and had some airflow through the mesh suit, it was actually quite comfortable. The suit was bulky, but it had previously, and would in the future, save me if I were to take a fall. Throughout my journey in India, I was constantly surprised by the number of people on the roads riding motorcycles and scooters without helmets or any other safety gear. My mantra was to prepare for the crash and walk out alive rather than risk it by getting seriously injured. I had fallen from sanDRina about 10 times on my journey but not had a single injury, except the occasional bruised ego. I never had any doubt regarding the value of my gear.

After a hard day's ride, I arrived in the small town of Khajuraho, which is famous for its unique temples that depict the Kama Sutra. At the crack of dawn, I crossed the road from my small hotel and entered the Western Group of temples in which the three big temples glowed in the early morning light. I was instantly mesmerized by the geometric shapes of these thousand-year-old temples, still so well defined in all their details. Some of the statues adorned on the exterior surfaces had been damaged over time, but most were still intact.

The temples are legendary for their vivid and erotic depictions but more than that, the stone craftsmanship was incredible. I spent some time staring at a figurine of a woman and noted how her expression of pleasure had been depicted by means of a smile and posture. One of the security guards there became my de facto guide and told me that the sexual imagery had many explanations. One was that the kings who commissioned these temples had wanted to please Indra, the god of lightning. Another reason was that 'kama' (desire in Sanskrit) is one of the 'purusharthas', or goals of life in Hinduism, which includes 'dharma' (righteousness), 'artha' (duty) and 'moksha' (liberation). A more practical reason might be that fertility rates were decreasing across the region and the king perhaps wanted to encourage his populace to increase their rates of procreation. I was intrigued by the fact that the conservative Hindu culture of today once had elements of very liberal attitudes toward sex.

I made an early start the next day to beat the heat, and continued north on country roads. I was happy to be away from the highways and about 400 km (249 miles) later, in the heat of the afternoon, I arrived in Agra. Located on the banks of the Yamuna River, this ancient city housed an icon that I was excited to see. I met up with the Royal Riders Bullet Club of Agra, and two of its members, Himanshu and Rajesh, who treated me to a pizza lunch; I was in a big city once again. After lunch, Himanshu was eager to take me to a special view point. Upon arriving at an open field, in the distance and through the haze, I could see the unmistakable shape of the Taj Mahal with its domed mausoleum and four minarets. It was the symbolic representation of India to the world, and I was only seeing it for the first time just then. I knew the Taj Mahal was special for being covered in white marble, but Himanshu revealed that its most endearing quality was the intricate use of marble inlays with thinly cut semi-precious stones. It so happened that Himanshu ran a marble inlay handicraft shop, and since the process intrigued me, I immediately accepted when he asked if I would like a tour. In a quiet part of bustling Agra, craftsmen sat by grinding wheels, slowly thinning out semi-precious stones that were to be used as inlays on marble tables and sculptures. This technique had come from Italy during the rule of Shah Jahan, who commissioned the Taj Mahal for his wife Mumtaz in the seventeenth century but it was in Agra that the workmanship had been perfected. Himanshu's family business, fifty years in the making now, had made it their mission to revive this artwork of marble inlaying by nurturing the skills of the artisans in Agra. What a good coincidence that my biker host also happened to be deeply tied to the culture of this famous city and its most-prized attraction.

In the morning, I woke up early and excited as I would finally get to see the Taj Mahal up close. My first stop was at Mehtab Bagh, a park on the opposite bank of the Yamuna River, right across the Taj. We arrived at sunrise, and the yellow glow of the early morning rays cast a warm embrace over the domed mausoleum. It was larger than I had expected, and my first impression was that it really was as magnificent as it is reputed to be. We proceeded to cross the river and enter the actual site. Security was tight, particularly about food items, with the guard asking me to throw away my mints that helped me stay cool in the dry heat. From the main red sandstone gate, the first sight of the Taj Mahal, framed by the arch, set me up for a mesmerizing view. Once inside, I felt privileged to be an Indian and have such a grand monument be our symbol to the world. Up close, it was even more impressive as the whiteness of the marble was enhanced by the sunlight hitting its eastern face. Looking at the intricate inlay of semi-precious stones, I thought back to how many hours it must have taken to build such a structure, that too almost four centuries ago. I wondered how many more centuries it would stand there for visitors to appreciate.

The marble was slowly yellowing due to the air pollution in Agra, and the Archaeological Survey of India had taken some measures to counter it, namely by enforcing a 500 m (1,640 ft) radius ban of conventional automobiles around the structure. From the car park, only battery-operated vehicles or camel carts were allowed to get close to the Taj. I couldn't comment on how much of an effect it had on the marble but it definitely gave the area a quiet feel, which makes the Taj Mahal experience all that much more special.

I rode out of Agra the next day with a big smile on my face. I was finally leaving behind the heat of the plains and beginning my climb into the foothills of the Himalayas. I took state highways northeast from Agra and passed through bustling towns and fertile farmlands that lay bare, ready for the promised monsoon. Uttar Pradesh is the most populous state of India with over 200 million people. All its little towns were awash with a cacophony of jarring honking, crazy driving, cows and buffaloes, and trucks of all sizes hauling goods all over the place. The frenetic energy and chaos of these towns was typical of India.

A little further north and I had reached the base of the Himalayas. The road became curvy and started climbing up to the hill station of Nainital. I had just entered Uttarakhand, a new mountainous state that had broken off from the rest of low-lying Uttar Pradesh a few years prior. I rose from 200 m (656 ft) to 2,000 m (6,562 ft) of elevation within an hour. It was refreshing to feel cool once again after frying for days in the plains. sanDRina was also happy to be leaning in and out of the well-designed cambered turns. I was greeted by the gorgeous sight of the Naini Lake set amidst its steep and dramatic mountains, just as the sun was slowly setting. I was delighted to finally be starting the Himalayan leg of my journey. From there on, it was to be narrow roads through the mountains until I would descend from Kashmir in the west.

I continued further north through hill stations that had a strong military presence, reminding me that I was getting closer to the border with China. I took breaks on empty stretches and enjoyed the peace and refreshing smell of the pine forests. It was a much-needed change from all the hustle and bustle of the plains. At times, I felt as though I was back in South America, particularly northern Peru and Bolivia, with all the small roads and mountain villages. The towns in India, of course, showed up more frequently and were a whole lot busier. I was sure that the similarities with the Andes would increase as I started seeing snow.

Stopping at a dhaba (highway restaurant), I satisfied my hunger with a fresh 'aloo paratha' (potato-filled flat bread) served with 'dahi' (yoghurt). It was interesting to taste all the different ways in which aloo parathas are made across north India. It is standard dhaba food, ready almost as soon as you arrive. Sometimes they're thick, sometimes very crispy, sometimes with lots of aloo whereas sometimes the aloo is just in the name. Either way, it's always tasty, especially with some 'achar' (pickle).

I spent the night in Rudraprayag, a small town at the confluence of the Alaknanda and Mandakini rivers as they flow from their glacier sources further upstream. I continued northwest through Uttarakhand tracking a route into the next state over – Himachal Pradesh. The main route would have taken me back down to the plains and its large cities, which I was not at all interested in. I found the secluded route I was seeking by using a combination of paper maps, my GPS and directions from truck drivers. While I was in Chennai, I had learnt of this route from other motorcycle travellers and I had immediately put it on my route plan. They said it would require some exploring as the narrow mountain roads were prone to landslides and closures, prompting U-turns and alternative routes. I was excited to be exploring obscure tracks through the Himalayas. From New Tehri, on the shores of the Tehri Dam Reservoir, I twisted my way through the small hamlet of Barkot to the northwest. I finally found the correct turn-off over a ridge towards the small town of Rohru in Himachal Pradesh, which was marked by an inconspicuous road sign. I had successfully found the way into Himachal Pradesh without going through any major cities. Chuffed with my progress, I picked up the pace on the empty roads ahead.

Just past the state border, I noticed my rear brakes squealing noisily. Upon inspection, I noticed that the brake pad material had worn through to the metal backing. I had not been paying attention to this part of sanDRina. Instead of it being a simple maintenance issue if addressed at an earlier stage, it now required immediate attention. Luckily, it wasn't too serious because I was carrying a spare set of brake pads and was able to switch them out in front of a mechanic shop by the roadside. Once again, a small crowd gathered to watch me, just like in South America and Africa.

Just outside Rohru, my trip odometer rolled over a major milestone. I had covered 100,000 km (62,150 miles) from Chicago, across five continents and thirty-three countries. When I had started the trip, I didn't have any particular goal in mind besides getting to India. With just that, I had managed to travel through some of the most exciting places on the planet and survived to tell the story. I was proud of sanDRina for hanging in there with me. Remarkably, we had only endured six flat tyres in all that distance, which I credited my high-quality Heidenau tyres with. sanDRina had been treated to seventeen oil changes, six sets of tyres and five sets of brake pads, not to mention the fifteen times we had to find a welder. She had also suffered eight breakdowns that were either simple roadside fixes or major kerfuffles, such as her destroyed engine near San Francisco and my running headless in Tanzania. Through it all, I was only left with the positive memories of how each incident turned out for the best and the wonderful people I met during those mini adventures. Isn't that why I started my journey in the first place? To be thrust into situations where I would learn about mental fortitude and being open-minded. It taught me that every ordeal can be approached as just another adventure.

The next morning, pouring over my maps and GPS, I couldn't seem to locate a road I was told about by other travellers that was heading north from Rohru, but the hotel proprietor said that there was, in fact, a road. Following his advice, I crossed a lone ridge blanketed by forests to Rampur, a large town down on the Sutlej River and on the Hindustan–Tibet Highway, designated as NH-22. This highway was built by the British Governor Dalhousie in the 1850s and many reasons have been cited for its construction. Some say it was as innocent as wanting to improve trade links with Tibet, while other claims are more malicious, such as the Governor's intent to build a sneaky route for an invasion into China. Regardless, the modern-day outcome was a road linking the once-isolated Kinnaur Valley to the rest of the world.

Rampur was the biggest town I had planned to cross before reaching the old Silk Road city of Leh in Ladakh, so I stocked up on cash, petrol and a spare jerrycan, just in case. From there, the NH-22 started out grand and wide, a beneficiary of the numerous hydroelectric projects along the Sutlej River. But once the dams ended, so did the smooth tarmac road, regressing to the natural rock and sand state of the region. And then finally, around a corner, I caught my first glimpse of snow-peaked mountains – my first since the Alps over two years ago. I was graduating from the foothills.

An hour from Rampur, I turned right and went south into the Baspa Valley heading for Sangla along a one-way road carved into the mountains. It was a short ride of only 18 km (11 miles), but it took me over an hour. While the road was rough, the views compelled me to stop at every other corner to soak in the stunning mountain views. The dust and haze of the plains had been replaced by crystal-clear air, sweeping mountain views and the perfume of the forest and soil. Snow-covered peaks were melting into waterfalls, cascading down through deodar forests to the Baspa River that flowed into the Sutlej. After an hour of basking in the majestic views, I arrived in Sangla, a small mountain town set at the base of the imposing Kinner Kailash mountain bedecked with a stunning vista of encircling snowy peaks.

I had plans to keep moving but the mountains had a different plan for me. I woke up the next morning to an overcast sky with thunder rolling in. Soon after, it started raining and that resulted in landslides further up the road. Moreover, the hotel owner informed me over breakfast that Kunzum Pass, which I had expected to journey through between the Spiti and Lahaul Valleys, wouldn't be open for another two weeks. Hence, I took the day off to allow the rains to pass while rethinking my route through Himachal Pradesh.

Sangla's heritage is the product of the Himalayas being left on the sidelines through the countless invasions that have swept through lowland India over the millennia. The inhabitants have skin that is more golden-brown with slightly narrower eyes, reflecting their Tibetan and north Asian origins. I spoke with many of them that afternoon as I wandered around town after the rain had passed. Unlike the aggression that is so typical of the plains, people in the hills are a lot friendlier and more amiable, almost certainly a result of the climate. I felt at ease with most of them. People would approach me every now and then and even ask for their photos to be taken, seeing the large SLR camera in my hand. I was impressed by an older lady sitting outside her shop who struck up a pose, resplendent in a flat, green felt hat characteristic of the Kinnauris. There was a distinct warmth and humour to these people. A little later, I enjoyed gazing at Kinner Kailash in the fading afternoon light over a plate of fried mutton momos. It's important to remember just how distinct every state and locality can be in India. More than a country, it is a grand commonwealth in which the people and languages are as distinct as their heritage. This would change again as I continued further north. I was still on the green side of the Himalayas. Ahead of me lay the high-altitude deserts; yet another instalment in India's history.

With the landslide cleared the next day, I backtracked to the Hindustan–Tibet Highway and headed out of Kinnaur Valley. I was a bit disappointed not to be riding into Spiti Valley but I'd learned to just take things as they come. Besides, it gave me an excuse to make another trip into the Himalayas sometime later. sanDRina and I cruised back through the valley and the countless mud and glacier streams that we had already crossed two days prior. sanDRina was in her element as we navigated diversions around landslides in sandy, rough soils. Fuelling up once again in Rampur, I continued west into central Himachal Pradesh, ascending and descending narrow tracks that shifted from dirt to tar and back. People were eking out a living in every possible space in these mountains with terrace farms visible all along the route. I passed through many 'hairpin towns', where the activity of a small town would be centred on just one hairpin, usually the summit of a ridge. It was not so different from some of the settlements and villages I had passed through in South America and Africa.

The next day, I merged in with the main highway heading to Manali, the primary entry point to the high Himalayas. It wasn't long before I found myself dodging the reckless tourist vans and buses attempting suicidal overtaking moves. I hadn't dealt with such ugly driving since I had left the plains for Nainital over 1,700 km (1,057 miles) ago. There was development all along the fast-flowing Beas River with restaurants and rafting units trying to attract the hordes of tourists heading to Manali.

With advice from Buddhi, a motorcyclist friend who leads expeditions into Ladakh, I rode into Old Manali and to the Himalayan Country House, which was right at the top of a hill. Next door was an old farmhouse covered in shale roof tiles where the residents still kept cows and lived off the land. Beyond the farmhouse, labourers were toiling through the fields, harvesting wheat to dry in great bundles. This was all taking place against the concrete backdrop of the New Manali town below, in which shops advertised PlayStations for rent, yoga classes and adventure trips of all sorts. Granted, I wasn't the one toiling in the field, but I had practically no interest in the material pleasures Manali had to offer. I yearned to get back into the wild Himalayas on sanDRina.

After a pleasant walk through the old farmhouses and hanging out with some old-timers with contagious smiles and laughs, I stocked up on supplies for the tough journey ahead. I started my intake of Diamox to help me acclimatize to the high altitudes and stashed handfuls of oral rehydration sachets in my panniers. I also bought small packets of walnuts, dried ginger and apricots, all harvested in the surrounding hills.

It was a bright morning in Manali as I began my journey to Leh. There were shops and kiosks selling all sorts of winter clothing for tourists heading up to Rohtang Pass, the first of five high-altitude passes on the way to Leh. The climb started immediately out of town and a series of hairpin bends took sanDRina and I higher and higher. We passed through orchards, grasslands and then rock fields before hitting the snowline. It took little more than an hour to pass through these zones, slowed only by the melee of tourist vehicles sending people up to the snowline where they would slide down slopes in adult romper suits. I couldn't criticize them for their childlike enjoyment; for almost all of them, it would have been their first time experiencing snow.

I was delighted to see snow banks at least 3 m (10 ft) high on either side of the pass at 3,979 m (13,055 ft), but this also meant that the snow was slowly melting and coating the road in a dangerous slush. Through the pass, the crowds disappeared, which is when the real journey began for me. I carefully descended through thick mud that had been washed down onto the unpaved roads by the melted snow. It was a challenge to move out of the way for the colourful and rickety trucks charging up the hill trying to keep their momentum, but I was in no hurry. In fact, I enjoyed extended breaks of the expansive view of the Lahaul Valley ringed with snow peaks before me. I was taking my time to enjoy these views and moments, keeping in mind that I was on the final chapter of my journey. However, I felt no sadness at all. My main priority was to soak in the details that passed through my eyesight – to follow the route of streams down the sides of mountains and the spiralled ascent of eagles, and to imagine the lives of those who farmed during the short summer months in the valleys below. I did so with the same diligence as when I first started out. Three years later, I would still marvel at these little details.

Once down at Gramphu, the route followed a river valley on good tarmac. At Tandi, I filled up at the last petrol station till Leh, 365 km (227 miles) away as indicated on a signboard plastered with stickers. Soon after came Keylong, the biggest town in the area, but I pushed a bit further north and got to the small dhaba junction of Darcha. There were no hotels there, only temporary dhabas built for the season. Along with serving food, they had a few beds in the back for travellers. Other motorcyclists had told me that staying in the dhabas, along with hearty servings of mutton curry with rice and fresh rotis, was part of the experience of journeying from Manali to Leh.

I had a restful sleep in the dhaba bed. Since there were no toilet facilities there, I did my morning rituals down by the river with an amazing view of snow peaks all around. I couldn't think of too many other ways to start the day in such an inspirational manner. The route slowly climbed from the 3,350 m (10,990 ft) that Darcha was at through a large field of snow banks to Baralacha La at a staggering 4,948 m (16,235 ft) – 'La' meaning pass in the Ladakhi language. It was incredible to be at such altitudes on a motorcycle since it made my experience truly immersive. The same route would've been constricted if I were in a four-wheeled vehicle. Stopping repeatedly for photos, I took it very slow while getting on and off sanDRina as I didn't want the altitude to get to my head. It was sublime to be winding on a tarmac road for kilometres on end with snow piled up on both sides. I had never experienced this kind of riding before. There was very little traffic and I felt lost in a winter wonderland. From the top of the pass, I looked back to see that I had ridden on a path cut through a mammoth snowfield. All these roads were maintained by the Border Roads Organization (BRO), a support unit of the Indian Army. They remain a stalwart and underappreciated warhorse of India's frontier forces, keeping roads open and driving development deeper into the valleys.

On the other side of Baralacha La, I rode past a frozen lake and was stunned by the stillness and astounding beauty of being surrounded by white all around, highlighted by the stark blue of the sky. With my helmet off, there was a tinny sensation in my ears given the pure absence of sound. Coming down from the pass, I met with a British couple, Henry and Klara, who had rented an Enfield from Manali for a two-week trip through Ladakh and into Kashmir. We had been passing each other throughout the day and eventually decided to travel in a convoy as we moved out of the endless snow banks beyond Baralacha La and into the Himalayan rain shadow.

We got to the remote outpost of Sarchu by early afternoon, a mere 80 km (50 miles) from Darcha. Instead of pushing ahead to the next dhaba junction over two more passes, we decided to call it a day and enjoy the afternoon in the high Himalayas. Situated on a ridge with a stunning view of mountains all around, Sarchu is the last post in Himachal Pradesh, sitting at a breathtaking altitude of 4,329 m (14,202 ft). We relished the day's ride sitting outdoors at the dhaba with warm cups of chai. Henry had quit his corporate job, Klara had engineered a leave of absence from work and now they were on a whirlwind world tour for one year. After India, they planned on heading to Southeast Asia and then onwards to South America. They were amazed that I had been on the road for three years and that too with the same bike. I was more shocked to find out that Henry had never ridden off-road before this trip and was now tackling one of the toughest rides on the planet, that too with his fiancée sitting right behind him. If there was ever a novice motorcycling couple that deserved a toast over a couple of beers, it was them. It became freezing cold that night with the temperature dropping mercilessly. We all eventually retired under two heavy blankets each in our corrugated metal shack. I wasn't worried about sanDRina though. She was starting easily in this cold weather and was actually running much better at high altitudes than on the hot plains. This was clearly her comfort zone.

From Sarchu, the route headed to the Gata Loops, a series of twenty-one hairpin bends that raise the elevation rapidly by 457 m (1,500 ft). The route led us to Nakee La at 4,919 m (16,138 ft), with gorgeous views of snow-capped peaks all around. The sky also seemed different now. It took on a deep cobalt blue creating a clear contrast with the brown valley floors and iron-rich red mountain rocks. Only ribbons of green clinging to solitary riverbanks broke this Mars-scape.

Coming down from Nakee La, the route rapidly spiralled back up to Lachung La at 5,079 m (16,663 ft). It felt incredible to cross 5,000 metres in elevation – my first time since the high Andes of Bolivia. The air was so rarefied that it wasn't exactly fit for humans, but here I was, on a road built to accommodate regular traffic to pass through. We figured that it was going to be another short day, so the three of us took a break by a glacial stream and just enjoyed being in the middle of nowhere surrounded by pristine beauty. We spent maybe an hour by the stream and saw it change dramatically in just that much time. When we had arrived, the water was clear and I filled up my water bottle with it and enjoying its pure unfiltered taste. By the time we left, it was infused with sediment as the meltwater grew in volume under the sun's unrelenting gaze.

From there, it was a short ride to Pang at 4,519 m (14,826 ft), a collection of temporary dhabas with a few beds in the back. Electing for a separate tent, the three of us squeezed in to escape the chill air and harsh sun. Relishing the altitude, we spent that afternoon relaxing over countless mugs of chai, playing cards and observing life as it was in this small gathering in the remote Himalayas. Most of the families running these dhabas were Nepalis who would set up each season and cater to truckers and passing travellers. In their spare time, they would knit woollen caps and gloves in an attempt to drive some further revenue and probably alleviate the monotony of an existence that was far from romantic. Pang was slightly more developed than Sarchu, perhaps because it was next to an army base. It had a concrete block of toilets, though it was nothing more than a hole in the ground. I knew this settlement would disappear with the snows, leaving behind just the toilets, the road and the trash that was building up behind the dhabas. The local authorities were making great efforts and advances in regulating these dhabas, especially with regards to their impact on the environment, but like most places in India, pollution came with the passage of people. Alas, it is something I have found to be far more pronounced in India than in most other countries I have visited. The mindlessness with which I would see people throw empty bottles, candy bar wrappers and plastic bags, regardless of the natural beauty they were in the midst of, remains an incomprehensible affront to our country. This bothered me even more because I know that Indians don't behave the same way abroad. Lamentably, it is getting steadily worse amongst the younger travellers whose lack of shame was all too evident. I saw a kid throw a chocolate wrapper out his jeep window as it left Pang. India's attitude toward its environment has become a national shame.

After a delicious breakfast of aloo parathas with omelettes, we set out for the last day's ride to Leh. Pang sits at the bottom of a plateau, from where a series of hairpin bends brought us up to 4,778 m (15,678 ft) onto the Morey Plains. It was bizarre that there is a 40 km (25 miles) stretch of almost flat terrain up at this extreme altitude. The capacious valley ahead with a brand new tarmac road made for a sublime ride in the morning chill. After days spent on tight roads, we were finally able to ride freely and enjoy the expanse of space. The pavement ended halfway across the plains, which is when we began off-roading to the northern end where the route started climbing to the last and highest pass of the Manali–Leh Highway, Taglang La, at an astonishingly high 5,348 m (17,548 ft).

Along the whole way, road construction workers were hammering away at rocks with hand tools to make gravel for the road. Machinery had been eschewed in favour of manual labour as a way of providing employment, but the conditions the workers endured were harsh. Their campsites were nothing more than cheap plastic tarpaulins stretched over a wooden A-frame, where they endured the extreme conditions and washed their clothes and themselves in the cold glacial streams. The last camp we passed was at an agonizing 5,030 m (16,500 ft). Most of the workers looked like migrants from other parts of India, but the harsh ultraviolet rays at this extreme altitude had darkened their skin such that it was difficult to tell a 'foreign' economic migrant from a local. Yet, the one quality they all had in common was a cheerful attitude. They all waved as we rode past, to which I would return a salute, thanking them for their back-breaking work.

After crossing Taglang La and starting our descent down to Leh, the view changed. There were no more stunning red mountains or crisp blue sky as the clouds were back. We rode past snow banks and slowly descended down to Rumtse, the first proper village with brick buildings that we had seen since Keylong. Besides aloo parathas, another staple of the dhabas of the Manali–Leh Highway was Maggi Noodles. Every dhaba stocks this signature Indian comfort food, providing the hungry traveller with a warm and filling meal. We enjoyed a bowl and then continued descending to the Indus River. Seeing trees and greenery was a welcomed relief after the high-altitude desert we had just been through. After passing a very large army base, we found ourselves back in the midst of civilization with the abrupt arrival of traffic and erratic driving.

Reaching Leh after crossing the Great Himalayan and Ladakh mountain ranges truly felt epic. One must consider that this old city sits on the Silk Route, and many others over the centuries must have felt the same as I did upon entering Leh. The streets were bustling with activity. We rode past the old town to Changspa for a hotel on the hilltop that had a grand view of the snow-capped mountains that we had just crossed. That night, Henry, Klara and I celebrated our successful traverse of the Manali–Leh Highway over local Godfather beers and a meal heavy with mutton kebabs, which was meant to replenish our energy as much as it was to offset a week's diet of parathas, noodles and veg momos. The Manali–Leh Highway is one of the most incredible rides on the planet and its popularity is well deserved. Taxing, inspiring and, at times, punishing, there aren't too many routes that offer such a vista of snow-capped peaks combined with constantly shifting off-road challenges. It had been a privilege for me to surmount it, and in such good company too.

We took a day off after the journey from Manali and wandered the streets of Leh at a relatively pleasant 3,500 m (11,484 ft), considering we had gone up to 5,000 m (16,405 ft) over the past few days. Leh lies on the northern banks of the Indus River ringed with snow-capped mountains. It has a thousand years of history to its name and was founded in the tenth century as a key staging post on the Silk Route. Pashmina and cashmere wool were still being hawked on the streets alongside the now ubiquitous smartphones. This hive of activity made the most of these short summer months. A local man named Sonam gave us a ride in a Maruti 800 hatchback, the stalwart of the Indian automobile industry, after we got lost during a walk to town. He told us that he preferred the winters when the town more or less closes down due to the extreme weather, because that's when every family just socializes to pass the months. I could see the appeal in that, but had no real interest in spending an eight-month-long winter there from September to May, with most of my time spent freezing.

There are many places to visit from Leh, but with sanDRina's chain not at its best, I decided to visit only the main attraction, Khardung La, which is said to be the highest motorable road in the world. We set off from Leh and the steep climb catapulted us out of town. The route snaked up one huge mountain with each hairpin bend elevating us higher and higher. The road was tarred for 24 km (15 miles) up to the checkpoint at south Pullu. Reverting to gravel, the road got very rough with bumps, mud and glacier stream crossings (known as 'nallahs') for the final haul up to the pass 15 km (9 miles) ahead. Traffic was also pretty heavy as most people who visit Leh make the same trip. For India, Khardung La is of national importance as it is the only supply route to the Siachen Glacier and the army camps there. India and Pakistan went to war over this glacier and its tributaries in 1984. It was a vicious campaign noted as one of the highest altitude conflicts ever fought. To this day, the area is heavily militarized even though more troops die from avalanches and exposure than in combat.

Stopped by some BRO road construction for almost an hour, the traffic was finally let through in a long burst onto Khardung La. I'm not sure how the BRO get their altitude readings, but their claim of Khardung La being at an elevation of 5,600 m (18,375 ft) is off by a large margin. My GPS, calibrated to satellites overhead, told me we were actually at 5,378 m (17,646 ft), which was still the highest I had been on this journey. There were Tibetan prayer flags at the pass, just like at all the other passes in Ladakh. I bought my own set in Leh and let it fly in the wind at Khardung La. I wished for a good end to my journey, because from there on, I would be tracking south to Delhi – my official finish line.

I wish I could've spent more time in Leh but I had to get back on the road. I bid farewell to Henry and Klara and stocked up on 'yos', a Ladakhi snack made of roasted barley and assorted nuts. National Highway 1 took me along the roaring Indus River and

towards Kashmir. I could only imagine what it must be like at the
end of summer with the full force of melting snow.

A few kilometres out of Leh, there's an odd place called
Magnetic Hill. It is said that if you park your car in the designated
spot and leave it in neutral, it will move uphill due to the way the
magnetic field is aligned at that point. Of course, it wouldn't have
worked on a motorcycle. After some time, the landscape changed
dramatically, resembling the surface of the moon with bleach-
white rocks tumbled all over the valley. Then came Lamayuru,
a Tibetan Buddhist monastery said to be a thousand years old.
Framed with enigmatic snow peaks all around, it was a handsome
stone and mud brick structure perched on top of a hill.

I crossed two more passes, Fotu La and Namika La, but after the
Manali–Leh Highway, these seemed like hills. And then it was down
into Kargil, the northernmost point of my trip around India. It was
near Kargil in 1999 that India and Pakistan fought their last war.
After reading so much about it and seeing those events transpire
in the news just when I was leaving India, it was wonderful to see
that Kargil was just a regular old mountain town now. Traffic was
busy, street vendors were selling all sorts of items and fresh bread
was being baked. It was a town that was quite different from the
image created by the war.

I left Kargil early the next morning and headed towards
Srinagar. I had been warned that the route could be rough and
unpredictable. It was a bright and beautiful morning, but one that
I could not enjoy because I was focused on safely navigating past
the long army convoys that regularly traverse that route. These
roads were principally for military use, which is why many routes
had restrictions for civilians, and stricter ones for foreigners. A
little ways out of Kargil, I came up to Dras and the Kargil War
Memorial. There was a museum on the site showcasing photos
from the war and the troubles the Indian Army went through in
securing victory. I paid my respects and continued on my way. The
route slowly climbed up to Zoji La, the last pass of my trip. It was

quite the dramatic gateway separating Ladakh's dry desert airs to the lush green of Kashmir, which I was pleased to see was exactly like the postcards and posters I had seen growing up.

Descending from the pass, I was blocked first by a fresh landslide, and then by women protesting in the lush green valleys near Srinagar. Traffic had been backed up for kilometres, but my arrival coincided with the protest being broken up, which allowed the bottleneck to suddenly flow freely once again. The protest was a response to the jailing of one of the male villagers, a fairly common occurrence in Kashmir, where the military's efforts to maintain peace often causes as much strife as they seek to defuse.

The road from Srinagar to Jammu the next day was very hectic being packed full of tourist, freight and army vehicles. The scenery was enjoyable at times, but with so much effort required to navigate the traffic, I could only steal the occasional glance at the freshly prepared fields of paddy, which denoted the transition from upland to lowland communities. While I stopped by some fields to take a break, an army soldier on foot patrol emerged out of the nearby woods. It was a reminder of the ever-present military presence in Kashmir. I asked if it was okay for me to be there and he said that it was. I got chatting with him and it turned out he was from Kerala and was pleased to meet a fellow south Indian. After the flat farmland near Srinagar, the road climbed up and over two small mountains, passing through the 2.5 km (1.5 mile) long Jawahar Tunnel, which was built in the 1950s. It was the first tunnel in the world that was drilled simultaneously from both sides to meet perfectly in the middle.

When I reached Udhampur a few hours from Srinagar, I was greeted by wide tree-lined boulevards of an Indian Army bastion. Being close to the foothills, this was the primary barrack for all army operations in the mountains. Luckily, with an introduction from a rider of the Madras Bulls motorcycling club, I was welcomed as a VIP at the 4th Battalion of the Madras Regiment, the oldest in the Indian Army, dating all the way back to the 1750s.

I rode through the white gates of the base knowing that ordinary citizens would not be welcome without special permission. Major Karoop, moustached and fit, welcomed me by firmly grabbing my shoulders. He was proud to learn that an Indian, and that too a boy from Madras, had undertaken such a journey.

After freshening up in a bungalow looking very much as it might have during British rule, based on its staid and ornate furniture, I entered the clubhouse and immediately realized that I was extremely underdressed. The major had rounded up his lieutenants, who were bedecked in crisp shirts and slacks for an evening of drinks and dinner to celebrate my journey. It was slightly overwhelming, but I soaked it in. Any doubts I had as to whether I was Indian enough to warrant my passport were dismissed as each of the officers offered praise in my accomplishment. I felt a slight tinge of nationalistic pride when Major Karoop said that I had probably done more to project India's image in faraway lands in one trip than decades of diplomacy and posturing could hope to. I didn't accept such an accolade, but I felt the officers took pride in thinking so. And who was I to deny them the very pride that powers militaries the world over. Over a very formal dinner of roast mutton, I regaled them with stories from my journey and they discussed their lives in an army regiment. The Major invited me to stay for longer but I was eager now to get to Delhi.

One of the lieutenants at the base informed me of a back route that would avoid passing through the busy city of Jammu and take me back into Himachal Pradesh. Hence, I headed east through small towns and found myself on desolate and sinuous roads that took me through rich groves of pine and eucalyptus. I gained some elevation, but anything below 1,500 m (4,921 ft) at this point felt hot like the plains. I had to keep reminding myself that I would have to get used to it – Delhi awaited me and summers there could top 50°C (122°F). I was out of Jammu & Kashmir and back in Himachal Pradesh. I quickly swung by Dharamsala and McLeod Ganj, the seat of his Holiness, the Dalai Lama, and the centre of the exiled Tibetan community. I avoided the crowds in McLeod Ganj – a circus of daytrippers from the plains, spiritual tourists, and unending traffic snarls – which had swept away the last vestiges of a quiet hill station. Instead, I opted to rest in Dharamsala, which had retained its forested charm.

I woke up to the sound of the cool rain, but the climate of the plains was waiting for me just as I descended a few hundred metres from Dharamsala; dry, hot and dusty. sanDRina and I pressed on through Himachal Pradesh, savouring the twisting hill roads and river views as we swung through the last of the foothills.

Finally, the Himalayas faded away and the plains of Punjab greeted us as we headed straight to the city of Chandigarh, where I was hosted on my last night by the local Royal Enfield club. After a night of celebrating with my new friends, I woke up early from a good night's sleep for the last day of my journey.

About fifteen riders from Chandigarh joined me for a short breakfast ride and then bid me adieu. Someone was looking out for me as it was a very cool day compared to the last few in the area. It was cloudy and grey and the temperature was in the low 30s°C (86°F) range. A part of me wished for a bright, blue sky for the last ride of my journey, but I had experienced many brilliant skies in Ladakh and was glad to welcome the cool ride into Delhi.

The six lane, 225 km (140 miles) highway from Chandigarh to Delhi was a breeze to ride and I relished getting sanDRina into fifth gear and leaning back with my feet up on her highway pegs. While paying attention to the traffic ahead, I was reminiscing about all the good rides I had had over the past three-plus years. I had visited foreign lands, experienced gorgeous places, met wonderful people and savoured exquisite food along the way. I was elated to have had the chance to do something like this ... and I actually made it happen! My tunes were turned up and I was jammin' on sanDRina.

Delhi greeted me with its customary traffic snarl on the outer ring road, but a welcoming party of Bullet riders, who had come to celebrate the ending of my journey, escorted me through. Together, we rode to India Gate at the very heart of the city, where we persuaded the police to allow us in for a triumphant journey-ending photo, which I posed for with my arms outstretched and a gleeful smile, standing by sanDRina.

The evening afterwards was one of celebration with new friends who had made me feel welcome in this new city. It was not until later in the night that reality hit. I was staying at another friend's house, so when sanDRina and I pulled up outside, I just sat there with the engine running for a minute. The road was dark and there was no traffic going by. Past the gentle throb of sanDRina's single-piston engine, I could hear the hot wind blow through the trees overhead. My mind played with the thought of just riding off again, but I had ridden far enough this time. I gently pushed sanDRina's kickstand down to the road and adjusted my weight, allowing her to rest. Removing my gloves and helmet, I smiled, satiated. With one last pat to my friend and companion, I turned the key and sanDRina's engine rumbled to a close. The leaves in the overhead trees rustled as sanDRina's engine clicked cool. I unzipped my jacket and dismounted. We were home.

ACKNOWLEDGEMENTS

I would like to thank Oliver Fall for helping tremendously with the editing of this book and Sangita Vyas for encouraging me during the writing. I would also like to thank Lavanya Kannaiyan, Allen Minnehan, Shridhar Reddy and Harjoth Singh, among others, who supported me during the trip. Finally, I'm very grateful to the wonderful hosts that took me into their homes along the way.

ABOUT THE AUTHOR

Growing up in Zambia and India, Jay Kannaiyan started seeking adventure from an early age. In pursuit of the 'Indian-American dream', he set off to the US, where he lived, worked and squeezed in as much motorcycle travel as possible. In 2010, he pointed his front wheel away from America and embarked on a three-year motorcycle journey that took him to India, where he started another adventure in entrepreneurship. Jay now lives with his wife in Austin, Texas. Learn more and connect with him at JayKannaiyan.com.